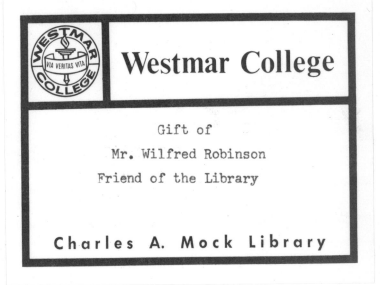

Logical Analysis and Contemporary Theism

LOGICAL ANALYSIS

and

Contemporary Theism

Edited by

JOHN DONNELLY

New York
Fordham University Press
1972

© Copyright 1972 by FORDHAM UNIVERSITY PRESS
Library of Congress Catalog Card Number: 77–168693
ISBN 0–8232–0940–7

Printed in the United States of America

To
JOY
and to
my MOTHER and FATHER

Contents

Editor's Preface

I can respect the men who argue that religion is true and therefore ought to be believed, but I can feel only profound reprobation for those who say that religion ought to be believed because it is useful, and that to ask whether it is true is a waste of time.—BERTRAND RUSSELL, *Why I Am Not a Christian*

. . . I nevertheless want to insist that any attempt to analyse Christian religious utterances as expressions or affirmations of a *blik* rather than as (at least would-be) assertions about the cosmos is fundamentally misguided.—ANTONY FLEW, "Theology and Falsification," *New Essays in Philosophical Theology*

In 1955 the academic world was introduced to what was soon to become the standard anthology in natural theology—Flew and MacIntyre's *New Essays in Philosophical Theology*. Much discussion has taken place in the interim, but most philosophers in the Anglo-American tradition remain nonetheless skeptical of the possibility of constructing a viable philosophical theology, as did, on the whole, the original contributors to *New Essays*. Ironically, the above remarks, so buoyant to the theist's intent to rejuvenate natural theology, were uttered by two of the most vituperative philosophical critics of the claims of natural theology. Nonetheless, they insightfully illustrate the folly of pragmatic or non-cognitive defenses of theism, which, however subtle in execution, cloak their meager underpinnings with the trappings of hypocrisy. It has been a lamentable fact that skilled practitioners of linguistic analysis often prove quite inept when directing their attention to matters of a theological nature. In brief, many friends of religion are enemies of theism.

The present volume intends to rectify such a pessimistic state of affairs, and, moreover, begin the necessary work, if a philosophical reconstruction of natural theology is to be a reality. To be sure, all the contributors to *Logical Analysis and*

Contemporary Theism philosophize utilizing the methodology of linguistic analysis. Ironically enough, such a philosophical technique is generally considered anathema (by non-analytic philosophers, as well as theologians) in the pursuit of a natural theology, but as James Ross so ably illustrates in Chapter 1, this is historically inaccurate, inasmuch as concern with the intricacies of logic and language was paramount in the thought of Aquinas, Scotus, etc. Whereas *New Essays* was covertly pessimistic in its verdict, the present volume is overtly tendentious. Yet the same concern for precise, well-delineated argumentation found in *New Essays* is, I believe, preserved in the present work.

Moreover, this ecumenical volume pretends no consensus on religious commitment by its individual contributors. A number of religious denominations are represented by some of the contributors; some are at best sympathetic to the claims of religious belief. However, all *qua* philosophers engage in apologetics of an epistemic nature for the Judaeo-Christian tradition.

In regard to content, Chapters 1 to 4 argue respectively for a modal proof of God's existence, present defenses of the cosmological and teleological arguments in light of atheological challenges, and conclude with the argument from religious experience. Chapters 5 to 7 focus attention on the concept of God while 8 deals with the formal requirements of theological predication, some problems of which are treated in detail in 9 to 15. Chapters 16 and 17 argue for the legitimacy of miracles, and 18 deals with the epistemological issue of religious verification. Chapter 19 defends the observability of the self, and removes certain conceptual difficulties from the theistic belief in immortality. To be sure, a theory of the self couched in the framework of dualism can be logically independent of the claims of theism. Nonetheless, I share Peter Geach's doubts concerning the possibility of disembodied survival for such a mental remnant, if only for the Thomistic reason that *anima mea non est ego,* and the consequent need of a God to resurrect the person. Lastly, in 20 I attempt to surmount the apparent absurdities inherent in Kierkegaard's famed illustration of "the teleological suspension of the ethical."

A. J. Ayer, following Gilbert Ryle, has suggested in *Language, Truth and Logic* that the philosopher's business "is rather to 'solve puzzles' than to discover truths." I would suggest that the logico-linguistic puzzles discussed in this volume are no idle conundrums, suitable only for philosophical leisure. Truth value attaches to such claims, and the specter of Cognitivity directs the philosopher to that recognition which is Wisdom.

Special thanks are due to the staff of Fordham University Press, particularly Professor Edwin A. Quain, Director, and H. George Fletcher, Editor, for their always generous assistance.

J. D.

Logical Analysis and Contemporary Theism

1

On Proofs for the Existence of God

JAMES F. ROSS

University of Pennsylvania

I. INTRODUCTION

FIRST, I SHALL SUMMARIZE A FEW POINTS which have been
explained and defended elsewhere.[1] Some may find these assumptions unacceptable; but it seems otiose to repeat arguments which I cannot at present improve.

1. Proofs for the existence of God cannot be characterized
usefully in terms of whether they are convincing, persuasive,
cogent, etc.; those predicates are person-relative and are cir-
cumstance-relative as well.

There are no arguments for any conclusion which could
reasonably be expected to be convincing, persuasive, or cogent

Reprinted from *The Monist,* 54 No. 2 (1970), Lasalle, Illinois, with the permission of the publishers and the author.

for everyone or even anyone, regardless of the circumstances in which they are encountered. An argument will prove its conclusion if it is sound, epistemologically straightforward (with premises epistemically prior to the conclusion), and has premises which are affirmatively decidable through philosophical analysis. Whether a given argument constitutes a proof or not can vary from time to time, depending upon the state of what is known by the community of scholars. So we are not able to give a useful analysis of what it is for an argument to prove its conclusion; though we do know what it is for an argument to prove its conclusion to *so and so*; but "being a proof," in general, is not a function of the number of persons for which an argument serves as a proof. It appears rather that, whether a sound argument is a proof or not depends primarily upon the status its premises hold within the body of human "scientific" knowledge at the time.

2. When we talk about proving the existence of God, we ought to be aware of the pragmatic inconsequentiality of good over bad arguments. In general, arguments have little or no effect on whether a person takes up, gives up, or continues his belief or disbelief in the existence of God; but insofar as they do have some effect, they have it not in virtue of their soundness or their objective goodness, but in virtue of their persuasive attractiveness which may be quite independent of their objective merits or defects when considered from the point of view of theoretical inquiry.[2] Knowing that, we shall restrict our critical consideration of proofs for the existence of God to a theoretical context: what are the conditions which a chain of reasoning must satisfy in order successfully to incorporate the existence of God among the body of things known by way of theoretical inquiry? We will require that it be sound, logically and epistemologically straightforward, and that it should survive philosophical scrutiny—not that every philosopher must accept its premises as true or that none may claim to have found them false—only that none shall have succeeded in showing the premises to be false or that the premises are inaccessible to our decision or that they are epistemically inaccessible to anyone who does not have prior knowledge of the conclusion.

3. I think we can take it as quite probable that the standard arguments from design, causality, motion, moral objectivity, and perfection have been found not to be proofs of the existence of God; not as they stand in the classical theological texts and not as they have been reformulated so far.

4. There is a difference between the *considerations* to which it is reasonable to attend when one is seeking to find out whether God exists or not (for instance, the origins of being, change, contingent things, the apparent hierarchy of perfections, and the orderliness and purposiveness of things in nature) and the *arguments* which have been formulated employing generalizations about these matters as premises and the existence of God as a conclusion. Such arguments have been variously criticized: as having false premises, as being invalid, as having premises which are epistemically posterior to the conclusion, etc. But the criticism of specific arguments will not preclude the formulation of new ones which begin with generalizations about those same considerations and argue that those generalizations could not be true if God did not exist. There is no *a priori* reason why such a new argument will not be discovered at any time. We shall, therefore, concede neither that cosmological, ontological, or teleological considerations are irrelevant to proving the existence of God nor that all arguments based upon such considerations have been found to be unsatisfactory; rather, only a few have been considered and rejected.[3]

5. We need to distinguish an argument from a given formulation of it. For instance, there have been many formulations of the argument from design or the argument for a first uncaused cause of motion, etc.[4] Formulations are classified as formulations of the same argument if they rest upon the same basic consideration (e.g., "that things acting purposefully but themselves incapable of knowledge, must be directed by an intelligent agent," or, "that motion arises from an external agent and that the chain of such causes cannot be without a beginning," etc.). The argument does not exist apart from its formulations, but is not identical with any of them. How-

ever, the argument is sound if any of its formulations is sound, unsound if none of them is, and is demonstrative if in at least one of its formulations the argument satisfies the conditions for proving its conclusion.

Thus, to show that in one or another formulation a given argument is unsound is not to show that the argument is unsound; there must be additional evidence that no formulation which does not alter the argument (by changing the central considerations) will be sound. Thus, refutation requires that we show the central consideration (which threads the different formulations together as formulations of one argument rather than as different but similar arguments) to be incorrect, cognitively inaccessible, or so related to the desired conclusion that no formulation will be valid and consistent.

The reason that I emphasize the distinction between an argument and its particular formulation is that not all the arguments called "modal arguments for the existence of God" have the same logical form or have the same semantical difficulties; some are better than others. Yet all seem to rest upon a common consideration: that whatever kind of thing God is, He is the sort of thing whose existing is consistent and whose nonexisting is excluded by the *sort* of thing He is. There is a further common consideration among the modal arguments: that the proper procedure is to offer some definition or characterization of God which, combined with the assumption that God does not exist, will yield a contradiction. The modal arguments which I employ depend upon the concept of explicability (the consistency of saying that there is an explanation for such and such), whereas some of Hartshorne's versions rest upon the concept of a perfect being; but these are preludes to different characterizations of God and do not, I think, essentially differentiate the arguments.

Insofar as two more proofs are known to share their central considerations, it seems reasonable to regard them as diverse formulations of the same argument; thus criticism tends to focus directly upon showing that upon *these* central considerations, no argument at all can be constructed which will yield the conclusion desired while satisfying the requirement of soundness, noncircularity, epistemic straightforwardness, public accessibility of the premises, and analytic (or, observational) decidability for its premises. Of course, according to this high standard of refutation, none of the traditional arguments for the existence of God has been refuted.

6. The modal arguments, which occur in different forms in Hartshorne's works and in my own, do, in my opinion, establish the conclusion that there is a being which exists necessarily and exists in virtue of what sort of thing it is (this point will be supported by a specific argument below). Some of the presuppositions of these arguments are interesting and worthy of further examination.

II. AN ARGUMENT

The question at issue is whether there can be a good *a priori* argument that God exists. I offer here a simplified formulation of an *a priori* argument which is presented more elaborately elsewhere.[5] The purpose of my stating the argument simply is not to persuade anyone that it actually establishes its conclusion or to excuse its defects by appeal to its simplicity, but to facilitate discussion of some ideas which are relevant to appraising whether it (in this formulation or in more elaborate logical form) establishes its conclusion. Simple statements, like the one to be offered, are, like the arguments of Aquinas in *Summa Theologica* I, q.2, a.3, to be regarded as schemata, as descriptions designed to communicate the basic idea and form but not necessarily the detailed content and most efficient logical formulation of the argument mentioned. We are substituting a line drawing for a photograph because the latter is inconveniently large and the point at issue does not depend upon the missing details.

Two preliminaries. *First,* the argument mentioned does not purport to establish that there is some thing which has all the divine attributes (the attributes which God actually has) but only that there is something which has certain of the divine attributes. That is the same as saying that it establishes that the being-which-is-God exists, but does not pretend to establish *that* it is God—not in a simple step. This is like establishing that the *x* which is president of the United States exists, but not that *x is* the president of the United States: such a thing could happen only if *x* is legitimately considered under some description which is not synonymous with "the president of the United States," but which is compatible with it.[6]

Secondly, the selection of that description is important; for while compatible with all the divine attributes, it will not be synonymous with them or their conjunction; yet it will have to represent a central element in our conception (both religiously and theoretically) of God, otherwise there will be no reason to regard a proof in which it figures as a proof of the existence of the being-which-is-God, rather than of some other being. The description I propose to use is this: "a being which is unproducible and unpreventable." Such a description logically implies that any such being has other attributes and that those other attributes logically exclude a cause of or external agent for the existence or nonexistence of such a being. In the case of God, there are a number of such attributes; I mention omnipotence only as an example. If a being, S, is omnipotent, then (by definition) for any logically contingent state of affairs p, "p is the case" is logically equivalent to "$_sWp$" (S effectively decides that p). If there is a being which is omnipotent (as the term is defined), then there cannot be anything else capable of causing it to be or preventing it from being. For if there were such a causing or preventing thing, the proposition that S exists would have to be inconsistent or contingent. We can assume that it is not inconsistent; if it is contingent, then its negation is contingent too; but if something prevented S from existing, it would (by the definition) have to be true that S willed that S did not exist; for we can substitute "S did not exist" for 'p'. If S were prevented from ever existing, the condition would still hold that if it is contingent, S would have to will it—with the result that a contradiction is yielded: for if "S never existed" were contingently true, it would have to be true that S willed that S never existed; but "S wills p" entails that S exists; hence the *falsity* of "S existed sometime" has as a necessary condition that S existed sometime. Thus all omnipotent beings (as the property is defined above) are uncausable and unpreventable. (It is, of course, also true that all omnipotent beings exist and exist necessarily.) The point here is that the properties involved in our description of the being whose existence is to be proved are themselves logically consequences of the traditional "divine attributes" and while all the traditional attributes are not connoted by the description, it is the being to which all those attributes were traditionally assigned whose existence is in question and whose existence is to be proved.

The summary of the argument is as follows

1. Every logically contingent state of affairs is heteroexplicable.
2. That there exists an uncausable and unpreventable being is not heteroexplicable.
3. Therefore, it is not a contingent state of affairs.
4. But it is a logically consistent state of affairs that there exists an unproducible and unpreventable being.
5. Whatever state of affairs is consistent but not contingent is logically necessary.
6. Hence it is a logically necessary state of affairs that there exists an uncausable and unpreventable being.
7. What is logically necessary is actually so; therefore, there exists an unproducible and unpreventable being.

This is an *a priori* argument based upon the exclusive disjunction of all states of affairs as necessary, impossible, or contingent. It is assumed that what is in question is not impossible and it is demonstrated that it is not contingent; from which it follows that it is necessary. Apart from the assumption that it is consistent to say that some thing which exists is unproducible and unpreventable, the two key assumptions of the argument are (1) that every contingent state of affairs is heteroexplicable and (2) that whether there exists an unproducible and unpreventable being is not heteroexplicable. We shall, therefore, consider each of these.

A. *Heteroexplicability*

Just as the concept attached to the name "God" is distilled from a consideration of the way the name has been used in the teaching and practice of Western Judaeo-Christian religion and in the theoretical commentaries on such teaching and practice which we find among philosophers and theologians, so too, the claim that all contingent states of affairs are heteroexplicable is justified by consideration of the way human inquiry is carried out and by attending to the commentaries upon the process of and nature of inquiry which we find among philosophers and scientists.

Take anything which might have been otherwise than the way it is; for example, that a railroad train does not leave Philadelphia for New York as scheduled on a certain day. If we inquire into that fact and are told that there is nothing whatever which accounts for its being so, we may be incredulous or skeptical; but we will not react with the same rebellion as when told "that the train did not leave on schedule is not only unexplained, it *could not* have been explained." Such a reply is utterly without foundation in any human experience; there is nothing about any contingent state of affairs which could ever be evidence that it is inexplicable; there is something about every contingent state of affairs which is evidence to the contrary: namely, that it is *consistent* to say of that state of affairs (however complete its description in terms of observable and inferable properties may be) that there could have been an explanation for its being the case—an explanation in some logically independent and logically distinct contingent state of affairs which involves an existent. The train could (logically) have been prevented from leaving by the choice of some human, by the advent of conditions making its leaving physically impossible, or by the caprice of its engineer, etc. It is simply inconsistent to say of any logically contingent state of affairs that some other state of affairs could not have occurred which would serve as its explanation. Were the world weird enough, anything (involving an existent) could explain the occurrence or the prevention of anything else. Contingency entails explicability. This can be generally proved in the following way: let p be any contingent state of affairs at all; let q be any other logically independent state of affairs distinct from p and involving the existence of something or another; then there is a logically contingent law-like universal of the form "if p then q" which is logically independent of the conjunction of p and q. (That is, the corresponding universal statement could be true if both 'p' and 'q' were false, or if 'q' were true and 'p' false, though not, of course if 'p' were true and 'q' false.) The state of affairs, q, is hypothetically-deductively heteroexplicable by way of the conjunction of p and the contingent natural law represented in the law-like universal statement "if p then q." If both the law and p were the actual and contingent states of the world then there would be an explanation for q's occurring, a heteroexplanation, an explanation by way of an independent state of affairs. Since p and q can be any two logically independent contingent states of affairs, it follows that every contingent state of affairs is heteroexplicable.

Notice that we are not claiming that there *is* actually a state of affairs involving an existent which can consistently be said to be the explanation of all contingent states of affairs—that would be inconsistent. We merely state that for any contingent but actual state of affairs it is logically consistent to say that there is some other state of affairs involving an existent, which is its explanation.

Again, all hypothetico-deductive explanations of contingent states of affairs are examples of heteroexplanation; since any contingent state of affairs is hypothetically-deductively explicable (provided that we will make wild enough law-like assumptions), it follows that every contingent state of affairs is heteroexplicable.

We therefore have two reasons, at least, for asserting premise (1) of the argument-schema: (*a*) that logical considerations disclose that it is *a priori* true; (*b*) that both the linguistic structure of discourse during and about inquiry and the way we think about contingent states of affairs require that we regard heteroexplicability as a logical consequence of contingency.

B. *Unproducibility and Heteroexplicability*

We can now turn to whether the fact that some thing, in virtue of *what* it is, has attributes which render its existence unproducible and unpreventable also excludes its existence from being heteroexplicable.

(1) Further examination of the assumption that *what* a thing is may render it unproducible and unpreventable, seems useful. The way I imagined the relation was illustrated with

the example of omnipotence—but this is only an example. For even though there may be a being whose omnipotence excludes its being producible or preventable, omnipotence is not a first-level property (a property which does not logically presuppose other properties or characteristics of the thing). Both "unproducibility" and "omnipotence" are *propria* in the technical sense of early logicians: they follow necessarily from the properties which are essential to the being which has them, but they are not its essence, nor, strictly speaking, essential to it; for instance, the capacity to laugh (risibility) was called a *proprium* of man because, although it follows necessarily from man's being a rational animal, and although there cannot be a man which does not have the property, it is not essential: an essential property or attribute is *both* necessary and *constitutive* of the thing. The essence, as Aquinas says, is that *a parte rei* which is signified by the definition. But not all necessary properties of a thing are given in its definition, only the attributes which are constitutive. A divine being is not constituted to be divine by its omnipotence; rather, its omnipotence is a consequence of its divinity.

This may be part of the reason some philosophers, like Aquinas, looked for a description of God which presupposed no other property to be attributed to God and entailed every other property which God is said to have by nature or necessarily. For instance, St. Thomas' description of God as *actus purus* and as *ipsum esse subsistens* (which are the same thing) was an attempt to describe (in a metaphysically general way) the first-level attribute of God which, if understood, would explain how God had by nature all and only the properties usually ascribed to Him.

A brief reconstruction of St. Thomas' reasoning may assist a reader unfamiliar with medieval metaphysics in grasping the idea which I also share but can explicate here only with such examples.

For Aquinas, act was contrasted with potency; act is the principle (or "origin") of nonlimitation, of realization, actuality, exercise, etc. with respect to a capacity; potency is the principle (or "origin") of limitation, of capacity (both passive and active) and relative nonbeing in comparison to act. Act is logically prior to potency: there can be no potency except in that which is otherwise in act, and no potency can be "reduced" to act (no capacity fulfilled or exercised) except through an agent in act. Act is also the principle (or "origin") of perfection; in fact "act" and "perfection" are logically equivalent (though not synonymous), just as potency and imperfection are equivalent.[7]

The positive attributes of things are called perfections. There are two kinds of perfections: those attributes which presuppose that the subject has some unfulfilled capacity or unexercised ability or some dependence upon external causes; these are limited or mixed perfections and are contrasted with the pure perfections. Pure perfections do not entail that the subject has an unfulfilled capacity, an unexercised ability, or any passive disposition at all to undergo alteration, and do not exclude any other attribute which satisfies those conditions; examples of pure perfections are: to be, to live, to know, to will, to be simple, to be eternal, to be omnipotent, to be omniscient, benevolent, omnipresent, good, etc.

A being in pure act (*actus purus*) is in no way in potency, having neither unfulfilled capacities to be or to become nor unexercised abilities or passive dispositions of any sort. It can have no predicate, therefore, which is not a pure perfection; for if it had a limited perfection, it would be in potentiality in some respect and, therefore, would not be wholly in act. Moreover, a being in pure act must have every pure perfection. This can be seen by our assuming that there is a being in pure act and that it lacks one or more pure perfections; we then derive a contradiction from those premises.

Assume that there is something *a* which is in pure act and has the pure perfections A through H but lacks K and L which are also pure perfections. Why does *a* lack K and L? It cannot be because of what *a* is, because pure perfections do not exclude one another; A–H does not exclude K and L. It cannot be that *a* lacks K and L because some external cause prevents *a*'s having K and L; for a being in pure act has no unfulfilled capacity to be or to become and to be *prevented* externally from having K or L would require that *a* be in potentiality to K or L. Hence, if *a* should lack K or L that state of affairs would be inexplicable by appeal to *what a* is and would be equally inexplicable by our postulating a preventing external cause. But any consistent state of affairs is in principle, at least, explicable. Hence it is not a consistent state of affairs that *a* would lack K or L. So, a being in pure act has all pure perfections—and it has them in virtue of its being in pure act which is its "first level" property, a property logically prior to and entailing each of its properties.

To determine which properties *a* has, one conducts a conceptual analysis of the predicates we ascribe to things in order to determine which satisfy the conditions for a pure perfection: they are all to be attributed to the being in pure act. That is how the elaborate list of divine predicates which we find in *Summa Theologica* can be derived from the metaphysicians' most general description of God; it is how the apparent *non sequitur* of St. Thomas' saying "and this is what everyone calls God" is shown to be justified.

Within Aquinas' metaphysical scheme a first-level property of God can be described from which the *propria* of God can be derived logically; that provides a way one can come to know *that* the *actus purus* is God. Moreover the unproducibility and unpreventability of God can be derived directly from that first-level property: *actus purus*. A being in pure act cannot be potential with respect to any other thing. It cannot have external causes because only composites, things with unfulfilled capacities, unexercised abilities, or passive dispositions can be externally caused to be or become; God cannot satisfy any of those conditions; therefore the being of God must be unproducible and unpreventable.

This discussion of Aquinas is not intended to persuade one that Aquinas was right or even satisfactory in his account of the being and nature of God, but only to illustrate what I mean by asserting that unproducibility and unpreventability are not first-level properties of a divine being but are the logical consequences of its essential (necessary *and* constitutive) attributes.

Moreover, this discussion of Aquinas should make clear that one does not have to rest much upon my example of omnipotence as a property which logically generates the unproducibility and unpreventability, because there are other attributes which will serve the same end. I do not pretend to have found a substitute for the family of basic metaphysical concepts which makes this derivation so easy within St. Thomas' terms; but one does not need a full-scale system of metaphysical discourse within which we can characterize the essence of God in order to make it plausible that unproducibility and unpreventability are not first-level properties but are derived and suitably characteristic properties of the being which is God. It appears that we have good *prima facie* evidence for accepting the assumption that *what*-a-thing-is can account for its being unproducible and unpreventable: that is, a being x, can be, because of *what x* it is, such that any statement of the form "There is a y ($y \neq x$) such that y produces x or prevents x from existing" is self-contradictory.

Reflection upon the theological metaphysics of Aquinas discloses that within his theoretical system unproducibility and unpreventability are logical consequences of his description of the divine nature. This theoretical system is just one example of the plentiful evidence within the theoretical discourse of Western religious speculation that God is to be regarded as a being which is unproducible and unpreventable through any agent or cause.

This view of the divine attributes is supported also by appeal to the ordinary religious discourse of religious believers, who are taught to regard the question "What produced God?" as an absurdity which discloses that its utterer is either not serious or is deficient in a grasp of *what* God is. When you ask a believer the more unfamiliar question "Do you think, granting that God does exist, that it *might* have happened that He did not?" he has difficulty grasping what you are asking; for he sees that, as he understands what God is, nothing could account for God's not existing; as a result, he cannot imagine the situation you inquire about. Appeals to ordinary discourse are, of course, only auxiliary in such cases as this, and serve only to reinforce the theoretical and historical evidence which indicates that it is appropriate to regard a divine being as a being which is unproducible and unpreventable and as a being which has prior properties from which those attributes are logical consequences. It is still a long step to justifying the claim that any unproducible and unpreventable being may be regarded as identical with God; it is not pretended that we shall do this and it is not necessary for one who sets out to show that the being which God is, exists.

(2) Now we can return to the question as to whether unproducibility and unpreventability exclude heteroexplicability. That this is so can be concluded from the fact that if a being is produced it is produced by another, and if it is prevented from being, it is prevented by another; and if it is heteroexplicable, it must be producible or preventable.

It is more convenient, perhaps, to regard production and prevention as relations among states of affairs; thus we speak of "its being produced or prevented that there is a being of a certain sort"; in this case, "that there is a being which has attributes which logically entail that its existing is unproducible and unpreventable." The contradiction inherent in the claim that such a state of affairs can be produced or prevented is evident.

When what is to be heteroexplained is the existence or nonexistence of something, there can be no other forms of explanation but prevention or production. How could some logically independent state of affairs, p, account for the actuality or nonactuality of some state of affairs q which *is* the state of affairs that a exists, unless p's being actual either brings it about or prevents its being so that q is actual? The existence or nonexistence of a thing is heteroexplicable only through states of affairs which cause or prevent it. It is, therefore, analytic that any state of affairs which is unproducible and unpreventable is not heteroexplicable.

c. *The Possibility of the Unproducible and Unpreventable*

Unfortunately, we cannot claim to have demonstrated step (4) of the argument. Some progress toward making the truth of the claim evident can be achieved, but the premise cannot be demonstrated because proofs of consistency are always relative to something which is presumed to be consistent and which can be questioned just on the ground that it leads to a proposition whose consistency is doubted. For example, the consistency of the proposition that there exists an unproducible and unpreventable being can be demonstrated if we are permitted to assume that it is consistent to say that there exists a being in pure act. But for a philosopher who doubts premise (4), the additional assumption will be even more suspect when it is found to yield the doubted premise (4) as a logical consequence. When we cannot prove the consistency of a proposition by producing the state of affairs it describes or confronting that state of affairs in experience, we have to acknowledge that there is no inherent terminus to a dispute about the consistency of the propositions in question.

Strategically, however, one can appeal to two other factors: (a) that centuries of discussion of the existence of God in terms closely resembling these have not resulted in the discovery of an inconsistency in the supposition that such a being exists; (b) that, as Duns Scotus pointed out, the propositions (i) every producer is produced; (ii) every chain of producers is infinite, and (iii) every producer is producible, are not thought to be necessarily true, are not thought to have self-contradictory negations; therefore, the hypothesis that there is a first unproducible producer is consistent.

III. "HOC EST QUOD OMNES VOCANT DEUM"?

Many philosophers, even those sympathetic to religion, think proofs for the existence of God will, no matter how carefully conceived and executed, inevitably founder, not necessarily upon the first and existential step, but upon the identificatory step; especially, they believe that it is a long and logically unassisted leap from the existence of some unproducible and unpreventable being (which might be the world as a whole or some evil demon, for all that has been shown) to saying "*hoc est quod omnes vocant Deum.*" The predicates involved in our ordinary concept of God exceed in logical content those predicates which are employed in the proof of existence, whether it be one of the classical arguments or a modal argument. In fact, if an *a priori* argument of the Hartshorne variety is employed, using a predicate like "a perfect being," and if certain assumptions about the necessity that such a being should be in process are attached to that notion, then a great number of religious believers will deny that the existence of God has been proved or even that the existence of the being which is God has been proved—because the description in terms of which the proof is constructed is incompatible with what these believers take God to be.

Metaphorically, we can say that the description of God is the "middle term" of the demonstration, it is that upon which the claim that it is God whose existence has been proved, pivots. (*i*) If the description is too thin, too limited in the list of predicates involved, there will be no ground for concluding that it is God whose existence has been proved, but only for saying that the existence of some being has been proved and that this being could, for all that is known so far, be God. (*ii*) If the description is too rich (and, some would think, Hartshorne's metaphysically baggaged concept of perfection is), it will be denied that it is a proof of God's existence because what it claims to exist is something with quite different properties which exclude the existence of God as God has traditionally been conceived.

Moreover, when the description is "rich," it is important to determine whether the intermediary premises and logical form of the argument justify one's allowing the entire description to appear in the conclusion. For instance, if I began the brief modal argument stated above with a description of the form "God is an uncausable, unpreventable, omniscient, omnipotent, benevolent, eternal being," and then in the conclusion asserted that God exists, it could rightly be objected that while I had proved the existence of something uncausable and unpreventable I had not proved the existence of such a being *and* that it is also omniscient, omnipotent, benevolent, and eternal; it therefore remains an open question as to whether the existence of a being *which* is uncausable, unpreventable, omniscient, omnipotent, benevolent, and eternal has been proved. That question cannot be settled without an additional argument which will show that if a being is uncausable and unpreventable it has those other properties.

The identificatory stage of proof of the existence of God encounters difficulty in relation to the elaborateness of one's metaphysical system. For instance, as I showed above, it was very easy for St. Thomas to go from the assertion that there exists a being which is in pure act to the conclusion that there is a being which, without any limitation at all, exists, lives, thinks, loves, chooses, and is therefore simple, eternal, good, omniscient, omnipotent, etc.

Without a metaphysical system to allow me to pass from the narrow group of predicates used in the proof of existence to the wider group used in the identification with God, it is very difficult to justify claiming that one has proved the existence of God (no matter how good the existential argument actually given may be); it is more nearly correct to say that one has established the existence of a being which may be God and, unless the world is quite different from the way we have imagined it, can only be God.

Even with a metaphysical system to allow one to pass from the existential to the identificatory stages of proof, strange things can happen which result in the falsity of the principle "but this is what everyone calls God." For instance, if one accepts Hartshorne's basic metaphysics of process, omnipotence is not power over all contingent states of affairs, exercised immediately and entirely (as I described it above). It is power over all beings, and power to have all things as objects of knowledge. In this system it will turn out that omnipotence is not what it is in the modernized-Scotist framework I employed above; yet both interpretations of the predicate will be compatible with the orthodox Christian religious talk about God as almighty. Still, one of us must be mistaken; there certainly cannot be two Gods, one as I describe Him and one as Hartshorne does. The disagreement arises from the way we understand and define different divine attributes in relation to the overall metaphysical framework in which we speak of necessity, contingency, explanation, perfection, power, knowledge, and goodness. The difference about God can be traced to differences which are more general.

Furthermore, in order to identify the being whose existence is established with God, the various predicates to be attributed to it must be analyzed. That process requires that what is indefinite in ordinary religious discourse concerning God's knowledge, power, will, and moral quality must be made determinate by way of theoretical considerations, some of them, as in Hartshorne's case, being the result of very general metaphysical hypotheses about the whole universe. (This was true of

Aquinas too, of course.) A religious believer may be quite surprised when he finds out what is involved in the attributes which are predicated of the basic existent in order to justify calling it God. Moreover, since the ordinary religious concept-set is incomplete and indeterminate, a theoretical establishment of the existence of God cannot escape a certain amount of legislation; with the result that there can be competing "proofs" of the existence of God which differ radically at the identificatory stage in their conceptions of the divine attributes. (I would imagine that this difference would be quite obvious between Hartshorne's theory and mine.)

Now, if my assumption is correct that one cannot pass from the existential to the identificatory phase of proving the existence of God without employing background metaphysical concepts, then the identification of a being whose existence has been proved with God will not itself be an object of demonstration but will also presuppose the justification of the metaphysical system as a whole. This suggests that because of the uneliminable element of legislation involved, we shall have to say that there cannot be a proof that any given existent is God; at best there can be a probable argument. That there can be a proof of the existence of a being which is God, I have no doubt; that we can *show* that such a being is God does not seem likely when it is God as conceived by religious believers (rather than metaphysicians) who is to be identified.

NOTES

1. Cf. my *Philosophical Theology* (New York: Bobbs-Merrill, 1969), Chapter 1, where these matters are argued in detail.

2. These points and a number of related points have, I think, been successfully argued by George I. Mavrodes in *The Concept of a Direct Experience of God* [University of Michigan Ph.D. thesis] (Ann Arbor, Michigan: University Microfilms, 1962).

3. There is nothing wrong with our speaking of the various proofs *for* the existence of God and denying that they are proofs of the existence of God. For to say of A "A is a proof for *p*" is to say that A purports to be a proof *that p* or a proof of 'p'. The standard arguments do not succeed in establishing their conclusions, though that is surely what they are *for*.

4. For instance, St. Thomas uses the argument from order in the world *ten* times (in slightly different formulations). They are (as determined by Fr. Jules Baisnée): "*In II Sent*; D. I., q. 1, ar. 1; *De Veritate*, q.V,a. 2; *Contra Gentiles*, I, 13 and 44; II, 43; *De Potentia Dei*, q. III, a. 6; *Summa Theologica*, I, q. 2

a.3; *In 12 Metaphysicorum,* lect. 12; *In Evangelium S. Joannis, Prologus;* *Super Symbolorum Apostolorum,* a. 1." St. Thomas offers seven formulations of the Argument based upon motion, five formulations of the argument *"ex gradibus perfectionis,"* four formulations of the contingency argument, three versions of the argument from the plurality of things, etc. A great deal of additional information on the various formulations of the arguments and their correlation with various periods of St. Thomas' life is to be found in the paper "St. Thomas Aquinas' Proofs of the Existence of God Presented in their Chronological Order" by Jules A. Baisnée, s.s., in *Philosophical Studies in Honor of Ignatius Smith,* ed. John K. Ryan (Westminster, Md., 1951).

5. Cf. Chapter III, *Philosophical Theology.*

6. Part III develops this further.

7. The pairs of terms are not synonymous because the members have partly different connotations which derive from the nontheoretical contexts from which the terms were extended to their theoretical uses.

Two Criticisms of the Cosmological Argument

WILLIAM L. ROWE

Purdue University

IN THIS PAPER I WISH TO CONSIDER TWO MAJOR CRITICISMS which have been advanced against the Cosmological Argument for the existence of God, criticisms which many philosophers regard as constituting a decisive refutation of that argument. Before stating and examing these objections it will be helpful to have before us a version of the Cosmological Argument. The Cosmological Argument has two distinct parts. The first part is an argument to establish the existence of a necessary being. The second part is an argument to establish that this necessary being is God. The two objections I shall consider are directed against the first part of the Cosmological Argument. Using the expression "dependent being" to mean "a being which has the reason for its existence in the causal

Reprinted from *The Monist,* 54 No. 3 (1970), LaSalle, Illinois, with the permission of the publishers and the author.

efficacy or nature of some other being," and the expression "independent being" to mean "a being which has the reason for its existence within its own nature," we may state the argument for the existence of a necessary being as follows:

1. Every being is either a dependent being or an independent being; therefore,
2. Either there exists an independent being or every being is dependent;
3. It is false that every being is dependent; therefore,
4. There exists an independent being; therefore,
5. There exists a necessary being.

This argument consists of two premises—propositions (1) and (3)—and three inferences. The first inference is from (1) to (2), the second from (2) and (3) to (4), and the third inference is from (4) to (5). Of the premises neither is obviously true, and of the inferences only the first and second are above suspicion. Before discussing the main subject of this paper—the reasoning in support of proposition (3) and the two major objections which have been advanced against that reasoning—I want to say something about the other questionable parts of the argument; namely, proposition (1) and the inference from (4) to (5).

Proposition (1) expresses what we may call the strong form of the Principle of Sufficient Reason. It insists not only that those beings which begin to exist must have a cause or explanation (the weak form of the Principle of Sufficient Reason) but that absolutely every being must have an explanation of its existing rather than not existing—the explanation lying either within the causal efficacy of some other being or within the thing's own nature. In an earlier paper I examined this Principle in some detail.[1] The objections I wish to consider in this paper are, I believe, independent of the Principle of Sufficient Reason. That is, these objections are meant to refute the argument even if the first premise is true. This being so, it will facilitate our examination of these two objections if we take proposition (1) as an unquestioned premise throughout our discussion. Accordingly, in this paper proposition (1) will function as an axiom in our reasoning. This, of course, should not be taken as implying that I think the first premise of the argument is true.

The inference from proposition (4) to proposition (5) is not considered in this paper. Indeed, for purposes of this paper we could have ended the statement of the argument with proposition (4). I have included the inference from (4) to (5) simply because it is an important element in the first part of the Cosmological Argument. Proposition (4) asserts the existence of a being which has the reason or explanation of its existence within its own nature. Proposition (5) asserts the existence of a necessary being. By "a necessary being" is meant a being whose nonexistence is a logical impossibility.[2] Many philosophers have argued that it is logically impossible for there to be a necessary being in this sense of "necessary being." Hence, even if the two objections I shall examine in this paper can be met, the defender of the Cosmological Argument must still face objections not only to the inference from (4) to (5) but to (5) itself. But again, this is a matter which I shall not pursue in this paper. Unlike proposition (1), however, which I treat as an unquestioned assumption, neither proposition (5) nor the inference from (4) to (5) will be appealed to in this paper. In what follows we may simply ignore that part of the argument. Indeed, our attention will be focused entirely on proposition (3), the reasoning which supports it, and the two major criticisms which have been advanced against that reasoning.

Proposition (3) asserts that it is false that every being is dependent. For what reasons? Well, if every being which exists (or ever existed) is dependent, then the whole of existing things, it would seem, consists of a collection of dependent beings, that is, a collection of beings each member of which exists by reason of the causal efficacy of some other being. This collection would have to contain an infinite number of numbers. For suppose it contained a finite number, let us say three, *a*, *b*, and *c*. Now if in Scotus' phrase "a circle of causes is inadmissible" then if *c* is caused by *b* and *b* by *a*, *a* would exist without a cause, there being no other member of the collection that could be its cause. But in that case *a* would not be what by supposition it is, namely a *dependent* being. Hence, if we grant that a circle of causes is inadmissible it is impossible that the whole of existing things should consist of a collection of dependent beings *finite* in number.

Suppose, then, that the dependent beings making up the collection are infinite in number. Why is it impossible that the whole of existing things should consist of such a collection? The proponent of the Cosmological Argument answers as follows.[3] The infinite collection *itself*, he argues, requires an explanation of its existence. For since it is true of each member of the collection that it might not have existed, it is true of the whole infinite collection that it might not have existed. But if the entire infinite collection might not have existed there must be some explanation of why it exists rather than not. The explanation cannot lie in the causal efficacy of some being outside of the collection since by supposition the collection includes every being which is or ever was. Nor can the explanation of why there is an infinite collection be found within the collection itself, for since no member of the collection is independent, has the reason of its existence within itself, the collection as a whole cannot have the reason of its existence within itself. Thus the conception of an infinite collection of dependent beings is the conception of something whose existence has no explanation whatever. But since premise (1) tells us that whatever exists has an explanation for its existence, either within itself or in the causal efficacy of some other being, it cannot be that the whole of existing things consists of an infinite collection of dependent beings.

The reasoning developed here is exhibited as follows:

1. If every being is dependent then the whole of existing things consists of an infinite collection of dependent beings;
2. If the whole of existing things consists of an infinite collection of dependent beings then the infinite collection itself must have an explanation of its existence;
3. If the existence of the infinite collection of dependent beings has an explanation then the explanation must lie either in the causal efficacy of some being outside the collection or it must lie within the infinite collection itself;
4. The explanation of the existence of the infinite collection of dependent beings cannot lie in the causal efficacy of some being outside the collection;

5. The explanation of the existence of the infinite collection of dependent beings cannot lie within the collection itself; therefore,

6. There is no explanation of the infinite collection of dependent beings (from 3, 4, and 5); therefore,

7. It is false that the whole of existing things consists of an infinite collection of dependent beings (from 2 and 6); therefore,

8. It is false that every being is dependent (from 1 and 7).

Perhaps every premise in this argument is open to criticism. I propose here, however, to consider what I regard as the two major criticisms advanced against this reasoning in support of proposition (3) of the main argument. The first of these criticisms may be construed as directed against premise (2) of the above argument. According to this criticism it *makes no sense* to apply the notion of cause or explanation to the totality of things, and the arguments used to show that the whole of existing things must have a cause or explanation are *fallacious*. Thus in his B.B.C. debate with Father Copleston, Bertrand Russell took the view that the concept of cause is inapplicable to the universe conceived of as the total collection of things. When pressed by Copleston as to how he could rule out "the legitimacy of asking the question how the total, or anything at all comes to be there," Russell responded: "I can illustrate what seems to me your fallacy. Every man who exists has a mother, and it seems to me your argument is that therefore the human race must have a mother, but obviously the human race hasn't a mother—that's a different logical sphere."[4]

The second major criticism is directed at premise (5). According to this criticism it is *intelligible* to ask for an explanation of the existence of the infinite collection of dependent beings. But the answer to this question, so the criticism goes, is provided once we learn that each member of the infinite collection has an explanation of its existence. Thus Hume remarks: "Did I show you the particular causes of each individual in a collection of twenty particles of matter, I should think it very unreasonable, should you afterwards ask me, what was the cause of the whole twenty. This is sufficiently explained in explaining the cause of the parts."[5]

These two criticisms express the major reasons philosophers have given for rejecting what undoubtedly is the most important part of the Cosmological Argument—namely, that portion of the argument which seeks to establish that not every being can be a dependent being. In this paper my aim is to defend the Cosmological Argument against both of these criticisms. I shall endeavor to show that each of these criticisms rests on a philosophical mistake.

The first criticism draws attention to what appears to be a fatal flaw in the Cosmological Argument. It seems that the proponent of the argument (*i*) ascribes to the infinite collection itself a property (having a cause or explanation) which is applicable only to the members of that collection, and (*ii*) does so by means of a fallacious inference from a proposition about the members of the collection to a proposition about the collection itself. There are, then, two alleged mistakes committed here. The first error is, perhaps, a category mistake—the ascription to the collection of a property applicable only to the members of the collection. As Russell would say, the collection, in comparison with its members, belongs to a "different logical sphere." The second error is apparently what leads the proponent of the Cosmological Argument to make the first error. He ascribes the property of having an explanation to the infinite collection because he *infers* that the infinite collection must have a cause or explanation from the premise that each of its members has a cause. But to infer this, Russell suggests, is as fallacious as to infer that the human race must have a mother because each member of the human race has a mother.

That the proponent of the Cosmological Argument ascribes the property of having a cause or explanation to the infinite collection of dependent beings is certainly true. That to do so is a category mistake is, I think, questionable. But before pursuing this point I want to deal with the second charge. The main question we must consider in connection with the second charge is whether the Cosmological Argument involves the inference: Every member of the infinite collection has an explanation of its existence; therefore, the infinite collection itself has an explanation of its existence. As we have seen, Russell thinks that Copleston has employed this inference in coming to the conclusion that there must be an explanation for the totality of things, and not simply for each of the things making up that totality.

Perhaps some proponents of the Cosmological Argument have used the argument which Russell regards as fallacious. But not all of them have.[6] Moreover, there is no need to employ such an inference since in its first premise the Cosmological Argument has available a principle from which it follows that the infinite collection of dependent beings must have an explanation of its existence. Thus one famous exponent of the argument—Samuel Clarke—reasons that the infinite collection of beings must have an explanation of its existence by appealing to the strong form of the Principle of Sufficient Reason. The principle assures us that whatever exists has an explanation of its existence. But if there exists an infinite succession or collection of dependent beings then that collection or succession, Clarke reasons, must have an explanation of its existence. Hence, we can, I think, safely dismiss the charge that the Cosmological Argument involves an erroneous inference from the premise that the members of a collection have a certain property to the conclusion that the collection itself must have that property.

We must now deal with the question whether it makes *sense* to ascribe the property of having an explanation or cause to the infinite collection of dependent beings. Clearly only if it does make sense is the reasoning in support of proposition (3) of the main argument acceptable. Our question, then, is whether it makes sense to ask for a cause or explanation of the entire universe, conceiving the universe as an infinite collection of dependent beings.

One recent critic of the Cosmological Argument, Ronald Hepburn, has stated our problem as follows:

When we are seriously speaking of absolutely everything there is, are we speaking of something that requires a cause, in the way that events *in* the universe may require causes? What indeed can be safely said at all about the totality of things? For a great many remarks that one can make with perfect propriety about limited things quite obviously can*not* be made about the cosmos itself. It cannot, for instance, be said meaningfully to be "above" or "below" anything, although things-in-the-universe can be so related to one another. Whatever we might claim to be "*below* the universe" would turn out to be just some more *universe*. We should have been relating part to part, instead of relating the whole to something not-the-universe. The same applies to "outside the universe." We can readily imagine a boundary, a garden wall, shall we say, round something that we want to call the universe. But if we imagine ourselves boring a hole through that wall and pushing a stick out *beyond* it into a nameless zone "outside," we should still not in fact have given meaning to the phrase "outside the universe." For the place into which the stick was intruding would deserve to be called a part of the universe (even if consisting of empty space, no matter) just as much as the area within the walls. We should have demonstrated *not* that the universe has an outside, but that what we took to be the whole universe was not really the whole.

Our problem is this. Supposing we could draw up a list of questions that can be asked about objects in the universe, but cannot be asked about the *whole* universe: would the question, 'Has it a cause?' be on that list? One thing is clear. Whether or not this question is on the proscribed list, we are not entitled to argue as the Cosmological Argument does that *because* things in the world have causes, therefore the sum of things must also have *its* cause. No more (as we have just seen) can we argue from the fact that things in the world have tops and bottoms, insides and outsides, and are related to other things, to the belief that the universe has its top and bottom, inside and outside, and is related to a supra-cosmical something.[7]

In this passage Hepburn (*i*) points out that some properties (e.g., "above," "below," etc.) of things in the universe cannot properly be ascribed to the total universe, (*ii*) raises the question whether "having a cause" is such a property, and (*iii*) concludes that ". . . we are not entitled to argue as the Cosmological Argument does that *because* things in the world have causes, therefore, the sum of things must also have *its* cause." We noted earlier that the Cosmological Argument (i.e., the version we are examining) does not argue that the sum of things (the infinite collection of dependent beings) must have a cause *because* each being in the collection has a cause. Thus we may safely ignore Hepburn's main objection. However, his other two points are well taken. There certainly are properties which it makes sense to apply to things within a collection but which it makes no sense to apply to the collection itself. What assurance do we have that "having a cause" is not such a property?

Suppose we are holding in our hands a collection of ten marbles. Not only would each marble have a definite weight but the collection itself would have a weight. Indeed, from the premise that each marble weighs more than one ounce we could infer validly that the collection itself weighs more than an ounce. This example shows that it is not always fallacious to infer that a collection has a certain property from the premise that each member of the collection has that property.[8] But the collection in this example is, we might say, *concrete* rather than *abstract*. That is, we are here considering the collection as itself a physical entity, an aggregate of marbles. This, of course, is not a collection in the sense of a class or set of things. Holding several marbles in my hands I can consider the *set* whose members are those marbles. The set itself, being an *abstract* entity, rather than a physical heap, has no weight. Just as the set of human beings has no mother, so the set whose members are marbles in my hand has no weight. Therefore, in considering whether it makes sense to speak of the infinite collection of dependent beings as having a cause or explanation of its existence it is important to decide whether we are speaking of a collection as a *concrete* entity—for example, a physical whole or aggregate—or an *abstract* entity.

Suppose we view the infinite collection of dependent beings as itself a concrete entity. As far as the Cosmological Argument is concerned, one advantage of so viewing it is that it is understandable why it might have the property of having a cause or explanation of its existence. For concrete entities— physical objects, events, physical heaps—can be caused. Thus if the infinite collection is a concrete entity it may well make sense to ascribe to it the property of having a cause or explanation.

But such a view of the infinite collection is implausible, if not plainly incorrect. Many collections of physical things cannot possibly be themselves concrete entities. Think, for example, of the collection whose members are the largest prehistoric beast, Socrates, and the Empire State Building. By any stretch of the imagination can we view this collection as itself a concrete thing? Clearly we cannot. Such a collection must be construed as an *abstract* entity, a class or set.[9] But if there are many collections of beings which cannot be concrete entities, what grounds have we for thinking that on the supposition that every being that is or ever was is dependent the collection of those beings would itself be a concrete thing such as a physical heap? At any rate our knowledge of the things (both past and present) comprising the universe and their interrelations would have to be much greater than it currently is before we would be entitled to view the *sum* of concrete things, past and present, as itself something *concrete*.

But if the infinite collection of dependent beings is to be understood as an abstract entity, say the set whose members include all the beings that are or ever were, haven't we conceded the point to Russell? A set or class conceived of as an abstract entity has no weight, is not below or above anything, and cannot be thought of as being caused or brought into being. Thus if the infinite collection is a set, an abstract entity, is not Russell right in charging that it makes no more sense to ascribe the property of having a cause or an explanation to the infinite collection than it does to ascribe the property of having a mother to the human race?

Suppose that every being that is or ever was is dependent. Suppose further that the number of such beings is infinite. Let A be the set consisting of these beings. Thus no being exists or ever existed which is not a member of A. Does it make *sense* to ask for an explanation of A's existence? We do, of course, ask questions about sets which are equivalent to questions about their members. For example, "Is set X included in set Y?" is equivalent to the question "Is every member of X a member of Y?" I suggest that the question "Why does A exist?" be taken to mean "Why does A have the members that it does rather than some other members or none at all?" Consider, for example, the set of men. Let M be this set. The question "Why does M exist?" is perhaps odd if we understand it as a request for an explanation of the existence of an abstract entity. But the question "Why does M exist?" may be taken to mean "Why does M have the members it has rather than some other members or none at all?" So understood the form of words "Why does M exist?" does, I think, ask an intelligible question. It is a contingent fact that Hitler existed. Indeed, it is a contingent fact that any men exist at all. One of Leibniz' logically possible worlds is a world which includes some members of M, for example Socrates and Plato, but not others, say Hitler and Stalin. Another is a world in which the set of men is entirely empty and therefore identical with the null set.

Why is it, then, that M exists? That is, why does M have just the members it has rather than some other members or none at all? Not only is this question intelligible but we seem to have some idea of what its answer is. Presumably, the theory of evolution might be a part of the explanation of why M is not equivalent to the null set and why its members have certain properties rather than others.

But if the question "Why does M exist?" makes sense, why should not the question "Why does A exist?" also make sense? A is the set of dependent beings. In asking why A exists we are not asking for an explanation of the existence of an abstract entity; we are asking why A has the members it has rather than some other members or none at all. I submit that this question does make sense. Moreover, I think that it is precisely this question which the proponents of the Cosmological Argument were asking when they asked for an explanation of the existence of the infinite collection or succession of dependent beings.[10] Of course, it is one thing for a question to make sense and another thing for there to be an answer to it.

The interpretation I have given to the question "Why does A exist?" is somewhat complex. For according to this interpretation what is being asked is not simply why does A have members rather than having none, but also why does A have just the members it has rather than having some other members. Although the proponents of the Cosmological Argument do seem to interpret the question in this way, it will facilitate our discussion if we simplify the interpretation somewhat by focusing our attention solely on the question why A has the members it has rather than having none. Hence, for purposes of simplification, in what follows I shall take the question "Why does A exist?" to mean "Why does A have the members it has rather than not having any?"

For any being to be a member of A it is necessary and sufficient that it have the reason of its existence in the causal efficacy of some other being. Imagine the following state of affairs. A has exactly three members: a_1, a_2, and a_3. a_3 exists by reason of the causal efficacy of a_2, and a_2 exists by reason of the causal efficacy of a_1. There exists an *eternal* being b which does not exist by reason of the causal efficacy of any other being. Since b is not a dependent being, b is not a member of A. At a certain time a_1 came into existence by reason of the causal efficacy of b. Clearly the question "Why does A exist?" when taken to mean "Why does A have the members it has rather than none at all?" makes sense when asked within the context of this imagined state of affairs. Indeed, part of the answer to the question would involve reference to b and its causal efficacy in bringing about the existence of one of the members of A, namely a_1.

What this case shows is that the question "Why does A exist?" is not always (i.e., in every context) meaningless. If Russell holds that the question is meaningless in the framework of the Cosmological Argument it must be because of some special assumption about A which forms part of the context of the Cosmological Argument. The assumption in question undoubtedly is that absolutely every being is dependent. On this assumption every being which is or ever was has membership in A and A has an infinite number of members.

Perhaps Russell's view is that within the context of the assumption that *every* being is dependent it makes no sense to ask why A has the members it has rather than none at all. It makes no sense, he might argue, for two reasons. First, on the assumption that every being is dependent there could not be such a thing as the *set* A whose members are all dependent beings. For the set A is, although abstract, presumably a being. But if every being is dependent then A would have to be dependent and therefore a member of itself. But apart from whatever difficulties arise when a set is said to be a member of itself, it would seem to make little sense to think of an abstract entity, such as a set, as being caused, as having the reason of its existence within the causal efficacy of some other being.

Second, Russell might argue that the assumption that every being is dependent and therefore a member of A rules out the possibility of any answer to the question why A has the members it has rather than none at all. For on that assumption our question about A is in effect a question about the totality of things. And, as Russell observes, "I see no reason whatsoever to suppose that the total has any cause whatsoever."[11]

Neither of these reasons suffices to show that our question about A is meaningless. The first reason does, however, point up the necessity of introducing some restriction on the assumption "Every being is dependent" in order that abstract entities like numbers and sets not fall within the scope of the expression "Every being." Such a restriction will obviate the difficulty that A is said to be both a member of itself and dependent. I propose the following rough restriction. In speaking of beings we shall restrict ourselves to beings that *could be caused* to exist by some other being or *could be causes* of the existence of other beings. God (if he exists), a man, the sun, a stone are beings of this sort. Presumably, numbers, sets, and the like are not. The assumption that every being is dependent is to be understood under this restriction. That is, we are here assuming that every being of the sort described by the restriction is *in fact* a being which exists by reason of the causal efficacy of some other being. The second reason given confuses the issue of whether a question makes sense, is meaningful, with the issue of whether a question has an answer. Of course, given the assumption that every being is a member of A we cannot expect to find the cause or reason of A's existence in some being which is not a member of A. If the explanation for A's existence cannot be found within A itself then we must conclude that there can be no explanation for the infinite collection of dependent beings. But this is to say only that on our assumption that every being is dependent there is no answer to the question "Why does A exist?" It is one thing for a question not to have an answer and quite another thing for the question to be *meaningless*.

We have been examining the first of the two major criticisms philosophers have directed at the reasoning the Cosmological Argument provides in support of the proposition that not every being is dependent. The heart of this criticism is that it *makes no sense* to ascribe the property of having a cause or explanation to the infinite collection of dependent beings. This criticism, I think, has been shown to be correct in one way, but incorrect in another. If we construe the infinite collection of dependent beings as an abstract entity, a set, it perhaps does not make sense to claim that something caused the existence of this abstract entity. But the question "Why does A exist?" may be interpreted to mean "Why does A have the members it has rather than none at all?" I have argued that taken in this way the question "Why does A exist?" is a *meaningful* question.

According to the Principle of Sufficient Reason there must be an answer to the question "Why does A exist?," an explanation of the existence of the infinite collection of dependent beings. Moreover, the explanation either must lie in the causal efficacy of some being outside of the collection or it must lie within the collection itself. But since by supposition every being is dependent—and therefore in the collection—there is no being outside the collection whose causal efficacy might explain the existence of the collection. Therefore, either the collection has the explanation of its existence within itself *or* there can be no explanation of its existence. If the first alternative is rejected then, since the Principle of Sufficient Reason requires that everything has an explanation of its existence, we must reject the supposition that every being is dependent. For on that supposition there is no explanation for why there is an infinite collection of dependent beings.

The second major criticism argues that the proponent of the Cosmological Argument is mistaken in thinking that the explanation of the existence of the infinite collection cannot be found within the collection itself. The explanation of the existence of the collection is provided, so the criticism goes, once we learn what the explanation is of each of the members of the collection. As we noted earlier, this criticism was succinctly expressed by Hume in his remark: "Did I show you the particular causes of each individual in a collection of twenty particles of matter, I should think it very unreasonable, should you afterwards ask me, what was the cause of the whole twenty. This is sufficiently explained in explaining the cause of the parts." Applying this objection to the infinite collection of dependent beings, we obtain the result that to explain the existence of the infinite collection, A, amounts to no more than explaining the existence of each of its members. Now, of course, A is unlike Hume's collection of twenty particles in that we cannot give *individual* explanations for each of the members of A. For since A has an infinite number of members we would have to give an infinite number of explanations. But our inability to give a particular explanation for each of the members of A does not imply that there is any member of A for whose existence there is no explanation. Indeed, from the fact that each member of A is dependent (i.e., has the reason of its existence in the causal efficacy of some other being), we know that every member of A has an explanation of its existence; from the assumption that every being is a member of A we know that for each member of A the explanation lies in the causal efficacy of some other member of A. But, so the criticism goes, if every member of A has an explanation of its existence then the existence of A has been sufficiently explained. For to explain why a certain collection of things exists it is sufficient to explain the existence of each of its members. Hence, since we know that the existence of every one of A's members is explained we know that the existence of the collection A is explained.

This forceful criticism, originally advanced by Hume, has gained wide acceptance in contemporary philosophy. Indeed, the only remaining problem seems to be to explain why the proponents of the Cosmological Argument failed to see that to explain the existence of all the members of a collection is to explain the existence of the collection. In restating Hume's criticism, Paul Edwards suggests that perhaps they may have been misled by grammar.

> The demand to find the cause of the series as a whole rests on the erroneous assumption that the series is something over and above the members of which it is composed. It is tempting to suppose this, at least by implication, because the word "series" is a noun like "dog" or "man." Like the expression "this dog" or "this man" the phrase "this series" is easily taken to designate an individual object. But reflection shows this to be an error. If we have explained the individual members there is nothing additional left to be explained. Suppose I see a group of five Eskimos standing on the corner of Sixth Avenue and 50th Street and I wish to explain why the group came to New York. Investigation reveals the following stories:
> Eskimo No. 1 did not enjoy the extreme cold in the polar region and decided to move to a warmer climate.
> No. 2 is the husband of Eskimo No. 1. He loves her dearly and did not wish to live without her.
> No. 3 is the son of Eskimos 1 and 2. He is too small and too weak to oppose his parents.
> No. 4 saw an advertisement in the *New York Times* for an Eskimo to appear on television.

No. 5 is a private detective engaged by the Pinkerton Agency to keep an eye on Eskimo No. 4.

Let us assume that we have now explained in the case of each of the five Eskimos why he or she is in New York. Somebody then asks: "All right, but what about the group as a whole; why is *it* in New York?" This would plainly be an absurd question. There is no group over and above the five members, and if we have explained why each of the five members is in New York we have *ipso facto* explained why the group is there. It is just as absurd to ask for the cause of the series as a whole as distinct from asking for the causes of the individual members.[12]

The principle underlying the Hume–Edwards criticism may be stated as follows: *If the existence of every member of a set is explained the existence of that set is thereby explained.* This principle seems to be a corollary of our interpretation of the question "Why does this set exist?" For on our interpretation, once it is explained why the set has the members it has rather than none at all it is thereby explained why the set exists. And it would seem that if a set A has, say, three members, a_1, a_2, and a_3, then if we explain the existence of a_1, a_2, and a_3 we have explained why A has the members it has rather than none at all. Thus the principle which underlies the second major criticism seems to be implied by our conception of what is involved in explaining the existence of a set.

The principle underlying the Hume–Edwards criticism seems plausible enough when restricted to finite sets, i.e., sets with a finite number of members. But the principle is false, I believe, when extended to infinite sets in which the explanation of each member's existence is found in the causal efficacy of some other member. Consider M, the set of men. Suppose M consists of an infinite number of members, each member owing its existence to some other member which generated it. Suppose further that to explain the existence of a given man it is sufficient to note that he was begotten by some other man. That is, where x and y are men and x begat y we allow that the existence of y is explained by the causal efficacy of x. On these suppositions it is clear that the antecedent of the principle is satisfied with respect to M. For every member of M has an explanation of its existence. But does it follow that the existence of M has an explanation? I think not. We do not have an explanation of the existence of M until we have an explanation of why M has the members it has rather than none at all. But clearly if *all* we know is that there always have been men and that every man's existence is explained by the causal efficacy of some other man, we do not know *why* there always have been men rather than none at all. If I ask why M has the members it has rather than none, it is no answer to say that M always had members. We may, I suppose, answer the question "Why does M have the *currently existing* members it has?" by saying that M always had members and there were men who generated the currently existing men. But in asking why M has the members it has rather than none at all we are not asking why M has the currently existing members it has. To make this clear, we may rephrase our question as follows: "Why is it that M has now and always had members rather than never having had any members at all?" Surely we have not learned the answer to this question when we have learned that there always have been members of M and that each member's existence is explained by the causal efficacy of some other member.

What we have just seen is that from the fact that the existence of each member of a collection is explained it does not follow that the existence of the collection is thereby explained. It does not follow because when the collection (set) has an infinite number of members, each member's existence having its explanation in the causal efficacy of *some other member,* it is true that the existence of every member has an explanation, and yet it is still an open question whether the existence of the set has an explanation. To explain the existence of a set we must explain why it has the members it has rather than none. But clearly if every member's existence is explained by some other *member,* then although the existence of every member has an explanation it is still unexplained why the set has the members it has, rather than none at all.

Put somewhat differently, we have seen that the fact (assuming for the moment that it is a fact) that there always have been men, each man's existence brought about by some other man, is insufficient to explain *why* it is a fact that there always have been men rather than a fact that there never have been any men. If someone asks us to explain why there always have been men rather than never having been any it would not suffice for us to observe that there always have been men and each man has been brought into existence by some other man.

I have argued that the second major criticism rests on a false principle, namely, that if the existence of every member of a set is explained then the existence of that set is thereby explained. This principle, so far as I can determine, is true when restricted to sets with a *finite* number of members. For example, if a set A has two members, a_1 and a_2, and if we explain a_2 by a_1 and a_1 by some being b that caused a_1, then, I think, we have explained the existence of A. In any case we have explained why A has members rather than none at all. Thus I am not claiming that the principle underlying Hume's objection is always false. Indeed, as I have just indicated, it is easy to provide an example of a finite set of which the principle is true. And perhaps it is just this feature of the principle— i.e., its plausibility when applied to finite sets such as Hume's collection of twenty particles and Edwards' five Eskimos— which has led Hume and many philosophers since Hume to reject the Cosmological Argument's thesis that even if every member of the infinite succession of dependent beings has an explanation the infinite succession itself is not thereby explained. If so, then the mistake Hume and his successors have made is to assume that a principle which is true of all finite sets also is true of all infinite sets.

We know, for example, that if we have a set B consisting of five members and a set C consisting of three of the members of B, the members of C cannot be put in one-to-one correspondence with those of B. In reflecting on this fact, we are tempted to conclude that for *any* two sets X and Y, if all the members of X are members of Y but some members of Y are not members of X then the members of X cannot be put in one-to-one correspondence with those of Y. Indeed, so long as X and Y are restricted to *finite* sets the principle just stated is true. But if we let X be the set of *even* natural numbers—2, 4, 6, . . . —and Y be the set of natural numbers—1, 2, 3, . . . —the principle is shown to be false. For although all the members of X are members of Y and some members of Y—the odd integers—are not members of X, it is not true that the members of X cannot be put in one-to-one correspondence with those of Y. What this example illustrates is that a principle which holds of all finite sets may not hold of all infinite sets. The principle underlying the second major criticism is, I have argued, such a principle.

One final point concerning my reply to the second major criticism needs to be made clear. In rejecting the principle on which the criticism rests I have contended that when a set has an *infinite* number of members, every one of which has an explanation of its existence, it *does not follow* that the existence of the set is thereby explained. In saying this I do not mean to imply that in explaining the existence of every member of an infinite set we never thereby explain the existence of the set, only that we *sometimes* do not. Specifically, we do not, I think, when we explain the existence of each member of the set by some other member of *that set*. Recall our example of M, the set of men. If we think of the members of this set as forming a temporal series stretching infinitely back in time, each member's existence explained by the causal efficacy of the preceding member, we have an example, I think, in which an explanation of the existence of each member of M does not constitute an explanation of the existence of M. Let us suppose that each man is produced not by another man but by some superior being, say a god. What we are supposing is that M is described as before except that instead of every member having the explanation of its existence in some preceding member of M the explanation is found in the causal efficacy of some member of the set of gods. From eternity, then, gods have been producing men. There have always been members of M and every member has an explanation of its existence. Here it does seem true to say that in explaining the existence of every member of M we have thereby explained the existence of M. If someone asks why there now are and always have been men rather than never having been any, we can say in response that there always have been men because there always have been gods producing them. This, if true, would explain why M has always had members.

In this paper I have examined two criticisms which have been advanced against that part of the Cosmological Argument which seeks to establish that not every being can be a dependent being. I have argued that each of these criticisms is mistaken and, therefore, fails as a refutation of the Cosmological Argument. If my arguments are correct, it does not follow, of course, that the Cosmological Argument is a good argument for its conclusion. But it does follow that those philosophers who have rejected the argument for either of the two criticisms discussed in this paper need to re-examine the argument and, if they continue to reject it, provide some *good* reasons for doing so.

NOTES

1. See "The Cosmological Argument and the Principle of Sufficient Reason," *Man and World,* 1, No. 2 (1968).

2. Not all versions of the Cosmological Argument employ the notion of a logically necessary being. It seems likely, for example, that in Aquinas' Third Way the expression "necessary being" is not used to mean a logically necessary being. (See P. Brown, "St. Thomas' Doctrine of Necessary Being," *Philosophical Review,* 73 [1964], 76–90.) But in the version we are considering, it is clear that by "necessary being" is meant a being whose existence is logically necessary. Thus Samuel Clarke, from whose work our version has been adapted, remarks: ". . . the only true idea of a self-existent or necessarily existing being, is the idea of a being the supposition of whose not-existing is an express contradiction" (Samuel Clarke, *A Demonstration of the Being and Attributes of God,* 9th edition, p. 17). David Hume also understands the notion of a necessary being this way. Thus in his statement of the argument, which he adapted from Clarke, he has Demea conclude, "We must, therefore, have recourse to a necessarily existent being, who carries the reason of his existence in himself, and who cannot be supposed not to exist, without an express contradiction" (*Dialogues Concerning Natural Religion,* Part IX).

3. See, for example, Samuel Clarke's discussion of Propositions II and III in his *Demonstration.* This discussion is summarized by Hume in Part IX of his *Dialogues.*

4. "The Existence of God, A Debate between Bertrand Russell and Father F. C. Copleston," in John Hick (ed.), *The Existence of God* (New York: Macmillan, 1964), p. 175. The debate was originally broadcast by the British Broadcasting Corporation in 1948. References are to the debate as reprinted in *The Existence of God.*

5. *Dialogues,* Part IX.

6. Samuel Clarke did not. Nor do we find Hume appealing to this inference in the course of presenting the Cosmological Argument in Part IX of the *Dialogues.*

7. Ronald W. Hepburn, *Christianity and Paradox* (London: Watts, 1958), pp. 167–168.

8. For a consideration of inferences of this sort in connection with the fallacy of composition see my paper "The Fallacy of Composition," *Mind,* 71 (January 1962). For some needed corrections of my paper see Yehoshua Bar-Hillel, "More on the Fallacy of Composition," *Mind,* 73 (January 1964).

9. Of course, the three members of this collection, unlike the members of the collection of dependent beings, presumably are causally unrelated. But it is equally easy to think of collections which cannot possibly be concrete entities whose members are causally related—e.g., the collection whose members are the ancestors of a given man.

10. Thus in speaking of the infinite succession, Hume has Demea say: ". . . and yet it is evident that it requires a cause or reason, as much as any particular object which begins to exist in time. The question is still reasonable, *why this particular succession of causes existed from eternity, and not any other succession, or no succession at all"* (*Dialogues*, Part IX; italics mine).

11. "Debate," p. 175.

12. Paul Edwards, "The Cosmological Argument," in Donald R. Burrill (ed.), *The Cosmological Arguments* (New York: Doubleday, 1967), pp. 113–114. Edwards' paper was originally published in *The Rationalist Annual for the Year 1959.*

3

The Argument from Design

R. G. Swinburne

University of Hull

THE OBJECT OF THIS PAPER[1] is to show that there are no valid formal objections to the argument from design, so long as the argument is articulated with sufficient care. In particular I wish to analyse Hume's attack on the argument in *Dialogues Concerning Natural Religion* and to show that none of the formal objections made therein by Philo have any validity against a carefully articulated version of the argument.

The argument from design is an argument from the order or regularity of things in the world to a god or, more precisely, a very powerful free non-embodied rational agent, who is responsible for that order. By a body I understand a part of the material universe subject, at any rate partially, to an agent's direct control, to be contrasted with other parts not thus subject. An agent's body marks the limits to what he can directly control; he can only control other parts of the universe by moving his body. An agent who could directly control any part of the universe would not be embodied. Thus ghosts, if they ex-

Reprinted from *Philosophy,* 43 (1968), 199–212, with the permission of the author and the publishers.

isted, would be non-embodied agents, because there are no particular pieces of matter subject to their direct control, but any piece of matter may be so subject. I use the word "design" in such a way that it is not analytic that if anything evinces design, an agent designed it, and so it becomes a synthetic question whether the design of the world shows the activity of a designer.

The argument, taken by itself, as was admitted in the *Dialogues* by Cleanthes the proponent of the argument, does not show that the designer of the world is omnipotent, omniscient, totally good, etc. Nor does it show that he is the God of Abraham, Isaac, and Jacob. To make these points, further arguments would be needed. The isolation of the argument from design from the web of Christian apologetic is perhaps a somewhat unnatural step, but necessary in order to analyse its structure. My claim is that the argument does not commit any formal fallacy, and by this I mean that it keeps to the canons of argument about matters of fact and does not violate any of them. It is, however, an argument by analogy. It argues from an analogy between the order of the world and the products of human art to a god responsible for the former, in some ways similar to man who is responsible for the latter. And even if there are no formal fallacies in the argument, one unwilling to admit the conclusion might still claim that the analogy was too weak and remote for him to have to admit it, that the argument gave only negligible support to the conclusion which remained improbable. In defending the argument I will leave to the objector this way of escape from its conclusion.

I will begin by setting forward the argument from design in a more careful and precise way than Cleanthes did.

There are in the world two kinds of regularity or order, and all empirical instances of order are such because they evince one or other or both kinds of order. These are the regularities of co-presence or spatial order, and regularities of succession, or temporal order. Regularities of co-presence are patterns of spatial order at some one instant of time. An example of a regularity of co-presence would be a town with all its roads at right angles to each other, or a section of books in a library arranged in alphabetical order of authors. Regularities of succession are simple patterns of behaviour of objects, such as their behaviour in accordance with the laws of nature—for example, Newton's law of gravitation, which holds universally to a very high degree of approximation, that all bodies attract each other with forces proportional to the product of their masses and inversely proportional to the square of their distance apart.

Many of the striking examples of order in the world evince an order which is the result both of a regularity of co-presence and of a regularity of succession. A working car consists of many parts so adjusted to each other that it follows the instructions of the driver delivered by his pulling and pushing a few levers and buttons and turning a wheel to take passengers whither he wishes. Its order arises because its parts are so arranged at some instant (regularity of co-presence) that, the laws of nature being as they are (regularity of succession), it brings about the result neatly and efficiently. The order of living animals and plants likewise results from regularities of both types.

Men who marvel at the order of the world may marvel at either or both of the regularities of co-presence and of succession. The men of the eighteenth century, that great century of "reasonable religion," were struck almost exclusively by the regularities of co-presence. They marvelled at the design and orderly operations of animals and plants; but since they largely took for granted the regularities of succession, what struck them about the animals and plants, as to a lesser extent about machines made by men, was the subtle and coherent arrangement of their millions of parts. Paley's *Natural Theology* dwells mainly on details of comparative anatomy, on eyes and ears and muscles and bones arranged with minute precision so as to operate with high efficiency, and Hume's Cleanthes produces the same kind of examples: "Consider, anatomise the eye, survey its structure and contrivance, and tell me from your own feeling, if the idea of a contriver does not immediately flow in upon you with a force like that of sensation." [2]

Those who argue from the existence of regularities of co-presence other than those produced by men to the existence of a god who produced them are, however, in many respects on slippery ground when compared with those who rely for their premisses on regularities of succession. We shall see several of these weaknesses later in considering Hume's objections to the argument, but it is worth while noting two of them at the outset. First, although the world contains many striking regularities of co-presence (some few of which are caused by human agency), it also contains many examples of spatial disorder. The uniform distribution of the galactic clusters is a marvellous example of spatial order, but the arrangement of trees in an African jungle is a marvellous example of spatial disorder. Although the proponent of the argument may then proceed to argue that in an important sense or from some point of view (e.g., utility to man) the order vastly exceeds the disorder, he has to argue for this in-no-way-obvious proposition.

Secondly the proponent of the argument runs the risk that the regularities of co-presence may be explained in terms of something else by a normal scientific explanation[3] in a way that the regularities of succession could not possibly be. A scientist could show that a regularity of co-presence R arose from an apparently disordered state D by means of the normal operation of the laws of nature. This would not entirely "explain away" the regularity of co-presence, because the proponent of this argument from design might then argue that the apparently disordered state D really had a latent order, being the kind of state which, when the laws of nature operate, turns into a manifestly ordered one. As long as only few of the physically possible states of apparent disorder were states of latent order, the existence of many states of latent order would be an important contingent fact which could form a premiss for an argument from design. But there is always the risk that scientists might show that most states of apparent disorder were states of latent order, that is, that if the world lasted long enough considerable order must emerge from whichever of many initial states it began. If a scientist showed that, he would have explained by normal scientific explanation the existence of regularities of co-presence in terms of something completely different. The eighteenth-century proponents of the argument from design did not suspect this danger, and hence the devastating effect of Darwin's Theory of Evolution by Natural Selection on those who accepted their argument. For Darwin showed that the regularities of co-presence of the animal and plant kingdoms had evolved by natural processes from an apparently disordered state and would have evolved equally from many other apparently disordered states. Whether all regularities of co-presence can be fully explained in this kind of way no one yet knows, but the danger remains for the proponent of an argument from design of this kind that they can be.

However, those who argue from the operation of regularities of succession other than those produced by men to the existence of a god who produces them do not run into either of these difficulties. Regularities of succession (other than those produced by men), unlike regularities of co-presence, are all-pervasive. Simple natural laws rule almost all successions of events. Nor can regularities of succession be given a normal scientific explanation in terms of something else. For the normal scientific explanation of the operation of a regularity of succession is in terms of the operation of a yet more general regularity of succession. Note too that a normal scientific explanation of the existence of regularities of co-presence in terms of something different, if it can be provided, is explanation in terms of regularities of succession.

For these reasons the proponent of the argument from design does much better to rely for his premiss more on regularities of succession. St. Thomas Aquinas, wiser than the men of the eighteenth century, did just this. He puts forward an argument from design as his fifth and last way to prove the existence of God, and gives his premiss as follows:

"The fifth way is based on the guidedness of nature. An orderedness of actions to an end is observed in all bodies obeying natural laws, even when they lack awareness. For their behaviour hardly ever varies, and will practically always turn out well; which shows that they truly tend to a goal, and do not merely hit it by accident." [4] If we ignore any value judgment in "practically always turn out well," St. Thomas' argument is an argument from regularities of succession.

The most satisfactory premiss for the argument from design is then the operation of regularities of succession other than those produced by men, that is, the operation of natural laws. Almost all things almost always obey simple natural laws and so behave in a strikingly regular way. Given the premiss, what is our justification for proceeding to the conclusion that a very powerful free non-embodied rational agent is responsible for their behaving in that way? The justification which Aquinas gives is that "Nothing . . . that lacks awareness tends to a goal, except under the direction of someone with awareness and with understanding; the arrow, for example, requires an archer. Everything in nature, therefore, is directed to its goal by someone with understanding, and this we call 'God'." [5] A similar argument has been given by many religious apologists since Aquinas, but clearly as it stands it is guilty of the grossest *petitio principii*. Certainly *some* things which tend to a goal, tend to a goal because of a direction imposed upon them by someone "with awareness and with understanding." Did not the archer place the arrow and pull the string in a certain way the arrow would not tend to its goal. But whether *all* things which tend to a goal tend to a goal for this reason is the very question at issue, and that they do cannot be used as a premiss to prove the conclusion. We must therefore reconstruct the argument in a more satisfactory way.

The structure of any plausible argument from design can only be that the existence of a god responsible for the order in the world is a hypothesis well-confirmed on the basis of the evidence—viz., that contained in the premiss which we have now stated, and better confirmed than any other hypothesis. I shall begin by showing that there can be no other possible explanation for the operation of natural laws than the activity of a god, and then see to what extent the hypothesis is well confirmed on the basis of the evidence.

Almost all phenomena can, as we have seen, be explained by a normal scientific explanation in terms of the operation of natural laws on preceding states. There is, however, one other way of explaining natural phenomena, and that is explaining in terms of the rational choice of a free agent. When a man marries Jane rather than Anne, becomes a solicitor rather than a barrister, kills rather than shows mercy after considering arguments in favour of each course, he brings about a state of the world by his free and rational choice. To all appearances this is an entirely different way whereby states of the world may come about than through the operation of laws of nature on preceding states. Someone may object that it is necessary that physiological or other scientific laws operate in order for the agent to bring about effects. My answer is that certainly it is necessary that such laws operate in order for effects brought about directly by the agent to have ulterior consequences. But unless there are some effects which the agent brings about directly without the operation of scientific laws' acting on preceding physical states bringing them about, then these laws and states could fully explain the effects and there would be no need to refer in explaining them to the rational choice of an agent. True, the apparent freedom and rationality of the human will *may* prove an illusion. Man may have no more option what to do than a machine and be guided by an argument no more than is a piece of iron. But this has never yet been shown, and, in the absence of good philosophical and scientific argument to show it, I assume, what is apparent, that when a man acts by free and rational choice, his agency is the operation of a different kind of causality from that of scientific laws. The free choice of a rational agent is the only way of accounting for natural phenomena other than the way of normal scientific explanation, which is recognised as such by all men and has not been reduced to normal scientific explanation.

Almost all regularities of succession are the result of the normal operation of scientific laws. But to say this is simply to say that these regularities are instances of more general regularities. The operation of the most fundamental regularities clearly cannot be given a normal scientific explanation. If their operation is to receive an explanation and not merely to be left as a brute fact, that explanation must therefore be in terms of the rational choice of a free agent. What, then, are grounds for adopting this hypothesis, given that it is the only possible one?

The grounds are that we can explain some few regularities of succession as produced by rational agents and that the other regularities cannot be explained except in this way. Among the typical products of a rational agent acting freely are regularities both of co-presence and of succession. The alphabetical order of books on a library shelf is the result of the activity of the librarian who chose to arrange them thus. The order of the cards of a pack by suits and seniority in each suit is the result of the activity of the card-player who arranged them thus. Among examples of regularities of succession produced by men are the notes of a song sung by a singer or the movements of a dancer's body when he performs a dance in time with the accompanying instrument. Hence, knowing that some regularities of succession have such a cause, we postulate that they all have. An agent produces the celestial harmony like a man who sings a song. But at this point an obvious difficulty arises. The regularities of succession, such as songs which are produced by men, are produced by agents of comparatively small power, whose bodies we can locate. If an agent is responsible for the operation of the laws of nature, he must act directly on the whole universe, as we act directly on our bodies. Also he must be of immense power and intelligence compared with men. Hence he can only be somewhat similar to men, having, like them, intelligence and freedom of choice, yet unlike them in the degree of these and in not possessing a body. For a body, as I have distinguished it earlier, is a part of the universe subject to an agent's direct control, to be contrasted with other parts not thus subject. The fact that we are obliged to postulate on the basis of differences in the effects, differences in the causes, men and the god, weakens the argument. How much it weakens it depends on how great these differences are.

Our argument thus proves to be an argument by analogy and to exemplify a pattern common in scientific inference. As are caused by Bs. A*s are similar to As. Therefore—given that there is no more satisfactory explanation of the existence of A*s—they are produced by B*s similar to Bs. B*s are postulated to be similar in all respects to Bs except in so far as shown otherwise, viz., except in so far as the dissimilarities between As and A*s force us to postulate a difference. A well-known scientific example of this type of inference is as follows. Certain pressures (As) on the walls of containers are produced by billiard balls (Bs) with certain motions. Similar pressures (A*s) are produced on the walls of containers which contain not billiard balls but gases. Therefore, since we have no better explanation of the existence of the pressures, gases consist of particles (B*s) similar to billiard balls except in certain respects—e.g., size. By similar arguments, scientists have argued for the existence of many unobservables. Such an argument becomes weaker in so far as the properties which we are forced to attribute to the B*s because of the differences between the As and the A*s become different from those of the Bs. Nineteenth-century physicists postulated the existence of an elastic solid, the aether, to account for the propagation of light. But the way in which light was propagated turned out to have such differences (despite the similarities) from the way in which waves in solids are normally propagated that the physicists had to say that if there was an aether it had very many peculiar properties not possessed by normal liquids or solids. Hence they concluded that the argument for its existence was very weak. The proponent of the argument from design stresses the similarities between the regularities of succession produced by man and those which are laws of nature and so between men and the agent which he postulates as responsible for the laws of nature. The opponent of the argument stresses the dissimilarities. The degree of support which the conclusion obtains from the evidence depends on how great the similarities are.

The degree of support for the conclusion of an argument from analogy does not, however, depend merely on the similarities between the types of evidence but on the degree to which the resulting theory makes explanation of empirical matters more simple and coherent. In the case of the argument from design, the conclusion has an enormous simplifying effect on explanations of empirical matters. For if the conclusion is true, if a very powerful non-embodied rational agent is responsible for the operation of the laws of nature, then normal scientific explanation would prove to be personal explanation. That is, explanation of some phenomenon in terms of the operation of a natural law would ultimately be an explanation in terms of the operation of an agent. Hence (given an initial arrangement of matter) the principles of explanation of phenomena would have been reduced from two to one. It is a basic principle of explanation that we should postulate as few as possible kinds of explanation. To take a more mundane example—if we have as possible alternatives to explain physical phenomena by the operation of two kinds of force, the electromagnetic and the gravitational, and to explain physical phenomena in terms of the operation of only one kind of force, the gravitational, we ought always—*ceteris paribus*—to prefer the latter alternative. Since, as we have seen, we are obliged, at any rate at present, to use explanation in terms of the free choice of a rational agent in explaining many empirical phenomena, then if the amount of similarity between the order in the universe not produced by human agents and that produced by human agents makes it at all plausible to do so, we ought to postulate that an agent is responsible for the former as well as for the latter. So then in so far as regularities of succession produced by the operation of natural laws are similar to those produced by human agents, to postulate that a rational agent is responsible for them would indeed provide a simple unifying and coherent explanation of natural phenomena. What is there against taking this step? Simply that celebrated principle of explanation—*entia non sunt multiplicanda praeter necessitatem*—do not add a god to your ontology unless you have to. The issue turns on whether the evidence constitutes enough of a *necessitas* to compel us to multiply entities. Whether it does depends on how strong the analogy is between the regularities of succession produced by human agents and those produced by the operation of natural laws. I do not propose to assess the strength of the analogy but only to claim that everything turns on it. I claim that the inference from natural laws to a god responsible for them is of a perfectly proper type for inference about matters of fact, and that the only issue is whether the evidence is strong enough to allow us to affirm that it is probable that the conclusion is true.

Now that I have reconstructed the argument from design in what is, I hope, a logically impeccable form, I turn to consider Hume's criticisms of it, and I shall argue that all his criticisms alleging formal fallacies in the argument do not apply to it in the form in which I have stated it. This, we shall see, is largely because the criticisms are bad criticisms of the argument in any form but also in small part because Hume directed his fire against that form of the argument which used as its premiss the existence of regularities of co-presence other than those produced by men, and did not appeal to the operation of regularities of succession. I shall begin by considering one general point which he makes only in the *Enquiry* and then consider in turn all the objections which appear on the pages of the *Dialogues*.

1. The point which appears at the beginning of Hume's discussion of the argument in section XI of the *Enquiry* is a point which reveals the fundamental weakness of Hume's sceptical position. In discussing the argument, Hume puts forward as a general principle that "when we infer any particular cause from an effect, we must proportion the one to the other, and can never be allowed to ascribe to the cause any qualities but what are exactly sufficient to produce the effect." [6] Now, it is true that Hume uses this principle mainly to show that we are not justified in inferring that the god responsible for the design of the universe is totally good, omnipotent, and omniscient. I accept, as Cleanthes did, that the argument does not by itself lead to that conclusion. But Hume's use of the principle tends to cast doubt on the validity of the argument in the weaker form in which I am discussing it, for it seems to suggest that although we may conclude that whatever produced the regularity of the world was a regularity-producing object, we cannot go further and conclude that it is an agent who acts by choice, etc., for this would be to suppose more than we need in order to account for the effect. It is, therefore, important to realise that the principle is clearly false on our normal understanding of what are the criteria of inference about empirical matters. For the universal adoption of this celebrated principle would lead to the abandonment of science. Any scientist who told us only that the cause of E had E-producing characteristics would not add an iota to our knowledge. Explanation of matters of fact consists in postulating on reasonable grounds that the cause of an effect has certain characteristics other than those sufficient to produce the effect.

2. Two objections seem to be telescoped in the following passage of the *Dialogues*. "When two *species* of objects have always been observed to be conjoined together, I can *infer* by custom the existence of one wherever I *see* the existence of the other; and this I call an argument from experience. But how this argument can have place where the objects, as in the present case, are single, individual, without parallel or specific

resemblance, may be difficult to explain." [7] One argument here
seems to be that we can only infer from an observed A to an
unobserved B when we have frequently observed As and Bs
together, and that we cannot infer to a B unless we have actually observed other Bs. Hence we cannot infer from regularities of succession to an unobserved god on the analogy of the
connection between observed regularities and human agents,
unless we have observed at other times other gods. This argument, like the first, reveals Hume's inadequate appreciation of
scientific method. As we saw in the scientific examples which I
cited, a more developed science than Hume knew has taught us
that when observed As have a relation R to observed Bs, it is
often perfectly reasonable to postulate that observed A^*s, similar to As, have the same relation to unobserved and unob-
servable B^*s similar to Bs.

3. The other objection which seems to be involved in the
above passage is that we cannot reach conclusions about an object which is the only one of its kind, and, as the universe is
such an object, we cannot reach conclusions about the regularities characteristic of it as a whole.[8] But cosmologists are reaching very well-tested scientific conclusions about the universe as
a whole, as are physical anthropologists about the origins of
our human race, even though it is the only human race of which
we have knowledge and perhaps the only human race there is.
The principle quoted in the objections is obviously wrong.
There is no space here to analyse its errors in detail, but suffice
it to point out that it becomes hopelessly confused by ignoring
the fact that uniqueness is relative to description. Nothing describable is unique under all descriptions (the universe is, like
the solar system, a number of material bodies distributed in
empty space), and everything describable is unique under some
description.

4. The next argument which we meet in the *Dialogues* is that
the postulated existence of a rational agent who produces the
order of the world would itself need explaining. Picturing such
an agent as a mind, and a mind as an arrangement of ideas,
Hume phrases the objection as follows: "a mental world or
Universe of ideas requires a cause as much as does a material

world or Universe of objects." [9] Hume himself provides the obvious answer to this—that it is no objection to explaining X by Y that we cannot explain Y. But then he suggests that the Y in this case, the mind, is just as mysterious as the ordered universe. Men never "thought it satisfactory to explain a particular effect by a particular cause which was no more to be accounted for than the effect itself." [10] On the contrary, scientists have always thought it reasonable to postulate entities merely to explain effects, so long as the postulated entities accounted simply and coherently for the characteristics of the effects. The existence of molecules with their characteristic behaviour was "no more to be accounted for" than observable phenomena, but the postulation of their existence gave a neat and simple explanation of a whole host of chemical and physical phenomena, and that was the justification for postulating their existence.

5. Next, Hume argues that if we are going to use the analogy of a human agent we ought to go the whole way and postulate that the god who gives order to the universe is like men in many other respects. "Why not become a perfect anthropomorphite? Why not assert the deity or deities to be corporeal, and, to have eyes, a nose, mouths, ears, etc." [11] The argument from design is, as we have seen, an argument by analogy. All analogies break down somewhere; otherwise they would not be analogies. In saying that the relation of A to B is analogous to a relation of A* to a postulated B*, we do not claim that B* is in all respects like B, but only in such respects as to account for the existence of the relation and also in other respects except in so far as we have contrary evidence. For the activity of a god to account for the regularities, he must be free, rational, and very powerful. But it is not necessary that he, like men, should only be able to act on a limited part of the universe, a body, and by acting on that control the rest of the universe. And there is good reason to suppose that the god does not operate in this way. For, if his direct control was confined to a part of the universe, scientific laws outside his control must operate to ensure that his actions have effects in the rest of the universe. Hence the postulation of the existence of the god would not explain the operations of those laws: yet to explain

the operation of all scientific laws was the point of postulating the existence of the god. The hypothesis that the god is not embodied thus explains more and explains more coherently than the hypothesis that he is embodied. Hume's objection would, however, have weight against an argument from regularities of co-presence which did not appeal to the operation of regularities of succession. For one could suppose an embodied god just as well as a disembodied god to have made the animal kingdom and then left it alone, as a man makes a machine, or, like a landscape gardener, to have laid out the galactic clusters. The explanatory force of such an hypothesis is as great as that of the hypothesis that a disembodied god did these things, and argument from analogy would suggest the hypothesis of an embodied god to be more probable. Incidentally, a god whose prior existence was shown by the existence of regularities of co-presence might now be dead, but a god whose existence was shown by the present operation of regularities of succession could not be, since the existence of an agent is contemporaneous with the temporal regularities which he produces.

6. Hume urges: why should we not postulate many gods to give order to the universe, not merely one? "A great number of men join in building a house or a ship, in rearing a city, in framing a commonwealth, why may not several deities combine in framing a world?" [12] Hume again is aware of the obvious counter-objection to his suggestion—"To multiply causes without necessity is . . . contrary to true philosophy." [13] He claims, however, that the counter-objection does not apply here, because it is an open question whether there is a god with sufficient power to put the whole universe in order. The principle, however, still applies whether or not we have prior information that a being of sufficient power exists. When postulating entities, postulate as few as possible. Always suppose only one murderer, unless the evidence forces you to suppose a second. If there were more than one deity responsible for the order of the universe, we should expect to see characteristic marks of the handiwork of different deities in different parts of the universe, just as we see different kinds of workmanship in the different houses of a city. We should expect to find an inverse square law of gravitation obeyed in one part of the

universe, and in another part a law which was just short of being an inverse square law—without the difference's being explicable in terms of a more general law. But it is enough to draw this absurd conclusion to see how ridiculous the Humean objection is.

7. Hume argues that there are in the universe other things than rational agents which bestow order. "A tree bestows order and organisation on that tree which springs from it, without knowing the order; an animal in the same manner on its offspring." [14] It would, therefore, Hume argues, be equally reasonable if we are arguing from analogy, to suppose the cause of the regularities in the world "to be something similar or analogous to generation or vegetation." [15] This suggestion makes perfectly good sense if it is the regularities of co-presence which we are attempting to explain. But as analogous processes to explain regularities of succession, generation or vegetation will not do, because they only produce regularities of co-presence—and those through the operation of regularities of succession outside their control. The seed only produces the plant because of the continued operation of the laws of biochemistry.

8. The last distinct objection which I can discover in the *Dialogues* is the following. Why should we not suppose, Hume urges, that this ordered universe is a mere accident among the chance arrangements of eternal matter? In the course of eternity, matter arranges itself in all kinds of ways. We just happen to live in a period when it is characterised by order, and mistakenly conclude that matter is always ordered. Now, as Hume phrases this objection, it is directed against an argument from design which uses as its premiss the existence of the regularities of co-presence. "The continual motion of matter . . . in less than infinite transpositions must produce this economy or order, and by its very nature, that order, when once established supports itself for many ages if not to eternity." [16] Hume thus relies here partly on chance and partly on the operation of regularities of succession (the preservation of order) to account for the existence of regularities of co-presence. In so far as it relies on regularities of succession to explain regu-

larities of co-presence, such an argument has, as we saw earlier, some plausibility. But in so far as it relies on chance, it does not—if the amount of order to be accounted for is very striking. An attempt to attribute the operation of regularities of succession to chance would not thus be very plausible. The claim would be that there are no laws of nature which always apply to matter; matter evinces in the course of eternity all kinds of patterns of behaviour; it is just chance that at the moment the states of the universe are succeeding each other in a regular way. But if we say that it is chance that in 1960 matter is behaving in a regular way, our claim becomes less and less plausible as we find that in 1961 and 1962 and so on it continues to behave in a regular way. An appeal to chance to account for order becomes less and less plausible, the greater the order. We would be justified in attributing a typewritten version of collected works of Shakespeare to the activity of monkeys typing eternally on eternal typewriters if we had some evidence of the existence of an infinite quantity of paper randomly covered with type, as well as the collected works. In the absence of any evidence that matter behaved irregularly at other temporal periods, we are not justified in attributing its present regular behaviour to chance.

In addition to the objections which I have stated, the *Dialogues* contain a lengthy presentation of the argument that the existence of evil in the world shows that the god who made it and gave it order is not both totally good and omnipotent. But this does not affect the argument from design which, as Cleanthes admits, does not purport to show that the designer of the universe does have these characteristics. The eight objections which I have stated are all the distinct objections to the argument from design which I can find in the *Enquiry* and in the *Dialogues,* which claim that in some formal respect the argument does not work. As well as claiming that the argument from design is deficient in some formal respect, Hume makes the point that the analogy of the order produced by men to the other order of the universe is too remote for us to postulate similar causes.[17] I have argued earlier that if there is a weakness in the argument it is here that it is to be found. The only way to deal with this point would be to start drawing the parallels or stressing the dissimilarities, and these are perhaps tasks more appropriate for the preacher and the poet than for the philosopher. The philosopher will be content to have shown that though perhaps weak, the argument has some force. How much force depends on the strength of the analogy.

NOTES

1. I am most grateful to Christopher Williams and to colleagues at Hull for their helpful criticisms of an earlier version of this paper.

2. David Hume, *Dialogues Concerning Natural Religion,* ed. H. D. Aiken (New York, 1948), p. 28.

3. I understand by a "normal scientific explanation" one conforming to the pattern of deductive or statistical explanation utilised in paradigm empirical sciences such as physics and chemistry, elucidated in recent years by Hempel, Braithwaite, Popper, and others. Although there are many uncertain points about scientific explanation, those to which I appeal in the text are accepted by all philosophers of science.

4. St. Thomas Aquinas, *Summa Theologiae,* Ia.2.3. Trans. Timothy Mc-Dermott, o.p. (London, 1964).

5. *Ibid.*

6. David Hume, *An Enquiry Concerning Human Understanding,* ed. L. A. Selby-Bigge (2nd ed., 1902), p. 136.

7. *Dialogues,* p. 23.

8. For this argument see also *Enquiry,* pp. 147f.

9. *Dialogues,* p. 33.

10. *Ibid.,* p. 36.

11. *Ibid.,* p. 40.

12. *Ibid.,* p. 39.

13. *Ibid.,* p. 40.

14. *Ibid.,* p. 50.

15. *Ibid.,* p. 47.

16. *Ibid.,* p. 53.

17. See, for example, *Dialogues,* pp. 18 and 37.

4

The Claims of
Religious Experience

H. J. N. Horsburgh
University of Victoria

AT ONE TIME THE BELIEVER COULD REST SECURELY on religious experience. The sceptics might nibble at the doctrinal frills of his religion; but they could not touch his seamless inner garment of truth, which was freshly woven in every generation by the experience of the Church's saints, and, to a lesser extent, even by the experience of the most vacillating and sinful Christian. But in our own century the sceptics have tried to set their teeth in this seamless garment. Psychologists have carried out what are commonly thought of as damaging researches into the nature of religious experience, and more recently philosophers have joined them in making difficulties for the believer—and not only the neanderthalers of the linguistic age in philosophy (the early logical positivists), but also *Homo sapiens* at his highest power, as represented by the fol-

Reprinted from *Australasian Journal of Philosophy*, 35 (1957), 186–200, with the permission of the author and the publishers.

lowers of the later Wittgenstein. It is with this recent philosophical onslaught that I am concerned in this article.

An attempt to estimate its force should be prefaced by a close study of what has actually been claimed for religious experience—particularly by the mystics, since it is with them that I am primarily concerned. But such an investigation is clearly impossible, as even the classics of Western mysticism form a literature of very considerable bulk. I shall therefore confine myself to the examination of some of the claims which might be made. These claims will be considered as they are suggested by the objections themselves.

My paper, then, has two aims: (*a*) to give a brief account of the main objections which have recently been brought against religious experience as either a source of, or as a means of confirming, religious beliefs; and (*b*) to consider what important claims they dispose of (if any). The first of these aims is rendered difficult by the fact that as the attack comes from a single school of philosophy the objections tend to run into one another. The three parts into which I divide it are therefore somewhat artificial. I shall call these (1) the psychological objection, (2) the verificationist objection, and (3) the objection from the ineffable nature of religious experience. These labels are mere conveniences: I claim no special aptness for them.

I

The psychological objection is the most popular at the present time. One can therefore find many accounts of it. I shall quote from three writers who have recently put it forward. ". . . I want to argue," says Mr. Alasdair MacIntyre, "that neither feeling-states nor mental images could provide evidence for religious belief. . . . The reason for this is that the point of the experience is allegedly that it conveys information about something other than the experience, namely, about the ways of God. Now an experience of a distinctively 'mental' kind, a feeling-state or an image cannot of itself yield us any information about anything other than the experience." [1] A much more elaborate account of the same objection is to be found in Mr. C. B. Martin's article, "A Religious Way of Knowing." [2] But at one place it is succinctly stated: "The only thing that I can establish beyond correction on the basis of having certain feelings and sensations is that I have these feelings and sensations." [3] Finally, an account of essentially the same objection is to be found in Professor R. B. Braithwaite's Arthur Eddington Memorial Lecture.[4] "If it is maintained," says Braithwaite, "that the *existence* of God is known by observation in the 'self-authenticating' experience of 'meeting God,' the term 'God' is being used merely as part of the description of that particular experience." At first sight this seems to be quite a different argument. But this impression is mistaken; for what Braithwaite is saying is that the term "God" can only be used, in such contexts, as part of one's description of a particular experience, for one is only referring to one's own feelings, images, etc., and these cannot be used to establish an existential claim.

In the above I have given pride of place to MacIntyre's statement of the objection because it reveals the nature of the argument most clearly. It is also the purest form of the argument, since both the other versions contain intrusive references to other issues. (I shall have something to say about these issues later without referring back explicitly to the passages I have quoted.)

I think it must be agreed that if mystical experiences consist merely of unusual feelings or peculiar sensations or images— i.e., if they are experiences of "a distinctively 'mental' kind" in MacIntyre's sense—they do not establish the existence of God or support any belief concerning His nature. Indeed, no massive apparatus of logic is needed to appreciate this point; it might be expected to lie within the range of even a mystic's mundane intelligence. But to say that mystical experiences are any of these things is to beg the most vital question at issue, namely, the nature of mystical experience. Admittedly, mystics do frequently use the words "feeling," "image," and "sensation" in connexion with their experiences. But linguistic philosophers are aware that the logical topography of these terms is most involved and should therefore be the first to appreciate that mystics may sometimes use them in different senses from those illustrated by such sentences as "I have a prickly sensation," "I am haunted by the image of Britannia," or "I have a numb feeling in my toe." In fact, it is obvious that more is claimed by mystics for their experiences than is allowed by those who urge the psychological objection; they would refuse to agree that their visions are visionary in the same sense as the dagger of Macbeth, or that their moments of ecstasy or illumination are ecstatic or illuminating in the same senses as the experience of a gardener confronted by a perfect rose or of a logician suddenly conscious of an interesting distinction. And their claim to have experienced something other than bizarre or beguiling feelings is borne out by the fact that their conduct in no way resembles the conduct of those who have devoted their lives to the cultivation of such feelings.

Braithwaite and MacIntyre do not even dismiss these claims: they ignore them. And Martin summarises the psychological objection in the sentence I have quoted before he has examined them. However, he later attempts to show that the logic of such statements as "I have direct experience of God and therefore know He exists" is "very, very like" the logic of such admittedly psychological statements as "I have a queer feeling and therefore know I have a queer feeling." I shall contend that Martin is wrong in this logical assertion. But at the moment I wish to make a different point, namely that even if these statements have a similar logic one can only rule out the existential claim with assurance by falling back (as all the writers quoted do, at least implicitly) on cast-iron assertions about the possibilities of experience. Thus Martin says: "Because 'having direct experience of God' does not admit the relevance of a society of tests and checking procedures it places itself in the company of the other ways of knowing which preserve their self-sufficiency, 'uniqueness,' and 'incommunicability' by making a psychological and not an existential claim." [5] In brief, the existential claim must be withdrawn. But it is quite conceivable that the world should be such that only some people can (in the empirical sense) discover certain things about it. For all that Braithwaite, MacIntyre, and Martin know to the contrary, this may describe the actual situation of the mystics. In other words, the existential claim can only be ruled out by applying logical distinctions (e.g., those between thoughts, feelings, sensations, images, etc.) which have arisen out of ordinary experience. But mystical experience is not

ordinary experience; therefore, it remains an open question
whether the distinctions which we ordinarily make would require to be either modified or changed altogether if account
were to be taken of it. There seems to be something scholastic
in its rigidity about this whole mode of argument. One can imagine, for example, the plight of a present-day scientist pitch-
forked without books or apparatus into the Middle Ages and
forced to engage in discussion with philosophers who applied
twentieth-century techniques to the elucidation of thirteenth-
century speech. At every turn he would be accused of unwar-
rantably extending the meanings of words, using misleading
analogies, falling into mislocations and distortions of logical
geography, etc., etc. What could he do if these philosophers
stood on their logic and refused to enlarge their experience in
the way that he might suggest? [6]

But in any case it is quite wrong to speak of the logic of
statements concerning religious experience as "very, very like"
the logic of psychological statements. There are several important differences. But, at the moment, so as not to trespass on
the ground of the next section, I shall mention only one. This
difference arises out of the fact that, whereas psychological
statements are always made with the same assurance, claims
based on religious experience are made with varying degrees
of assurance. Thus, it does not make sense to ask "Is A less
sure he has the sensation x than B is sure he has the sensation
y?" On the other hand it makes perfectly good sense to ask
"Which of them is the more sure that he has had direct experience of God, A or B?"

To point out further differences would be to pass on to the
verificationist objection. Indeed, the psychological objection is
to be regarded as a special or disguised form of the verificationist objection, in that, if subjected to sufficient scrutiny, it
turns into that objection. Thus, when someone claims to have
intuitive or clairvoyant powers and refuses to admit that his
"hunches" are mere feelings, images, etc., we test his claims,
and the retention or withdrawal of the word "mere" turns on
the results of these tests. In advancing the psychological objection, therefore, one is maintaining either that such tests
have been applied to the mystic and his claims shown to be

unfounded or that (as Martin suggests) no tests can be applied to him and therefore his claims *must* be unfounded.

II

Martin raises the verificationist objection in as telling a way as any when he asks "How do we know that someone has had direct experience of God or that we ourselves have had such an experience?" In other cases in which existential claims are made "a whole society of tests and checking up procedures are available"; in this case, according to Martin, it does not exist. He sharpens the objection by drawing attention to two interesting possibilities. The first of these is the possibility of a full description of an alleged direct experience of God. He writes:

> . . . the theologian discourages[7] any detailed description of the required experience ["apprehension of God"]. The more naturalistic and detailed the description of the required experience became, the easier would it become to deny the existential claim. One could say, "Yes, I had those very experiences, but they certainly did not convince me of God's existence." The only sure defence here would be for the theologian to make the claim analytic—"You *couldn't* have those experiences and at the same time sincerely deny God's existence."[8]

The second possibility is that those who used to make the existential claim should cease to do so, while maintaining that their experiences have not changed. "Perhaps they still attend church services and pray as often as they used to do, and perhaps they claim to have the same sort of experiences as they had when they were believers, but they refuse to accept the conclusion that God exists."[9]

I want to begin what I have to say by way of comment on this objection with some remarks on the subject of self-authentication, the topic raised by the question "How do I know that I have had direct experience of God?"

Martin and Braithwaite pay no heed to the most remarkable feature of self-authentication in religious experience—namely, that it is not self-authenticating in the same way as it has sometimes been claimed that moral intuitions are self-authenticating. Thus, if asked "Why is murder wrong?," the ethical intuitionist would reply "One just *knows* that it is." This is not a slowly-dawning moral perception; it is something which strikes one as soon as one thinks about it. But mystical experience does not seem to be self-authenticating in its beginnings; or, at any rate, not so self-authenticating as to be destructive of doubt. Many religious people can set themselves the question "Have I had direct experience of God?" and be forced to answer either "I don't know" or "I think so, but I'm not sure." Only the experiences of the greatest mystics would seem to be fully self-authenticating. As I have already shown, this growth of self-authentication serves to distinguish the logic of statements about mystical experience from the logic of ordinary experiential statements. It is also important in connexion with the testing of the mystic's claims, as I hope to show.

No one who emphasises the importance of religious experience would wish to deny that this self-authentication is mysterious; indeed, for reasons different from those of the sceptic he would wish to stress its mystery. Nevertheless, something can be said to dispose us more favourably towards it. For example, it can be pointed out, many everyday assertions are mysterious in a somewhat similar way. Thus, when looking for a friend's house one may be told: "Keep straight on and you can't miss it." Painfully aware of one's capacity to miss the obvious, one may fail to be reassured by this prophecy. Yet it may be justified; and when one sees one's friend's house one may appreciate why it could be made. Similarly, one must have had certain experiences to appreciate why some experiences have been called self-authenticating.

It can also be pointed out that at least an element of self-authentication attaches to many of our cognitive experiences. Thus, we may set out to look for something without knowing what it is, impelled by an indeterminate longing. Yet faced by an object, an occupation, or an activity, we may instantly recognise that it is what we have been looking for. Our response to what we find guarantees that it is the true object of our search. The religious man goes in quest of God, either alone or supported by the beliefs and practices of a religious commu-

nity; and he knows when he has found Him by the overwhelming religious significance of the encounter. He has met
God when it is only God whom he could have met, i.e., when
he has met the Being in whom he can find his fulfilment.[10]
This may sound like the perfect vindication of the psychological objection, since it can at once be suggested either that
the mystic's voyage is one of disguised self-discovery (similar
to that which reaches its completion when a man suddenly discovers that what he really wants to do is to paint), or that the
whole voyage is a self-deception like that of an ancient mari-
ner setting sail in his dreams for the wonderful port which
he has never visited. The response of the mystic, it will be
said, is like that of the dying man to the mirage; God is the
oasis which should, which must exist—which would exist if
thought really had the omnipotence which children and primi-
tives ascribe to it. But just as the ordinary romantic youth is
prepared to trade in his dreams for any pretty girl of flesh
and blood (discovering that his response to the pretty girl is
very different from, and goes far beyond, his response to any
figure of fantasy), so the overwhelming power of the mystic's final encounter argues the Presence of a Being who is
more than a figment of his own imagination. Moreover, it is
not the sickly and the highly emotional who, in contemplative
orders, have sometimes reached the level (as they claim) of
fully self-authenticating experience; the greatest mystics appear to have been eminently sane men with a handsome dis-
respect for the phenomena of hysteria, self-hypnosis, and the
like. Nobody, for example, can read St. John of the Cross
with an open mind without being checked between facile explanations. Indeed, it may be asserted more generally that one
can turn to the writings of the mystics after forty years of
Freudian investigation without receiving an impression of
psychological naïveté. In brief, the mystery of self-authentication is more than sheer mystification, and a comparison of the
mystic's claims with those of a man who is pronouncing on the
peculiarities of his after-images is simply fatuous.

Finally, it is instructive to consider other cases in which
the hideous cry of "Self-authentication" would echo just as
deafeningly among the ivory towers of philosophy. Let us suppose that there is a community consisting of three people, A,

B, and C. They are all blind but otherwise normal. Their scientific knowledge has reached a very high level so that they have been able to develop scientific aids which fulfil all the functions of eyes with a single exception. Let us now suppose that A suddenly discovers that he can see. He tries to tell B and C about his extraordinary experiences but finds them intransigently sceptical when it is discovered that his alleged new sense gives him no predictive advantages which can be appreciated by the others. Thus as his visual experience increases he can predict colour changes which they cannot predict; but they are unimpressed by these predictions, since they question the existence of colours in A's sense. (However, they discover that his alleged colour predictions are correlated with predictable changes in what we call light waves. Thereafter they are inclined to say in the manner of Braithwaite that A's colour words function as parts of his descriptions of the anomalous experiences caused by these changes.) Inevitably, A becomes a target for the psychological and verificationist objections. He then discovers that he can often make the same predictions as the others with fewer scientific aids. After protracted tests B and C agree that he can. But when he makes existential claims on the basis of his visual experiences they immediately look stern and warn him against "self-authentication." He insists that looking at things is itself a way of verifying that they exist and have certain properties, but this they refuse to admit; and the logic of use supports them since, in this community, verification has nothing whatever to do with seeing. I suggest that the objection to mystical experience on the ground that it is self-authenticating may be as pointless as this objection to A's "self-authenticating" visual experiences.

The same point can be brought out by considering another case—the impact of a stranger with extraordinary clairvoyant powers on a community of normal men. P, Q, and R—the local intellectuals—are forced to admit after extensive tests that Z can describe things which are out of sight as accurately as a normal man describes things which are fully visible and close at hand. Nevertheless, they refuse to allow him to make existential claims on the basis of these powers alone, on the ground that this would mean that his clairvoyant experiences were to be regarded as self-authenticating. Z points out that he "makes sure" before asserting anything, "looking" again and again as a man might look at something near him; but they insist that what Z "sees" in this way must be checked by what he and others see in the ordinary way. But surely P, Q, and R are being unreasonable? A community in which men had reliable clairvoyant powers would have a logic which permitted them to test existential and all other cognitive claims by the use of those powers. Indeed, clairvoyant perception might count for more than seeing, since it might give rise to fewer errors, e.g., those caused by the refraction of light, etc.[11]

To all this it may be objected, however, that A and Z do not claim certainty for the statements they make on the basis of their visual or clairvoyant experiences, whereas the mystic does. But such a criticism fails to distinguish between logical and empirical certainty. A and the mystic both say they are certain; but neither is making his claims analytic—as Martin suggests. Thus, the mystic does not say "You *couldn't* have these experiences and at the same time sincerely deny God's existence." It remains logically possible for the mystic to stop short of the existential claim. But it appears to be empirically impossible. In this it is similar to the run of everyday assertions. Thus, a man may have smelt, felt, and seen hundreds of lampreys, yet his dying words, after he had eaten a surfeit of them, may still be "there's no such animal." This is logically possible; but in a sincere, sane man with a good knowledge of the language it is empirically impossible.

Turning now to the charge that there are no tests in the field of religious experience, I first wish to point out that one can only reasonably ask for those tests which take account of the general nature of the field in which a claim is being made. The claims that A can see, that he is less anxious as a result of psychotherapeutic treatment, that he loves B, and that he has added a column of figures correctly are all different in important ways; and therefore the procedures by which they are tested must also be significantly different. Philosophers, in recent times, have often been unreasonable in what they have said about verification, insisting on paradigm procedures which they knew to be inapplicable to the field in which certain claims had been made. Some, for example, impugned the objectivity of history because its hypotheses could not be shown to be objective in the same ways, or in the same sense, as the hypotheses of science. But history was too respectable a study to be safely attacked for long, particularly by those with the built-in conventionality which comes from basing oneself on the ordinary usages of language. Religion has therefore become a popular object of old-style attack—even though no one has ever supposed that the methods of verification used in scientific work can also be used to test religious claims.

But are there any tests whatsoever in the field of religious experience? In my view there are. Something can be done to understand these tests by returning to A, B, and C. A is clearly extending the meaning of the term "exist" when he claims that it should have no closer connexions with what we hear than with what we see. He is unimpressed by C's ingenious objections to this extension, knowing that they represent "the empiricism of one who has had little experience." [12] Let us now suppose that the blindness of A, B, and C has been caused by some psychological disorder, and that A does not suddenly develop the power of sight but accidentally undergoes some mildly therapeutic experience as a result of which he manages to detect the faintest glimmerings of light. He then slowly develops a therapeutic technique which eventually enables him to achieve normal vision. B and C can now test A's claims by using the technique which A has developed. With his assistance they may also improve it, so that, if we now suppose the community to be a larger one in which this form of blindness is endemic, a greatly improved therapeutic technique may eventually come into general use. Much may also be learnt about the stages in which correct vision is developed and the steps which have to be taken to ensure that misleading visual phenomena— such as "seeing stars," etc.—are not cultivated instead of those which A, and other competent judges, know to be desirable.

The position of the mystic is somewhat similar to A's. His claims can be tested only if others, observing the changes in him or recognising that he has travelled farther along the same road as they, are induced to follow him. But following the mystic is a very much more complex and arduous undertaking than following A. To begin with, he insists that the religious quest is one in which progress is made only by those who give it pride of place in their lives. It therefore involves a commitment with pervasive and sometimes distasteful implications. Furthermore, one requires to have faith not only in those things which bear some resemblance to a technique— i.e., religious exercises and forms of worship—but also in the creeds and codes of behaviour which are also deemed essential.[13] It is not to be wondered at, therefore, that few who live outside the religious communities make a sustained and intensive effort to test these claims. Within the religious communities, on the other hand, they have been continuously tested over the centuries, and the stages through which the believer must pass—which vary with the nature of his religious gifts, etc.—have been very fully charted in relation to his goal. At the same time, experience has exposed the pitfalls and cul-de-sacs which he must avoid and the dangerous places where he must travel with special care. As a result, a spiritual director can make confident judgments regarding the extent and depth of the experience of those whom it is his duty to guide, basing them partly on what they have to tell him about their religious life and partly on how they behave.

All this would seem to be a perfectly adequate system of testing—one that can be studied in a very extensive literature which shows a continuous interest in, and awareness of, the problems of verification.

NOTE. There are other points which I might make about testing which I do not feel justified in elaborating in this paper. The most important of these is that verification is affected not only by the nature of the field in which claims are to be tested but also by the dominant concepts and interests of the society in which they are made. The whole subject is therefore much more complex than it has sometimes been made to seem in the more parochial pronouncements of the logical positivists and their successors.

III

The objection which bases itself on the ineffable or inexpressible nature of religious experience is even more important than it is common, not least because the mystics and their followers are concerned to stress the same facts as the critics and sceptics. The objection is as trenchantly stated by A. J. Ayer as by any other contemporary writer:

> . . . To say that something transcends the human understanding is to say that it is unintelligible. And what is unintelligible cannot be significantly described. . . . If one allows that it is impossible to define God in intelligible terms, then one is allowing that it is impossible for a sentence both to be significant and to be about God. If a mystic admits that the object of his vision cannot be described, then he must also admit that he is bound to talk nonsense when he describes it.[14]

It would seem to be obvious that this objection is likely to have more force against some claims than against others. I propose briefly to consider its impact on the following sorts of claims so far as they rest on religious experience:

(*i*) That God exists.
(*ii*) That God has certain attributes.
(*iii*) That one's religious experiences provide one with reasons for conceiving God in certain ways rather than in others.

The objection strikes at the second sort of claim with greater force than at either of the others. In fact, at first sight it seems quite fatal to claims of this kind. But a second look may dispose one to think otherwise. Thus, it might be maintained that such claims are risky but possible inductions. Consider A's claim that B loves him. "What makes you think so?" someone asks. "Because with her I've felt—well, I can't describe it." "If you can't describe it, how does it help?" "But that's just it —you can be sure when you feel like that that they really love you." It might be said that the claim that God loves us is founded on experience in just the same way as A's claim. But such an answer is inadmissible since it overlooks the fact that A can only use his indescribable feelings as a test of B's love because there are many women and he has been able to establish the reliability of this test by first using other tests of women's feelings for him. The mystic cannot make such inductions, first, because there is only one God, and secondly because, *ex hypothesi,* he has no non-experiential methods of establishing God's love for him.

But what if it should be said—perhaps by someone who recalls the abundance of negations in the writings of the mystics—that ineffable experiences may be negative guides to what something is like? Suppose we say that the position of the mystic is similar to that of B when something brushes against her in the darkness and she finds she cannot describe it. "Did it seem hard?" A asks. "No." "Then did it seem soft?" "No, it didn't seem soft either. Oh, I can't describe it. It just felt—funny." But while such cases show that one can reject a description without being able to offer another in its place, one's disavowals are useless if they extend to every possible description—and it is certainly the case that the mystic refuses to accept any description of his experiences. (He writes about them in ways which prove to be evocative to his fellow mystics.) Therefore, this defence must also be rejected. However, experiences such as B's are useful because they help to remind us that when one says that x is indescribable one is not saying that it is featureless; for that which cannot be described may still be recognised when it recurs. Thus, although mystics insist that their experiences are ineffable they do classify them to some extent and are sometimes prepared to say that they have had a certain kind of experience a definite number of times.

It seems, therefore, that the ineffable character of mystical experience rules out claims of the second kind. But I fail to see how it can be used against the assertion that God exists. As I have already tried to show, experience may give us sufficient warrant for extending the meaning of the word "exist" (or any other word); and even in ordinary life existential claims are made when one cannot describe what it is that one is affirming the existence of. Thus, when B says "something bumped into me," she will not withdraw the existential claim when she finds she can neither identify the object nor accept any suggested description of it. But to make such a comparison is calculated to stir the critic. "Yes," he may say, "B persists in making an existential claim. But she only does so—and other people are only interested in her claim—because she

thinks that something unidentified is present and wishes to en-
list other people's assistance in identifying it, lest it should
prove to be dangerous or otherwise important. If, after repeated efforts, it cannot be identified, she will either withdraw
the existential claim or say combatively 'Well, I know that
something bumped into me.' In either case other people will
cease to take an interest in it; and if B often has such experiences
they will quickly come to the conclusion that she is mentally
deranged. The mystic, on the other hand, is asserting the existence of something and at the same time insisting that it
cannot be identified. This is very different." Much of what I
am supposing the critic to say about B's experience seems to
me sound. But he is neglecting certain possibilities. Thus, it
might transpire that other people had had experiences similar
to B's when walking in the same locality and that in no case
had it been found possible to identify what it was that bumped
into them. In such circumstances an existential claim might
continue to be made without any description of what it is that
is being asserted to exist. "But," I will be told, "this claim will
only be made for the same reason as before—namely, the
possibility that further investigation will uncover the nature of
this mysterious something-or-other. If no amount of investigation serves to advance our knowledge, the claim will be withdrawn and the experience will be regarded as of a 'distinctively
mental kind'." I should agree that this is the probable course
of events; but I should want to stress its unsatisfactoriness.
However, even if one ignores this unsatisfactoriness an alternative remains—namely, that which is embodied in the
mystic's claims. Thus, it might be found that the unknown x,
which bumps into people, eludes description not because it
cannot be identified but because it can only be identified in a
special way. This is what mystics have said about God. Thus,
it is not pointless for them to say that God exists even when
they admit that He cannot be described, since they also affirm
that He can be apprehended in a special way by those who
seek Him. Of course, one can rule out the special non-con-
ceptual form of apprehension spoken of by mystics as nonsensical. But if one does, one is denying the meaningfulness
and appositeness of an expression without having had the experiences which give it meaning and establish its appositeness

—a procedure which puts one in reach of the criticism which
J. S. Mill levelled at Bentham.

Again, I do not think the objection has any force against
claims of the third kind, e.g., against the claim that it is best
to think of God as a loving God. The mystic, in his highest
spiritual flights, does not require a conception of God: at such
times (if we believe him) he enjoys direct communion with
God, and the special form of consciousness to which he has at-
tained is one which has no use for concepts. But for the ordinary course of his life, and for the instruction of others, the
mystic requires a conception of God. Clearly, it is a good reason for conceiving God in this way rather than in that, that it
has been found that this way is the more conducive to spiritual
progress, i.e., to more profound and indubitable encounters
with God. Of the conceptions and descriptions which are the
most useful of all it can be said that they are as true as truth
can be, the point of this unfashionable statement being that
they are the best spiritual ladders available, but that one comes
to the end of the longest ladder and must therefore eventually
discard them. Ayer simply ignores the possibility of claims of
this kind.

In my view, therefore, the force of the objection which Ayer
raises depends on the nature of the claim against which it is
directed. It is as fatal to claims of the second variety as it is
harmless when brought against claims of the first and third.
But it is these later sorts of claims which are vital to mysticism. Claims of the sort which cannot be sustained in the face
of this attack are precisely the sort of claims which are clearly
inconsistent with even the most obvious and familiar features
of mysticism.

It has become obvious that I do not think that the recent
philosophical critics of mysticism have succeeded in dislodging
the believer from what I take to be his ultimate stronghold.
But I recognise that my rebuttals are most unlikely to convince those who are not sympathetically inclined towards
mysticism. This is partly the result of such factors as my own
intellectual deficiencies. But it is also caused by the difficulty of
bringing critic and believer into effective touch with one another. One feels this in the course of reading even *New Essays
in Philosophical Theology,* although the contributors (Chris-

tian and non-Christian) have a common philosophical method; and it is still more obviously true when the believer is either a mystic or one who follows him from afar. In such a case the critic is like an elephant, the believer like a whale, and their combat is apt to have the unreality of a schoolboy frolic in which "dead" and "living" dispute which is which. In a disagreement of this kind there must come a point when the whale can only tempt the elephant by hinting at the marvels of underwater life, and the elephant can only stamp his feet, indicating that it is he who stands on solid ground. But there is a vital difference between them; for Leviathan, the father of the whales, will only be found—if he is found at all—by those who venture from the land.

NOTES

1. Flew and MacIntyre, *New Essays in Philosophical Theology* (London, 1955), pp. 255–256.

2. Martin, "A Religious Way of Knowing," *Mind*, 61 (1952), 497–512; reprinted in *New Essays*, pp. 76–95.

3. *New Essays*, p. 79.

4. Braithwaite, *An Empiricist's View of the Nature of Religious Belief* (Cambridge, 1955), p. 4.

5. *New Essays*, p. 85.

6. The cult of failing to understand one's opponents has reached such proportions in some quarters that it gives rise to curious flickers of apprehension. Thus I have never heard a philosopher complain that he cannot understand those stories of Edgar Allan Poe's in which the spirit of someone dead returns to inhabit or share the body of someone living. Yet in discussions of immortality, many philosophers fail to understand similar notions. One can only grieve when the hallmark of philosophical acumen becomes an incapacity to understand.

7. Martin produces no evidence whatsoever to justify the use of the word "discourage." This would seem a peculiarly disingenuous attack, coming from one who would probably also wish to urge the objection from the ineffable nature of mystical experience.

8. *New Essays*, p. 80.

9. *New Essays*, p. 87.

10. As P. T. Geach says, "in 'God exists' we are not predicating something of God, but predicating the term 'God' itself; 'God exists' means 'something or other is God'" (*Proceedings of the Aristotelian Society*, 15 [1954–1955], 266).

11. To this it might be objected that my use of the word "reliable" refers back to such tests as creatures like me are able to employ. But this criticism misses a big point in order to make a small one. The big point is that one's native constitution might be such that clairvoyance provided one with part of one's criteria of reliability.

12. J. S. Mill's criticism of Bentham. Cf. *Mill's Essays on Literature and Society*, ed. J. B. Schneewind (New York: Macmillan, 1965).

13. The "experiment" has certain features which are not fully paralleled in any other. Thus, one has to commit oneself not only to making a certain outcome; one must have faith in the mystic and in the God whom he is inviting one to seek. Of course, men have often staked their lives on the result of an experiment. But the same experiment might have been successfully conducted—or another experiment designed to test the same claims—with less at stake. When the stakes are less than this in the religious experiment its results are invariably negative. Some "experiments" in the field of human relations are somewhat similar. I am indebted to Mr. Arthur Burns for stressing this vital difference to me in discussion.

14. *Language, Truth, and Logic* (New York: Dover, 1952), 2nd ed., p. 118.

5

Ineffability

WILLIAM P. ALSTON

Rutgers University

It [the Godhead] is free of all names and void of all forms.
It is one and simple, as God is one and simple, and no man can
in any wise behold it.—MEISTER ECKHART

Brahman has neither name nor form, transcends merit and de-
merit, is beyond time, space, and the objects of sense-experience.
. . . Supreme, beyond the power of speech to express. . . .
—SHANKARA

In them [mystical states] the mysterium is experienced in its
essential, positive, and specific character, as something that bestows upon man a beatitude beyond compare, but one whose real
nature he can neither proclaim in speech nor conceive in
thought.—RUDOLPH OTTO

That Soul is not this, it is not that. It is unseizable, for it cannot be seized.—BRIHAD ARANYAKA UPANISHAD

No form belongs to Him, not even one for the Intellect. . . .
What meaning can there be any longer in saying: "This and
this property belongs to Him"?—PLOTINUS

PHILOLOGOS: How can anyone seriously make statements like
this? They seem to be self-defeating. For in making such a

Reprinted from *The Philosophical Review*, 65 (1956), 506–522, with the permission of the author and the publishers.

statement as "Brahman has neither name nor form . . . [and is] beyond the power of speech to express," isn't one doing (or purporting to do) the very thing which the statement declares to be impossible, namely, attach a name or ascribe a form to Brahman or "express" it in speech? Of course we cannot press this charge until we know the authors' exact intentions. Perhaps they are indulging in rhetorical exaggeration, as I would in saying, "Oh, Jane is impossible." If I said this, you wouldn't charge me with self-contradiction on the ground that I was on the one hand implying that "Jane" names an actually existing person and on the other hand asserting that it is impossible (logically or causally) that this person exists. You would take me to be saying, hyperbolically, that Jane is very difficult to get along with, and/or expressing my irritation at her. (Cf. "That outcome is unthinkable," "I *always* say the line 'Scarf up the tender eye of pitiful day' wrong.") Similarly, Shankara may be hyperbolically saying that it is difficult to find the right words to talk about Brahman, and/or expressing the frustration he meets in such attempts. Or perhaps the authors are using terms like "name," "form," "express," and "property" with unstated restrictions and qualifications such that their statements do not involve naming, expressing, attributing forms or properties, and so on, in their use of these terms. On neither of these interpretations would their statements be logically objectionable. But the oracular style of these writings makes it very difficult to know what interpretation to give them.

MYSTICUS: It is true that most religious writers are rather obscure, on this point as on others. But there is at least one exception—Professor W. T. Stace. In his recent book, *Time and Eternity*,[1] Stace puts forward the proposition that God is ineffable and takes considerable pains to explain exactly what he means, thereby, so it seems to me, giving a precise expression to what the people such as you cited were getting at. He makes it quite clear that he is not speaking hyperbolically, and he makes it quite explicit that the assertions are to be taken unqualifiedly, without any sort of restriction. And yet I cannot see that they are self-defeating in the way you suggest. Here are some of his statements of the thesis:

> To say that God is ineffable is to say that no concepts apply to Him, and that He is without qualities. . . . And this implies that any statement of the form "God is *x*" is false.[2]

> Thus to the intellect He is blank, void, nothing. You cannot attach any predicate to Him . . . because every predicate stands for a concept, so that to affirm a predicate of Him is to pretend that He is apprehensible by the conceptual intellect.[3]

> It is not merely *our* minds which cannot understand God, nor is it merely *our* concepts which cannot reach Him. No mind could understand His Mystery—so long as we mean by a mind a conceptual intellect—and no concepts could apprehend Him. And this is the same as saying that He is, in His very nature, unconceptualizable, that His Mystery and incomprehensibility are absolute attributes of Him.[4]

PHILOLOGOS: These utterances sound uncompromising enough. But there is something very queer about some of them, for example, "He is, in His very nature, unconceptualizable." Is this as if I should say, in speaking of a very bright but intractable student, "He is, by his very intelligence, incapable of learning"? Note that I *couldn't* be denying, in a literal sense, that he can learn. For my statement presupposes that he has intelligence, and we wouldn't say of anything that it has intelligence unless we suppose that it could learn something. Any evidence that it was in a strict sense incapable of learning would equally be evidence that it had no intelligence. In actually using this sentence I would be employing hyperbole to express vividly the fact that the very intelligence which makes him capable of learning is so quick-triggered that it is *difficult* for him to submit to the prolonged discipline which is essential for thoroughly learning anything. So in the same spirit I might say of an acquaintance that "He is, in his very nature, unconceptualizable" (cf. "His nature is an absolute enigma to me"), thereby exaggeratedly saying that he is hard to understand and expressing my puzzlement at his dark and devious ways. But again I could not mean "unconceptualizable" in a strict sense here;[5] for in ascribing to him a nature, I have already admitted that he is conceptualizable, that is, that concepts can be applied to him. We speak of the nature of *x* only where we suppose ourselves able to say various things about *x*. We wouldn't talk about human nature unless we supposed we could apply certain concepts to men. Hence I can suppose only that Stace in saying "He is, in His very nature, unconceptualizable" is hyperbolically expressing the *difficulty* of forming concepts which apply strictly to God. And so we are back to something like "Jane is impossible." [6]

MYSTICUS: No, I can't agree that Stace is just exaggerating. But I must admit that the statements you cite are not happy ones. However, I don't believe that they are essential for the statement of his thesis. He doesn't have to speak of God's *nature,* or of something being an absolute attribute of God. He used those locutions in order to emphasize that God is unconceptualizable not just by the human mind but by any mind whatsoever. But he could have made the point by saying just that (as he also does), and thereby have avoided tripping himself up in this way.

P.: Let's see what is left after the purge. "To say that God is ineffable is to say that no concepts apply to Him, . . . that any statement of the form 'God is x' is false." "Thus you cannot attach any predicate to Him." But if in saying "God is ineffable" we are making a true statement, haven't we applied a concept to Him, viz., the concept of ineffability? Haven't we attached a predicate to Him, viz., "ineffable"? Haven't we made a true statement of the form "God is x"? Aren't we in the position of being able to make a true statement only by doing the very things which the statement declares impossible, thereby falsifying it? Is this like a man saying "I can't speak English"? (Cf. the case of a town crier who cries that crying has been outlawed.)

M.: Surely you aren't serious. When I say, "God is ineffable," I am not attempting to apply a concept to Him or attach a predicate to Him, and so if the statement is true it would not be correct to say that I have succeeded in doing these things. I am denying that any concepts of predicates can be applied to Him. Of course, the grammatical form of "God is ineffable" is misleading. It looks like a positive statement, such as "Jones is ill" or "Susie is pretty," but actually it doesn't involve attaching any predicate to anything. Its logical form would be more clearly exhibited if it were formulated: "It is not the case that any predicate can be attached to God." This shows that "God is ineffable" is not really of the *logical* form "God is *x*," although it looks as if it were. Similarly, saying "King Arthur is fictitious" does not constitute attaching a predicate to King Arthur, although it looks as if it did. Hence to say truly "God is ineffable" we are not required to do what we are declaring to be impossible.

P.: So the man who said "I can't speak English," if charged with falsifying his own statement, might retort (in French) that he didn't mean that he couldn't say what he was saying. (And if the town crier were arrested, he might complain, "But surely the law doesn't forbid my crying *it*. It's the only way of publicizing it.") In both these cases the speaker trusts us to make the sort of qualification which would make his statement intelligible and proper. If we are tempted to interpret them in a paradoxical way, we draw back and say "They couldn't have meant that," and look for some qualification which will remove the paradox. So Stace perhaps trusted to the circumstances to make it plain that he wouldn't count "ineffable" as a predicate because it is negative. But wouldn't it be better to make this explicit and restate the principle as: "No *positive* predicates can be applied to God"?

M.: This qualification is unnecessary. "Ineffability" is not a predicate, in the strict sense of the term. For to "predicate" ineffability of *x* is really to deny something of *x*.

P.: If a pupil who had been directed to give an example of a subject–predicate sentence were to present "Freedom is intangible" or even "God is ineffable," wouldn't he get credit for his answer? And isn't "the concept of impossibility" a proper phrase? So whatever the "strict" sense might be, the point is that Stace is deviating from common usage and, in the interests of intelligibility, had best make his deviation explicit.

But now I want to bring out another feature of "God is ineffable" which puzzles me. Let me approach this by asking "What is it of which ineffability is being predicated or, if you prefer, of which 'effability' is being denied?"

M.: God, of course.

P.: Ah. But what do you mean by "God"?

M.: Stace identifies God with mystical experience. But that seems to me unduly restrictive. I would rather say that God is that toward which we direct religious activities of any sort: worship, prayer, and so forth.

P.: But when you and Stace explain in this way the meaning you attach to "God," aren't you thereby attaching predicates to Him, or at least putting yourself in a position to do so? In other words, in using "God," aren't you presupposing that you can predicate of God whatever phrase you would give to explain your meaning?

M.: There does seem to be something odd here. Perhaps we are overlooking some peculiarity in the way a proper name like "God" is used. Now that I recall, Stace says:

> As every logician knows, any name, any word in any language, except a proper name, stands for a concept or a universal. . . . Neither God nor Nirvana stand for concepts. Both are proper names: It is not a contradiction that Eckhart should use the name God and yet declare Him nameless. For though He has a proper name, there is for Him no name in the sense of a word standing for a concept.[7]

P.: This theory does not tally with the way you, and Stace, were just now explaining the meaning of "God." But never mind that. Let's look at this conception of proper names for a bit. And first I want to ask: "How do we determine whether a given person understands a given proper name?"[8] Let's start with something a little simpler than "God." Suppose I say to you, "Jane is a spiteful wench." You nod, but for some reason I suspect that you are bluffing. So I say, "I don't be-lieve you know who I am talking about." What could you do to vindicate yourself?

M.: I might point out a girl in the room and say, "That is Jane." Or I might just go over and address her by name.

P.: Yes. But this obviously doesn't apply to our problem, since one can't, in a literal sense, point out God, or go over and address Him. And so for our purpose we had better stipulate that I make my statement when Jane is not present and that for some reason we can't go to where she is. Or take the case of a historical figure, for example, "Richard II of England," where pointing out is *logically* impossible. How would you prove your understanding in these cases?

M.: In the case of Jane, I might reply to your charge by saying something like "She's Fred's sister-in-law" or "She's the girl with the auburn hair Bob introduced me to last night." In the case of Richard II, I might say, "He was the king deposed by Bolingbroke," or, "He was ruler of England from 1377 to 1399."

P.: Good. But doesn't this show that a condition of your understanding me, when I use the proper name of something you cannot point out, is your capacity to provide some such identifying phrase? If you were unable to provide any such phrase, would we say you understood the name?

M.: I suppose not.

P.: And isn't the same true of "God"? Suppose I say to you, "God is a very present help in time of trouble." You nod piously, but for some reason I suspect a failure of communication; perhaps I have reason to think you use the word differently. And so I ask, "What do you mean by 'God'?" You might reply, "The first cause," or "The necessary being," or "The supreme mind holding moral relations with mankind," or "He who revealed Himself to the prophets," or "The father of Jesus Christ," or "The judge of our sins." If you were unable to give *any* such answer, wouldn't I be justified in concluding that you didn't understand the word "God" in any way? This means that a condition of your understanding any statement containing "God" is your capacity to supply some such identifying phrase, and any such phrase would constitute a predicate which could be attached to God. Hence

"God is ineffable" asserts that an essential condition of its meaningfulness does not hold.

M.: Hold on. I might agree with your premise that I couldn't be said to understand a sentence containing "God" unless I could supply an identifying phrase. But your conclusion doesn't follow. Suppose that in order to identify Jane I use the phrase "the girl whose picture was on the back page of last night's paper," or in order to identify Richard II, I use the phrase "the protagonist of Shakespeare's play of that name." Would these responses be sufficient to convince you that I had understood your statements containing those proper names?

P.: I suppose so.

M.: But to say that a picture of Jane was on the back page of last night's paper is not to predicate anything of Jane or characterize her in any way. You might well complain that I had not told you what she is like and that you still can't form a concept of her. And still less have I predicated anything of Richard II when I have said that Shakespeare wrote a play about him.

P.: Maybe not. But you have said something about them.

M.: True. But to say that x is ineffable is obviously not to say that we can't say anything about x in any sense of "say something about." It is to say that we can't say anything which would involve attaching a predicate to x or characterizing it.

P.: You have overlooked one point, I fear. Even if you can't use those identifying phrases to characterize x, the information contained in these phrases gives you clues how to go about characterizing x. You can look at the back page of last night's paper, and on the basis of what you see, you can tell me all sorts of things about Jane. You can read Shakespeare's play and/or study his sources and thereby discover many characteristics of Richard II. Hence it isn't true that you could provide identifying phrases of this sort and yet *not be able* to characterize that which the phrase identifies.

M.: Perhaps. But what about "God"? That's the case we're really interested in. Couldn't I demonstrate my understanding of "God" by saying something like "the object of religious experience," or "the object of worship"? And surely saying that doesn't lead to any characterization of God. In the other cases there was perhaps a minimal characterization lurking in the very *mode* of identification. For in identifying *x* as the protagonist of a drama, I am presupposing that *x* is a human being; and to identify *x* as that a picture of which . . . is to presuppose that *x* is a visible thing. But to identify *x* as the object of religious experience or worship is not to imply anything about what sort of entity it is. It does not involve any limitation on what can and cannot be said about it. It is like saying of something that it is an object of thought. That tells us nothing. *Anything* can be thought about.

P.: But doesn't your identifying phrase tell us where to look for more information, just as in the other cases? If you actually use "object of religious experience" as a criterion for identifying God (and aren't just mechanically repeating the phrase), you can find other things to say of God by reflecting on your own religious experience and/or reading what other people have said on the basis of theirs. Thus, depending on what you are willing to call "religious experience," you could discover that God is infinite bliss, a consuming fire, the ground of all being, the spirit of love, and so on. Or if your criterion is "object of worship," you could examine what you take to be cases of worship and discover what is said of God there, for example, that He is our father, King of Kings, creator of heaven and earth, judge of all men, and so forth.

M.: Ah, but the language we use to describe what we meet in religious experience or to address the object of our worship is metaphorical language. We don't mean that God is literally a fire, a father, a King, and so forth. Hence in saying these things we aren't really predicating anything of God.

P.: The standards for *real* predication seem to be steadily stiffening. Do you really wish to say that when the poet says

> There is a garden in her face
> Where roses and white lilies grow,

he is not predicating anything of his lady fair?

M.: Not in the strict sense.

P.: What would you take to be a case of predication in the strict sense?

M.: "This cup is blue."

P.: "God is a consuming fire" is certainly different from that. But until you have said just how it is different, that is, until you have given some criteria for recognizing *real* predication, your general thesis that no predicate can be applied to God doesn't come to much.

M.: Surely such criteria could be given. But there is something else we have overlooked. There are cases in which we would say that someone understands a sentence even though he doesn't know who is named by a proper name occurring in the sentence. Suppose you are rambling on about your acquaintances and you say, "John Krasnick is a queer duck." Perhaps we are interrupted then, and I don't have a chance to ask you who John Krasnick is. Or perhaps I am just not interested in following up this facet of the conversation. It would be strange, wouldn't it, to say that I didn't understand what you had said?

P.: Yes, it would. But note why. If I were called away just after uttering this sentence, and someone asked you, "Who is John Krasnick?" you would reply, "Oh, I don't know, one of P.'s acquaintances," or perhaps, "Someone P. was just talking about; that's all I know about him." You would have to supply at least this much of an identification if you are to be said to understand my remark.

M.: But if the ability to supply an identifying phrase like "the *x* named '*N*'" or "the *x* *A* calls '*N*'" is sufficient for understanding a sentence containing a proper name, then I can certainly understand such a sentence without being able to characterize the nominatum. Surely not even you would hold that saying, "X is named by 'N' " constitutes a characterization of x.

p.: No, I wouldn't. But note what is going on here. Insofar as the only identifying phrase you gave for N is "the x called 'N'," we are hesitant about saying that you understand, or fully understand, what is being said. If, when I said "John Krasnick is a queer duck" you had nodded, assented, let it pass, or given other indication that you had understood me, and then it turned out later that the only identifying criterion you could give is "the man P. called 'John Krasnick'," I could accuse you of practicing deception. I might say, "Why didn't you tell me you didn't know who I was talking about?" In other words, when we give the usual indication of having understood a sentence containing a proper name, we are purporting to be able to say more about the nominatum than this.

This is also brought out by the fact that if, after the interruption, someone were to ask you "Who was P. talking about?," it would be misleading for you to reply "John Krasnick." For in *using* the proper name, you would be representing yourself as knowing more about him than that I called him—"John Krasnick." If that is all you know, the natural thing for you to say would be, "Oh, somebody named 'John Krasnick'." Thus we put this case into a special category.

And this means that the philosopher who *says* "God is ineffable" could not be interpreted as understanding "God" in this very weak sense. If I were to *say* "John Krasnick is queer," and couldn't tell you anything about him (except for queerness), apart from the fact that his name is "John Krasnick," you could justifiably accuse me of shamming. You might retort, "You weren't really saying anything." And there is a good reason for this usage. There would be no point in my saying anything about John Krasnick or God or anyone else unless I had some way of identifying them in addition to their being so named. Why should I bother to say of God that He is ineffable rather than effable, why should I care whether He is omnipotent or limited, loving or cruel, conscious or unconscious, if

I know Him only as what people call "God"? It is not only that in this case I would have no *basis* for saying one thing rather than the other. More fundamentally, I could have no interest in doing so. People are interested in saying things, and raising questions, about God because they identify Him as the source of their being, the promulgator of their moral laws, the judge of their sins, the architect of their salvation, the object of their worship, or (with Stace) mystical experience. It is because they identify God in such ways that they consider it important to ask and answer questions about Him.

M.: Perhaps you are right. But there is something else which has been worrying me. People differ enormously in verbal ability. Is it not possible for a man to understand a proper name and yet not be able to put this understanding, at least with any adequacy, in a formula?

P.: Perhaps. *Formulation* of an identifying phrase is not the only device for explaining one's understanding of a proper name, though it is the simplest. If the speaker lacks verbal facility, we might try to smoke out his criterion in some other way. We might, for example, present him with various passages from religious literature and note which ones he recognizes as describing God. Or we might describe (or present) various forms of worship and note which he considers appropriate. With sufficient pains we could, in this way, piece out a criterion which he would on reflection recognize as the one he actually uses. And if the most thorough attempts of this sort were persistently frustrated, wouldn't we again be justified in concluding that he wasn't using the word meaningfully?

Another thing. This point doesn't depend on any special features of *intersubjective* communication. I might be doubtful about whether I really understood a certain name. If so, I would have to use the same devices to assure myself that I did (or didn't).

But let's forget all these difficulties for the moment and suppose that one can say "God is ineffable" without thereby defeating one's purpose. We are still faced with the question why anyone should accept the statement. Isn't it amply refuted by the facts? Religious literature is crammed full of sentences attaching predicates to God, and there are many men who devote their lives to making such predications.

M.: Oh, no doubt there are many sentences which have a declarative grammatical form and contain "God" as subject. But if you examine them they will all turn out to be either negative or metaphorical. None of them express *conceptions* of God, and so none constitute predication in the strict sense of the term.

P.: Perhaps. But what positive reasons can be adduced for the position?

M.: Mystics, who are in the best position to know, have repeatedly declared God to be ineffable. Just consider, for example, the statements you cited at the beginning of our discussion.

P.: It is true that many mystics have said things which could be interpreted in this way. But if it is a question of authority, many deeply religious men who are not mystics have expressed themselves to the contrary. Of course you could rule out their testimony by defining "God" as what one encounters in mystical experience, or even (with Stace) simply as mystical experience.

M.: I would hesitate to do that. But if we approach God through mystical experience, without ruling out the possibility of other approaches, we can use a different line of argument. We can see that mystical experience has certain features which prevent it, or anything discovered in it, from being conceptualized. For example:

It is of the very nature of the intellect to involve the subject-object opposition. But in the mystic experience this opposition is transcended. Therefore the intellect is incapable of understanding it. Therefore it is incomprehensible, ineffable.[9]

But the oneness of God is indivisible and relationless. Now this relationless indivisible unity is precisely the character of the mystic intuition as described by all mystics. . . . To say this is only to say that the mystic experience is beyond the capacity of the intellect to handle, since it is the very nature of the intellect to operate by means of separation, discrimination, and analysis.[10]

P.: Leaving aside questions about the adequacy of the analysis of "intellect" employed here, there is something very strange about these arguments. The conclusion is "Mystical experience is unconceptualizable," and in order to prove it we adduce various characteristics of mystical experience. That is, we have made our success in conceptualizing mystical experience in a certain way a condition for proving that it can't be conceptualized. But how could a successful completion of a task ever enable us to prove that the task is impossible? Wouldn't it rather prove the opposite? Isn't this like giving an inductive argument for the invalidity of induction? Or presenting a documentary film to show that photography is impossible?

M.: You keep making the same mistakes. To say that God is an indivisible unity is not to apply any concept to Him. It is simply to *deny* that there is any distinction of parts in Him.

P.: I begin now to see the situation more clearly. Several times I have pointed out that in saying or defending "God is ineffable" you were saying, or implying your ability to say, something about God. And each time you deny that what is being said involves attaching any predicate to God, applying any concept to Him, or characterizing Him, either because it is negative, or because it is metaphorical, or because it is an extrinsic denomination, and so forth. It begins to appear that you are prepared to deny of anything you are committed to saying of God that it is a predicate, and so on. But if this is your tack, then in uttering "God is ineffable" you are just exhibiting a certain feature of your use of "ineffable" (and "predicate," "concept," and so on), rather than saying anything about God. You are expressing your determination not to count as a predicate and so on anything which is said of God. You are like a man who says that "Only empirically testable sentences are meaningful" (cf. "Only scientific method gives us knowledge") and then, whenever presented with a sentence which can't be empirically tested, denies that it is meaningful, without giving any reason for all these denials except the lack of empirical testability. After a while we will begin to suspect that he is just showing us how he uses "meaningful," rather than ascribing some property to all the members of a class which has been defined in some independent way.

M.: But I am just using "predicate," "concept," and so on, in their ordinary senses. The only statements which you showed I was committed to making would not ordinarily be thought to involve applying concepts or predicates to God. Similarly *if* the positivist just accepts or rejects examples of meaningful statements according to our ordinary discriminations, he is saying something about the class of statements which would ordinarily be called meaningful.

P.: I'm not at all sure that you are using "predicate" and so on in just the way we ordinarily do, if, indeed, there is any one such way. At least you haven't made that out. Of course, it is only if you are taking "having 'God' as subject" as your sole and sufficient criterion for saying that a sentence doesn't involve predication and so on that you can be accused of uttering a tautology in the strict sense. Insofar as you have other criteria, you are not uttering a tautology. But if you don't state your criteria, and if, whenever you are forced to admit that certain statements containing "God" as subject can be made, you rule these out as examples of "predication" and so on, either without any justification or on the basis of a principle which looks tailor-made for the occasion, we can be excused for suspecting that your utterance approximates to a tautology. Of course alternatively I might suppose that you have no criterion. But then your utterance becomes so indefinite as to assert almost nothing.

If you want to prevent your thesis from oscillating in this limbo between tautology and maximum indefiniteness, you had better include a specification of the senses in which you wish to deny that concepts and predicates can be applied to God. With such a specification the thesis might well be significant and worthy of serious consideration. For example, you might restate the position: "God cannot be positively characterized in literal terms." This assertion need not lead to such frustrations as we have been considering. For the speaker could use a nonliteral phrase to identify God; and although the statement itself is presumably literal, it is not positive. And, given a sufficiently precise explication of "literal," this is a thesis well worth consideration. Or you might wish to say, "We can speak only of extrinsic features of God, not of His intrinsic nature," or "God can never be characterized with the precision we can attain in science," or "We can speak of God only in a highly abstract way." None of these utterances need be self-defeating; for (1) in each case the sentence itself does not fall within the class of those declared impossible, and (2) a speaker or hearer can use a criterion for identifying God which does not involve attributing to Him a predicate of the sort which is ruled out. If you are interested in unambiguously communicating a definite thesis and avoiding tripping yourself up in the process, you would be well advised to make such specifications.

M.: Yes, I see that would be better. But how does it happen that so many philosophers make ineffability statements without qualification?

P.: Perhaps something like this is involved. There are many "un . . . able" words which can be applied with all sorts of qualifications, diminishing to an unqualified application. Thus I can say that our baseball team is unbeatable in our league; or unbeatable by any other college; or unbeatable by any other amateur team; or well-nigh unbeatable (by any team); practically unbeatable; or, simply, unbeatable; or even, to make it still stronger, absolutely unbeatable. The final term in this series, "unbeatable" (or "absolutely unbeatable"), is logically just as respectable as any of the others. Though it may be wildly improbable that our baseball team is unbeatable (without qualification), there is no logical self-stultification involved in saying so. (Cf. "unattainable," "unbreakable," "uncontrollable.") With such cases in mind it is easy to feel logically comfortable about saying of God without qualification that He is unconceptualizable or ineffable. But we still might feel more squeamish about this latter case were it not for the fact that there are contexts where we can employ even these terms (or terms very close to them) without qualification. For example:

(*a*) "A fall in the stock market is inconceivable"; (*b*) "John is unspeakable." Of course as (*a*) is actually used, it doesn't imply that we can't apply a concept to the falling of the stock market. It simply means that we have every reason to suppose it won't happen. But the verbal similarity between this and "God is unconceptualizable" (where this is intended to imply that we cannot form a concept of God) helps us to suppose that the latter is as legitimate as the former. Similarly (*b*) is simply a way of saying that John is despicable. But the fact that it has a use helps us to suppose that the verbally similar utterance "God is ineffable" (taken to imply that God cannot be spoken of) also can be given a use. But to untangle fully the muddle in "God is ineffable," we should have to make explicit all the similarities and differences in the ways sentences of this sort function.

If we want to avoid such muddles, we must make explicit the sorts of conception, predication, characterization, and so forth we are asserting to be impossible with respect to God in contrast to the sorts we are admitting as possible. To label something ineffable in an unqualified way is to shirk the job of making explicit the ways in which it *can* be talked about; just as unqualifiedly to label an expression (which is actually used) meaningless is to shirk the job of making explicit the sort of meaning it *does* have in these uses. There may be something in the world which can't be talked about in any way, but if so we can only signalize the fact by leaving it unrecorded.

NOTES

1. Princeton, 1952.
2. *Ibid.*, p. 33.
3. *Ibid.*, p. 42.
4. *Ibid.*, pp. 48–49.
5. A terminological note for the whole paper: I take Stace, and those who talk about this matter in the same way, to be using "concept" within the philosophical tradition in which we can be said to apply a concept to *x* whenever we predicate anything of *x* (or attach a predicate to *x*); and in which to say that we can apply concepts to *x* is equivalent to saying that *x* is conceptualizable, capable of being apprehended by concepts or by the conceptual intellect, etc. These equivalences are implicit in the second of the three above quotations from Stace and in the quotation on p. 81. Therefore, although I hold no brief for this double-barreled lingo, I shall in the following use "apply a concept to *x*" as

synonymous with "attach a predicate to *x*" (or "predicate something of *x*"). And, for stylistic purposes, I shall sometimes add as a further synonym "characterize *x*." I am under no illusion that the boundaries of these three terms are precisely drawn in the tradition. In fact a good part of this paper hinges, in part, on exhibiting their vagueness. But I think that within the tradition they oscillate together for the most part.

6. The same sort of considerations apply to "His Mystery and incomprehensibility are absolute attributes of Him."

7. Stace, p. 24.

8. We do not ordinarily speak of "understanding a proper name." But we do speak of understanding sentences and using them meaningfully; and one of the conditions of understanding or using meaningfully a sentence in which a proper name occurs is knowing who the proper name is a name of (with certain qualifications which are noted, p. 84). Hence, in the absence of any other compendious expression, I shall speak of "understanding a proper name, 'N,'" as synonymous with "knowing who (or what) 'N' is the name of" or "knowing who (or what) 'N' is." This extension of the use of "understanding" will not cause confusion unless it is allowed to obscure the important differences involved.

9. Stace, p. 40.

10. *Ibid.*, pp. 40–41.

6

The Divine Simplicity

Daniel C. Bennett

Swarthmore College

THE IDEA THAT GOD IS ONE, as expressed, for example, in the Shema Yisrael: "Hear O Israel, the Lord thy God, the Lord is One," comes in part to this: there is but one God (if there is any at all). But it also comes to this: God is a unity, not a "heap."

Insofar, God's oneness does not differ from the oneness of, say, legs attached to my right side; there is just one, and it is a unity, not a "heap."

However, God's uniqueness is, presumably, not accidental, whereas the uniqueness of legs on my right side is. The sense of the term "God," supposedly, requires that there be at *most* one (as it would require that there be at *least* one, if the ontological argument in one of its forms is sound), whereas the sense of "leg attached to my right side" does not require that there be at most one.

In that way God's uniqueness might be unique.

Is there anything unique about God's unity?

Reprinted from *The Journal of Philosophy*, 66 (1969), 628–637, with the permission of the author and the publishers.

According to some theologians, God's unity is unique in that God is absolutely simple. The unity of my right leg involves its being an organization of proper parts. According to the theologians in question, God has no proper parts.

"There cannot be any belief in the unity of God except by admitting that He is one simple substance, without any composition or plurality of elements; one from whatever side you view it, and by whatever test you examine it; not divisible into two parts in any way and by any cause" (Maimonides).

In this paper I want to try to clarify somewhat the idea that God is thus absolutely simple and to try to show that certain difficulties which might be or have been thought to follow from it can be gotten around, if certain dubious metaphysical assumptions are not made.[1]

I

A composite thing is either a heap or an organization of proper parts.

All the parts of a heap are essential to its existence. Take away a part of a heap and you get a different thing. Heaps have no accidental parts (though they have accidental properties).

A thing which is an organization of proper parts has among its parts states or activities or episodes of the thing. Some of these states or activities or episodes of a composite organization are essential or necessary to the thing, and some of them are accidental or incidental to the thing.

A composite thing, be it a heap or an organization, is not identical with its essential parts, and its essential parts are not identical with its existence.

A simple thing is an organization of parts, parts which include states and activities and episodes of the thing, but a simple thing is *identical* with its parts. Thus, a simple thing, like a heap, has no accidents, but, unlike a heap, it is identical with its essential parts, and its essential parts are identical with its existence. A simple thing is, literally, what it has and does and undergoes.

The idea we are examining is that God is simple in that sense.

To clarify the idea we need to say something about essence or necessity, accident or contingency,[2] possibility, and existence or actuality, and also a little about part–whole.

1.1. There are at least five ways of ascribing necessity, possibility, and contingency:

i. *Truth*: That spinsters are unmarried is a necessary truth. That some spinsters are philosophers is a contingent truth.

ii. *Exemplification* (quantified): Deity is a property which is necessarily exemplified by something (if the ontological argument in another of its forms is sound). Humanity is a property which is contingently exemplified by something. Being a physical entity is a property which is possibly exemplified by everything.

iii. *Empropertyment*: Being human is a necessary property of Socrates. Sitting is a contingent property of Socrates.

iv. *Existence*: God and properties are (according to the usual views) necessary beings; i.e., if they exist at all they are imperishable. Socrates is a contingent being.

v. *For the existence of*—: Socrates' humanity is necessary for his existence. His wisdom is contingent for his existence, i.e., is an accident of his.

Necessity, possibility, and contingency ascribed in the first three ways are "modalities." Type i modalities are *de dicto*. Type iii modalities are *de re*. Type ii modalities are modalities *in sensu composito*. Type iii modalities are modalities *in sensu diviso*. This classification is based only on surface features of the ascriptions. I will not discuss their interpretation in this paper.[3]

Necessity, possibility, and contingency, when they are ascribed in the last two ways, are (fragments of) properties of individuals. Being a necessary being is the property of imperishability or omnitemporality. A contingent being is a perishable being or one which comes to be or passes away. Type v are relational properties. They sometimes relate an individual and its states, activities, or episodes. The essence of a thing is a state or activity or episode of it necessary to its existence. An accident of a thing is a state or activity or episode of it contingent (incidental) to its existence.

It is a necessary truth that (type i ascription) if there are properties, they are necessary beings. The property of being red would (on the hypothesis) be a necessary being (type iv ascription) which is contingently exemplified by something (type ii ascription) and which is a contingent property of a certain rose (type iii ascription). Further, the redness of the rose is not necessary to the existence of the rose (type v ascription), and the rose itself is a contingent being (type iv ascription).

The property of being a rose would be a necessary being (type iv) which is contingently exemplified (type ii), but which is a necessary property of a certain rose (type iii). Further, the roseness of the rose is necessary to the existence of the rose (type v), though the rose itself is a contingent being (type iv).

The property of Deity would be a necessary being (type iv) which is necessarily exemplified (type ii) and which (on the orthodox view) is a necessary property of what exemplifies it (God) (type iii). Further (orthodoxly) the Deity of God is necessary to Him (type v), and He is a necessary being (type iv).[4]

Are the redness of the rose, the roseness of the rose, the Deity of God identical or not with (respectively) the property of redness, the property of being a rose, and the property of Deity? I shall return to this question later. It is fundamental to the topic of Divine Simplicity.

1.2. Can ways comparable to the five ways of ascribing necessity, possibility, and contingency be made out for existence or actuality?

i. *Truth* is the expression of the idea of actuality or existence *de dicto*.

ii. *Exemplification* (i.e., having *instances*) is the expression of the idea of actuality or existence *in sensu composito*.

iii. *Empropertyment* (i.e., having *properties*) is the expression of the idea of actuality or existence *in sensu diviso* or *de re*.

What about type iv and v ascription?

The property of existence belonging to Socrates may be either the property of self-identity or the property of being identical with Socrates. Self-identity is a transcendental prop erty, i.e., fails to sort a thing of which it is true from anything; and being identical with Socrates is an individuative property, i.e., sorts Socrates from everything. I do not think that it matters much which of these we decide on. Each of them, like the property of being a contingent being, is a necessary property of Socrates (in the type iii manner).

iv. *Self-identity* (either as common or as peculiar) is the expression of the idea of existence or actuality as a property of things.

The existence of Socrates, his *esse,* is his total biography or life, i.e., the whole space-time slab which is the Socrates-event. This event has events as parts. It is itself a contingent being (in type iv sense) which has elements some of which are necessary to it and some of which are contingent to it (in type v sense). Socrates' essence, if it is a state or activity or episode of Socrates, is a necessary part of his *esse,* but his wisdom or justice are contingent to his *esse.*

Since it has accidental parts, Socrates' *esse* is an accident of Socrates.

v. The *esse* of a thing is the expression of the idea of actuality or existence as a relation of the thing and its states or activities or episodes.

1.3. Spatial concreta (physical objects, substances) sometimes have spatial concreta as proper parts. If there are spatial concreta which do not have spatial concreta as parts, they are old-style atoms.

Temporal concreta (events) sometimes have temporal concreta as proper parts. If there are temporal concreta which do not have temporal concreta as proper parts, they are newer-style atoms (?).

Spatial abstracta (points, lines, planes, solids, etc.) sometimes have spatial abstracta as parts. Points are spatially abstract atoms.

Temporal abstracta (instants, durations) sometimes have temporal abstracta as parts. Instants are temporally abstract atoms.

Nonspatiotemporal abstracta (properties, propositions, classes, etc.) sometimes have nonspatiotemporal abstracta as parts. For example, classes contain other classes.

Things get aporetic when we feel the pressure to stretch part–whole across categories.

Are abstracta parts of concreta?

Especially:

a. Are spatiotemporal abstracta parts of spatiotemporal concreta?

b. Are nonspatiotemporal abstracta (especially properties) parts of concreta?

These aporia are as old as metaphysics.[5] I have assumed in this paper that temporal concreta, including states, activities, and episodes of spatial concreta, are parts of spatial concreta. The *crucial* question in discussing Divine Simplicity is:

b'. Are properties parts of concreta?

If they are, and God is a simple concretum, He is unintelligible.

II

That God is simple is equivalent to any one of the following four propositions:

1. God is identical with His essence.
2. God's essence is identical with His *esse*.
3. God has no accidents; i.e., every state or activity or episode of God is necessary to His existence.
4. Every state or activity or episode of God is identical with God, and so is identical with every other state or activity or episode of God.

So, if the Deity of God is His essence, then:

1'. The Deity of God is identical with God.

And, if the *esse* of God is His life or biography, then:

2'. The Deity of God is identical with the life of God.

If, say, God's knowledge of what I will eat for breakfast is a state of God's, then:

3'. God's knowledge of what I will eat for breakfast is necessary to God's existence.

And, on the same assumption, then:

4'. God's knowledge of what I will have for breakfast is identical with the Deity of God. And, if God's knowledge of what you had for lunch is a state of God's, then it is identical with His knowledge of what I will have for breakfast, and both are identical with God!

I will not comment on these consequences in this paper.[6]

II.1. We should now return to the question we deferred, i.e., Are the redness of the rose, its roseness, and the Deity of God properties or not?

More generally put:

Are the states, activities, and episodes of a thing properties of the thing?

Let us assume that they are, and see what becomes of the idea that God is simple.

If the redness of the rose is identical with the property of redness, then the redness of the rose is identical with the redness of someone's nose. The redness of the rose becomes "one over many" and a necessary being. Also, on the assumption, the contingency of the redness of the rose to the existence of the rose is just the property of redness being a contingent property of the rose. Similarly, the necessity of the roseness of the rose to its existence is just the property of being a rose being a necessary property of the rose.[7]

In general, if states (or activities or episodes) are properties, then states contingent to a thing (accidents) are contingent properties, and states necessary to a thing (including essences) are necessary properties. That is, type v ascriptions of necessity and contingency would just be type iii ascriptions.

The *esse* of a thing, on the assumptions, becomes the totality of properties true of the thing.

God's simplicity on the assumption now looks like this:

1″. God is identical with the properties necessarily (or essentially) true of Him.

2″. The properties necessarily true of God are identical with the totality of properties true of Him.

3″. Every property of God is a necessary property of Him.

4″. Every property of God is identical with God.

The assumption that the states (or activities or episodes) of a thing are properties, and the view that God is simple, lead to the consequence that God is a property! This is devastating to commonly held views about God.

A. If God has no accidents in the sense now given the claim, i.e., whatever properties He has, He necessarily has, as 3″ says, then, e.g., God necessarily elects Abraham. He necessarily wills what He wills. This is Spinozism.

If being referred to by me is a property of God's, then, according to 3″, it is a necessary property of God's. Thus, 3″ leads to a kind of Idealism.

B. If God is identical with His properties, as 4″ says, then the properties He has are identical with one another. Thus, if Wisdom and Justice and Mercy are different properties, then God cannot have more than one of these properties. But, if He has the property of Oneness, and Oneness is a different property from Wisdom, Justice, and Mercy, He cannot be either wise or just or merciful!

Further, if existence is a property (say, self-identity) and if it is a different property from Oneness, then if God is One He cannot also exist! He must be "above existence." This is the *via negativa* with a vengeance. 4″ seems to be the metaphysical basis for Pseudo-Dionysianism. On the assumptions, God becomes a self-participating property—the highest sort of being for Platonizers.

Incidentally, if God is identical with His properties, then He is a property, and if He is the property of Oneness, He is a transcendental property, i.e., a property which fails to sort a thing of which it is true from anything whatsoever. Thus, Pseudo-Dionysianism provides an efficient, if weird, account of God's universal providence. God becomes provident by being true of everything, including Himself!

C. If God is identical with all His properties, then He is identical with His essential properties, and all His properties must be essential properties, and, since there is just one of Him, there is just one property of Him.

It is a commonly held view that God is unknowable in His essence. We may put this idea as follows:

There is some property which is an essential property of God, but which we (composite beings) cannot know to be a property of Him.

That, as it stands, is an intelligible idea if the idea of essential property is intelligible, but, combined with the assumptions that God is simple and that states, activities, or episodes are properties, it makes God completely unknowable.

On the assumptions, we can know *no* property to be true of God, not even the property of having at least one property; not even the property of being referred to by me.

This is the Dark Night of Theology.

I think that we have made enough trouble.

II.2. The difficulties come from the assumptions that God is simple and that states, activities, and episodes are properties. Is there any independent reason for rejecting the latter assumption? I think that there is.

a. Falling downstairs and making someone laugh are different properties, each of which may belong to more than one episode. My falling downstairs yesterday and your falling downstairs today are both instances of one and the same property (this is usually put in terms of descriptions. My way of speaking is material mode for that).

The set of episodes which are fallings downstairs and the set of episodes which are makings of someone to laugh are not identical sets. There are fallings which make no one laugh and makings to laugh which are not fallings. However, a *particular* falling may be just what makes you laugh.

Just as, though the property of being a morning star and being an evening star are not identical, the morning star is the evening star, so, though the property of falling and making laugh are not identical, a falling may be a making laugh.

b. The property of redness is not identical with the property of coloredness (though it may be in some sense part of it), but the redness of her cheeks and the coloredness of her cheeks are identical.

The redness of her cheeks, unlike the property of redness, may spread and may fade.

The redness of her cheeks may be caused by an episode. It may be identical with various activities of capillaries.[8]

If we treat the states, activities, and episodes of a thing as concreta, we need not be constrained by the identity conditions which hold for properties when making such a claim as that, e.g., God's wisdom is His justice, any more than we are when we make such a claim as that, e.g., my falling down is the thing which made you laugh, or, e.g., my headache is a certain brain-state. Concreta are terms in spatial, temporal, and/or causal relations. Being a term of such relations is (it seems likely) a necessary property of concreta. Thus, the identity conditions for concreta are functions of these relata, and not of the necessary properties of abstracta.

If states, etc., are not properties, we can get around the difficulties A, B, and C.

A′. It does not follow from the assumption that God has no accidental *states* that there are no properties accidentally true of Him. Thus, God might have the accidental property of being referred to by me or of having chosen Abraham, and not be in an accidental state corresponding to the property. There are, of course, cases in which, when a property is accidentally true of an individual, the individual is in a corresponding accidental state. Thus, when Socrates is accidentally wise, there is part of his life which is his wisdom. But we need not hold that there is always such a correspondence, if type iii and type v attributions are kept distinct.

B′. We need not hold that God is identical with His properties, though we hold that He is identical with His states, activities, and episodes. The wisdom of God and the justice of God and the mercy of God are not identical with the properties of Wisdom, Justice, and Mercy, respectively. We may then hold that, though a plurality of properties is true of God, nevertheless, there is not in Him a corresponding plurality of states.

God's uniqueness need not be thought of as a function of a weirdness in His manner of instantiating properties. God might be wise and just in *exactly* the way and sense in which Socrates is wise and just. The uniqueness should be this: in the case of Socrates, because he is a composite, the properties of wisdom and justice correspond to and are exemplified in different states, but in the case of God they correspond to and are exemplified in the same state, which is God Himself. That is weird enough.

C′. There is no inconsistency in holding both that there is a property which is an essential property of God known only to Him and that we know a great deal about God, including some things which are necessarily true of Him, as well as some things which are contingently true of Him; that is, once the assumption that states, etc., are properties is given up.

That God has an unknown essential property is not unlike the idea that subatomic particles have an unknown essential property. To know the essence of a thing is to know the properties which sort it necessarily from other things. The only thing we *might* know about subatomic particles is that they are causal terms needed to account for certain manifest concreta. The difference would be that it is only a contingent ignorance in the case of subatomic concreta, whereas it is a necessary ignorance in the case of God.

III

Maimonides' point was that God cannot have *any* parts. There seems to be no serious difficulty in maintaining some of the familiar views about God together with the view that God *is* His parts, as long as the parts we are considering are concreta.[9] But a doubt remains. Suppose that states, activities, and episodes are not properties; might not properties still be parts of concreta?

There is some pressure to hold that states, activities, and episodes are parts of Socrates, for the assumption enables us to account for his *unity*—just as there is some pressure to say that a concretum like Socrates is part of an abstractum like the class of philosophers, because that enables us to account for the *unity* of the class. A pressure, then, for holding that properties are parts of things like Socrates would be the assumption's helping to account for his unity. There *is* a philosophical tendency which seeks such an account, i.e., the Platonizing tendency, but that is in conflict with seeking the account in terms of concrete parts.

In other words, properties should be taken to be parts of concreta if and only if concrete states, activities, and episodes should not.

NOTES

1. There are difficulties with the view that God is absolutely simple which I think cannot be gotten around, but which I shall not consider in this paper. I

am mostly interested here in exposing some of the metaphysical machinery needed to discuss the topic.

2. There are differences between essence and necessity and between accident and contingency which I have discussed in "Essential Properties," *Journal of Philosophy*, 66, No. 5 (1969), 487–499.

3. I have proposed an extensional interpretation of type iii ascriptions in "Essential Properties."

4. There are theologies which imply that the property of Deity, though perhaps itself a necessary being, is contingently exemplified, and/or is a contingent property of what exemplifies it, and/or is exemplified in contingent beings. S. Alexander and other emergentist theologians, as well as some Buddhists, seem to hold that Deity is an accident of contingent beings. An emergentist or Buddhist may yet believe that the property of Deity is necessarily exemplified and, thus, accept the ontological argument in one of its forms. I have argued all this in "Deity and Events," *Journal of Philosophy*, 64, No. 24 (1967), 815–824.

5. In Beta, *Metaphysica*, Aristotle wonders about the connections between (*i*) concreta (substances) and (*ii*) intermediaries (mathematicals), which include spatial abstracta, and (*iii*) genera and species, i.e., nonspatiotemporal abstracta.

6. It is consequences like 3′ and 4′ which Hume thought indicative of the unacceptability of the view that God both is simple and has a mind. "A mind, whose acts and sentiments and ideas are not distinct and successive; one, that is wholly simple, and totally immutable, is a mind which has no thought, no reason, no will, no sentiment, no love, no hatred; or, in a word, is no mind at all" (*Dialogues Concerning Natural Religion*, sec. 578). A determination of whether or not Hume is right would require clarification of identity conditions for mental states, activities, and episodes.

7. This is the view, which Aristotle considers in Zeta, which identifies the τὸ τί ἦν εἶναι, the "what it is to be" of a thing, with the universal, the Platonic Form (*Metaphysica*, 1038B–1039B, 19).

8. Aquinas argues as follows, roughly, in chapter 2 of *De Ente et essentia*: Being rational and Being animal are not identical, considered as genus and difference, i.e., as abstracta, but they are identical in a particular man. This is the same sort of argument which I have sketched for the accident of color, but applied to essence.

9. There is, of course, Hume's objection, noted earlier.

7

Necessary Being

JOHN H. HICK

University of Birmingham

I

"NECESSARY BEING" IS ONE OF THE TERMS by means of which Christian thought has sought to define the difference between God and man. The notion of necessary being, applied to God and withheld from man, indicates that God and man differ not merely in the characteristics which they possess but more fundamentally, in their modes of being, or in the fact that they exist in different senses of the word "exist."

That such a distinction, however it may be best expressed, is essential to the Christian concept of God is agreed virtually on all hands. Paul Tillich in our own day emphasises the distinction to the extent of using different terms to refer to the reality of God and of man respectively. Human beings and other created things exist; God, on the other hand, does not exist, but is Being-itself. This is the most recent way of formulating a discrimination which has been classically expressed in

Reprinted from *Scottish Journal of Theology,* 14 (1961), 353–369, with the permission of the author and of Cambridge University Press.

the history of Christian thought by the idea of the necessary being of God in contrast to the contingent being of man and of the whole created order.

There are, however, two importantly different concepts which may be, and which have been, expressed by the phrase "necessary being." "Necessity," in a philosophical context, usually means logical necessity, and gives rise in theology to the concept of a being such that it is logically impossible that this being should not exist. But this is not the only kind of necessity referred to in philosophical literature. The non-logical concepts of causal, empirical, and material necessity can be grouped together as forms of *factual* necessity. The distinction between logical and factual necessity first appears, as far as I know, in the *Critique of Pure Reason,* where Kant treats of the three modal categories of possibility, existence, and necessity. The category of necessity is derived by him from the necessary or analytic proposition in formal logic. But its schema in time is the existence of an object throughout all time;[1] and the corresponding "postulate of empirical thought" is called by Kant *die materiale Notwendigkeit* and is equivalent to what is often described as causal necessity, i.e. being part of the universal causal system of nature.[2] The schema of necessity as existence throughout all time suggests the notion of a temporally unlimited being, and this is an important part, though not the whole, of the concept of God as a factually necessary being. I shall argue that the notion of factual necessity, when appropriately spelled out, is an essential element in the Christian doctrine of God, but that the notion of logical necessity is both philosophically and religiously profitless, and indeed even dangerous, to theology.

It is important to distingush explicitly between logical and factual necessity, not only for the elucidation of the doctrine of God within the Church, but also in the interests of apologetics. For, a number of contemporary philosophers of the analytical school have assumed that Christian theology requires the notion of logically necessary being, and, having noted that this idea is rendered meaningless by the modern understanding of the nature of logical necessity, have rejected what they suppose to be the Christian concept of God. They are, however, I believe, mistaken in their initial assumption.

My thesis thus has a threefold bearing. I wish to suggest, as a matter of theology, that the idea of the divine being as factually necessary is more adequate to the data of Christian faith than the idea of God's being as logically necessary; and as a matter of philosophy, that the idea of factually necessary being is immune from the criticisms which have rightly been levelled against the notion of logically necessary being; and as a matter of history, that the notion of God's being as factually necessary has a stronger claim to be regarded as the normative Christian use of the term "necessary being" than has its interpretation in terms of logical necessity.

Let us begin with the idea of logically necessary being. To say that God has logically necessary being, or that His existence is logically necessary, is to say that it is logically impossible that God should not exist; or that the concept of God is such that the proposition "God exists" is a logical, analytic, or *a priori* truth; or again that the proposition "God does not exist" is a self-contradiction, a statement of such a kind that it is logically impossible for it to be true. Such a claim, however, contravenes one of the fundamental positions of empiricist philosophy—that an existential proposition (i.e., a proposition asserting existence) cannot be logically necessary. For, modern empiricism is largely founded upon the distinction between, in Hume's phrases, "the relations between ideas" on the one hand, and "matters of fact and existence" on the other. Given this distinction, logical necessity clearly belongs exclusively to the sphere of the relations between ideas. The ideas of "larger" and "smaller," for example, are such that it is a logically necessary truth that if A is larger than B, then B is smaller than A, the necessity arising from the meanings which we have given to the words "larger" and "smaller." On the same principle, such propositions as "God is omniscient" and "God is omnipotent" express necessary truths, if "God" has been defined as "a being who is omniscient and omnipotent" or, compendiously, as "unlimited Being." Given this definition, it is not only a truth but an analytic truth that God is omniscient and omnipotent; for the definition renders it incorrect to call a Being "God" who is other than omniscient and omnipotent. But, on the other hand, "God exists" cannot be treated in the same way. God cannot be *defined* as existing. For, in the familiar slogan which has emerged from the critiques of the Ontological Argument, existence is not a predicate. To say that *x* exists is not to define, or to expand the definition of, the term "*x*," but is to assert that this term refers to some object. And whether a given description has a referent or, to use another terminology, whether a given term has denotation, is a question of fact which cannot be settled *a priori*.

The logical doctrine involved, which had been previously clearly delineated by Hume and Kant, has been formulated definitively in our own time by Bertrand Russell in his theory of descriptions.[3] Russell showed that the question "Does *x* exist?" does not imply that in some prior sense the *x* of which we speak is, or subsists, or has being; and further, that the assertion that *x* exists is not an attribution to a subsisting *x* of the further characteristic of existence. It is rather the assertion, with regard to a certain description (or name as standing for a description) that this description has a referent. Thus "horses exist" has the logical structure: "there are *x*'s such that '*x* is a horse' is true." Such an analysis exorcises the puzzle which has tended since the time of Plato to haunt negative existential propositions. "Unicorns do not exist" does not entail that unicorns must first in some mysterious sense *be* in order that we may then say of them that they do not exist; it means simply that "there are no *x*'s such that '*x* is a unicorn' is true." And "God exists" means "there is one (and only one) *x* such that '*x* is omniscient, omnipotent, etc.' is true." This Russellian analysis makes plain the logical structure of propositions asserting existence. Their structure is such that they cannot be true by definition, or therefore by *a priori* necessity. Hence the concept of a being such that the proposition asserting its existence is a logically necessary truth, is a self-contradictory concept. There cannot—logically cannot—be a being whose non-existence is logically impossible. I conclude then that we must on philosophical grounds repudiate all talk of God as having necessary being, when the necessity in question is construed as logical necessity.

Granting then that the notion of God's existence as *logically* necessary has to be ruled out as untenable, it is perhaps worth asking, as a matter of history, whether this notion has in fact figured at all prominently in Christian thought.[4] The first great thinker of the Church who comes to mind in this connexion is Anselm. The ontological argument, to the effect that the concept of God, as the concept of the greatest conceivable being, entails the existence of God, appears to be an attempt to show that the proposition "God exists" is a logically necessary truth. Certainly Descartes' version of the ontological argument has this character. According to Descartes, as the concept of a triangle entails the truth that its internal angles are jointly equal to two right angles, so the concept of God entails the truth that God exists.[5] But in Anselm himself there is another line of thought which stands in conflict with such an interpretation. In the second formulation of the ontological argument, in the third chapter of the *Proslogion,* we read that "it is possible to conceive of a being which cannot be conceived not to exist" (*potest cogitari esse aliquid, quod non possit cogitari non esse*). On the face of it this statement would seem to confirm the view that Anselm has in mind what we would today call the notion of logically necessary being. For the most natural interpretation of his words, at any rate by a twentieth-century reader, is that a being which cannot be conceived not to exist means a being whose non-existence is logically inconceivable, that is to say, logically impossible. However, when we turn to Anselm's reply to Gaunilo we find that he states explicitly what he means by the notion of beings which can and which cannot be conceived not to exist.

> All those objects, and those alone, can be conceived not to exist, which have a beginning or end or composition of parts: also . . . whatever at any place or at any time does not exist as a whole. That being alone, on the other hand, cannot be conceived not to exist, in which any conception discovers neither beginning nor end nor composition of parts [*nec initium nec finem nec partium conjunctionem*], and which any conception finds always and everywhere as a whole.[6]

Here we have something quite different from the claim that "God exists" is a logically necessary truth. We have instead the essence of the contrasting notion of factual necessity—the notion, that is, of God as sheer, ultimate, unconditioned reality, without origin or end. Another aspect of the concept of factual necessity, namely *aseity,* is contributed by Anselm in the *Monologion,* where he draws the distinction between existence *a se* and existence *ab alio.* He says of God:

> The supreme Substance, then, does not exist through any efficient agent, and does not derive existence from any matter, and was not aided in being brought into existence by any external causes. Nevertheless, it by no means exists through nothing, or derives existence from nothing; since, through itself and from itself, it is whatever it is [*per seipsam et ex seipsa est quidquid est*].[7]

The relation between this aspect of Anselm's thought and his ontological argument is another and difficult question into which I do not propose to enter; I only wish, for the present purpose, to point to the presence, often I think unnoticed, of the notion of factually necessary being in his discussions.

Let us now turn the centuries to Thomas Aquinas, who explicitly uses the term "necessary being." [8] The conclusion of his Third Way argument is that "there must exist something the existence of which is necessary" (*oportet aliquid esse necessarium in rebus*).[9] But he also, I believe, like Anselm, uses the idea of necessary existence in the sense of factually, and not logically, necessary existence. For in the Third Way passage the mark of contingency is transiency, or temporal finitude—having a beginning and an end in time. And by contrast the mark of non-contingency, or of the necessary being of God, must be not having a beginning or an end in time—in other words, *eternal* being.

Can we then perhaps equate contingent with transient existence, and necessary with eternal existence? The answer which must be given, which is also the answer implicit in Thomas, is No. Eternity is one of the ingredients of the necessary being of the Godhead, but is not by itself sufficient. For it is possible to conceive of something existing eternally, not because it is such that there is and could be no power capable of abolishing it, but only because, although there are powers capable of abolishing it, they always refrain from doing so. Such a being would be eternal by courtesy of the fact that it is never destroyed, but not by the positive virtue or power of being indestructible. And it is surely integral to the Christian concept of

God that God, as the ultimate Lord of all, is not capable of being destroyed.

We must add at this point that, as the ultimate Lord of all, God is also incorruptible, in the sense of being incapable of ceasing either to exist or to possess His divine characteristics by reason of an inner decay or discerption. God can neither be destroyed from without nor suffer dissolution from within.

Indestructibility and incorruptibility, however, even taken together, cannot replace but must supplement the notion of eternal being. For it is possible to conceive of something being both indestructible and incorruptible and yet not eternal in the sense of being without beginning or end. Such a being would exist only if created, but once created would be indissoluble and indestructible.

In Thomist theology, angels and human souls are held to have precisely this character, on the ground that they are simple substances. They have a beginning by divine creation, but once created they exist for ever, unless of course destroyed by omnipotent divine action. As incorruptible, such beings are described as necessary beings, and it is presumably these, and perhaps especially angels, which Thomas has in mind when he distinguishes in the Third Way passage between necessary beings which have their necessary existence caused by another and ultimately necessary being which does not have its necessary existence caused by another, but which is uncreated and is God. Some Thomist theologians describe these two kinds of necessary being as, in the one case, intrinsically but not extrinsically necessary, and in the other case, both intrinsically and extrinsically necessary. These definitional refinements do not concern us here except as emphasising that in Thomist thought the notion of necessary being is not an all-or-nothing logical concept but is a factual notion, capable of degrees and qualifications; so that the distinction between necessary and contingent being is not to be correlated with the distinction between logically necessary and contingent truths. Necessity is for Thomas a factual or ontic and not a logical characteristic.

I conclude then, concerning Thomas, that whilst he does not explicitly make the distinction between logical and factual necessity, in practice he cleaved so consistently to one side of the distinction that he was not led into any important ambiguity or confusion by the lack of an explicit separation of the two notions. However, some Thomist writers of our own day do fall into the ambiguity which their master avoided. M. Maritain, for example,[10] uses an instance of logical necessity to illustrate the idea of existence *a se,* thereby revealing that he is not conscious of the difference between these two notions. He first defines necessary existence in these terms: "a thing is necessary when it *cannot* be prevented, contingent when it *can* be prevented. A thing is *absolutely necessary* when nothing can prevent it from being." This is a clear enough account of the notion of existence *a se.* But in the next sentence Maritain offers an example from mathematics. "Thus the properties of the sphere," he says, "are absolutely necessary" (p. 27). Now the properties of a sphere—for example, the fact that every point on its surface is equidistant from the centre—are indeed absolutely necessary; that is to say, there could not possibly be a sphere which lacked these properties. But the reason for this is not that there is nothing which can *prevent* a sphere from having these properties, but simply that these properties belong to the definition of "sphere." There is nothing to prevent there being objects which approximate in varying degrees to this particular set of properties, but such objects would not be called spheres for the simple reason that we have chosen to confine the name "sphere" to objects which fit certain specifications, which thus constitute the defining and necessary properties of a sphere.

II

If a skilled theologian can suppose that the Christian concept of God requires the notion of logically necessary existence, we can hardly blame secular philosophers if they make the same assumption and proceed to draw damaging conclusions from it. I should like in this connexion to refer to the much discussed article by Professor J. N. Findlay of London University, entitled "Can God's existence be disproved?" [11] in which he derives from the self-contradictory nature of the idea of logically necessary being what he regards as a strict disproof of divine existence. To see what is amiss with Findlay's argument is by contrast to see a little more clearly the outlines of a religiously and philosophically acceptable account of the unique mode of being of the Godhead.

Professor Findlay is, as far as I know, the first philosopher to have proposed an *a priori* proof of the non-existence of God. He puts the ontological argument into reverse by contending that the concept of deity, so far from guaranteeing the existence of an object corresponding to it, is such as to guarantee that no object corresponds to it.

Findlay defines the concept of God as that of the adequate object of religious attitudes, a religious attitude being described as one in which we tend "to abase ourselves before some object, to defer to it wholly, to devote ourselves to it with unquestioning enthusiasm, to bend the knee before it, whether literally or metaphorically";[12] such an attitude is rationally adopted only by one who believes that the object to which he relates himself as worshipper has certain very remarkable characteristics. Findlay lists the most important of these characteristics. First, an adequate object of religious attitudes must be conceived as being infinitely superior to ourselves in value or worth. (Accordingly Findlay refers to this object as "he" rather than as "it.") Second, he must be conceived as being unique: God must not merely be one of a class of beings of the same kind, but stand in an asymmetrical relationship to all other objects as the source of whatever value they may have. Third, says Findlay, the adequate objects of religious attitudes must be conceived as not merely happening to exist, but as existing necessarily; if he merely happened to exist he would not be worthy of the full and unqualified attitude of worship. And fourth, this being must be conceived as not merely happening to possess his various characteristics, but as possessing them in some necessary manner. For our present purpose we may conflate these two necessities, necessary existence and the necessary possession of properties, and treat them as one. It should be borne in mind throughout that in Findlay's argument "necessary" means "logically necessary."

It is the last two in his list of requirements which provide the ground for Findlay's ontological disproof of theism.

For if God is to satisfy religious claims and needs, he must be a being in every way inescapable, One whose existence and whose possession of certain excellencies we cannot possibly conceive away. And modern views make it self-evidently absurd (if they don't make it ungrammatical) to speak of such a Being and attribute existence to him.[13]

For, as we have already noted, post-Humean empiricism can assign no meaning to the idea of necessary existence, since nothing can be conceived to exist which cannot also be conceived not to exist. No propositions of the form "x exists" can be analytically true. Hence, Findlay argues, the concept of an adequate object of religious attitudes, involving as it does the notion of a necessarily existent being who possesses his characteristic in some necessary manner, is a self-contradictory concept. We can know *a priori,* from inspection of the idea itself, that there is and can be no such being.

We may distinguish in Findlay's argument a philosophical premise to the effect that no existential propositions can be necessary truths, and a theological premise to the effect that an adequate object of religious worship must be such that it is logically necessary that he exists. Of these two premises I wish to accept the former and reject the latter. I deny, that is to say, the theological doctrine that God must be conceived, if at all, in such a way that "God exists" is a logically necessary truth. I deny this for precisely the same reason as Findlay, namely that the demand that "God exists" should be a necessary truth is, like the demand that a circle should be square, not a proper demand at all, but a misuse of language. Only, whereas Findlay concludes that the notion of an adequate object of religious attitude is an absurdity, I conclude that that of which the idea is an absurdity cannot be an adequate object of religious attitudes; it would on the contrary be an unqualifiedly *in*adequate object of worship.

Let us then ask the question, which seems highly appropriate at this point, as to how religious persons actually think of the Being whom they regard as the adequate object of their worship. What aspect of the Christian experience of God lies behind the idea of necessary being?

The concept of God held by the Biblical writers was based upon their experience of God as awesome power and holy will confronting them and drawing them into the sphere of His ongoing purpose. God was known as a dynamic will interacting with their own wills; a sheer given reality, as inescapably to be reckoned with as destructive storm and life-giving sunshine, or the fixed contours of the land, or the hatred of their enemies and the friendship of their neighbours; indeed even more ineluctably so, as the Book of Jonah emphasises. God was not for them an inferred entity; He was an experienced reality. The Biblical writers were (sometimes, though doubtless not at all times) as vividly conscious of being in God's presence as they were of living in a material environment. Their pages resound and vibrate with the sense of God's presence, as a building might resound and vibrate from the tread of some great being walking through it. They thought of this holy presence as unique—as the maker and ruler of the universe, the sole rightful sovereign of men and angels, as eternal and infinite, and as the ultimate reality and determining power, in relation to whom His creatures have no standing except as the objects of His grace. But nowhere in the Biblical thought about God is use made of the idea of logical necessity. The notion is quite foreign to the characteristically Hebraic and concrete utterances found in the Bible, and forms no part of the Biblical concept or concepts of God.

But, it might be said, was it not to the Biblical writers inconceivable that God should *not* exist, or that He should cease to exist, or should lose His divine powers and virtues? Would it not be inconceivable to them that God might one day go out of existence, or cease to be good and become evil? And does not this attitude involve an implicit belief that God exists necessarily, and possesses His divine characteristics in some necessary manner? The answer, I think, is that it was to the Biblical writers psychologically inconceivable—as we say colloquially, unthinkable—that God might not exist, or that His nature might undergo change. They were so vividly conscious of God that they were unable to doubt His reality, and they were so firmly reliant upon His integrity and faithfulness that they could not contemplate His becoming other than they knew Him to be. They would have allowed as a verbal concession only that there might possibly be no God; for they were convinced that they were at many times directly aware of His presence and of His dealings with them. But the question whether the non-existence of God is *logically* inconceivable, or *logically* impossible, is a purely philosophical puzzle which could not be answered by the prophets and apostles out of their own first-hand religious experience. This does not of course represent any special limitation of the Biblical figures. The logical concept of necessary being cannot be given in religious experience. It is an object of philosophical thought and not of religious experience. It is a product—as Findlay argues, a malformed product—of reflection. A religious person's reply to the question "Is God's existence logically necessary?" will be determined by his view of the nature of logical necessity; and this is not part of his religion but of his system of logic. The Biblical writers in point of fact display no view of the nature of logical necessity, and would doubtless have regarded the topic as of no religious significance. It cannot reasonably be claimed, then, that necessary existence was part of their conception of the adequate object of human worship.

What, we must therefore ask, has led Findlay to hold so confidently that logically necessary existence is an essential element in the religious man's concept of God? His process of thought is revealed in these words: "We can't help feeling that the worthy object of our worship can never be a thing that merely *happens* to exist, nor one on which all other objects merely *happen* to depend." [14] The reasoning here is that if a being does not exist by logical necessity, he merely happens to exist; and in this case he ought not to be worshipped as God. But in presenting the dilemma "either God exists necessarily, or he merely happens to exist," Findlay makes the very mistake for which he has criticised the theologians. Findlay should be the last person to use this dichotomy, since he has himself rendered it inoperative by pointing out that one-half of the dichotomy is meaningless. And to remove half a dichotomy is to remove the dichotomy. If for example it is said that all human beings are either witches or non-witches, and it is then discovered that there is no such thing as a witch, it becomes pointless, and indeed misleading, to describe everyone as a non-witch. Likewise, having concluded that the notion of necessary existence has no meaning, to continue to speak of things merely *happening* to exist, as though this stood in contrast to some other mode of existing, no longer has any validity. From an empiricist standpoint, there are not two different ways of existing, existing by logical necessity and merely happening to exist. A thing either exists or does not exist; or to be more exact a description either has or does not have a referent. But Findlay, after ruling out the notion of necessary existence, in relation to which alone the contrasting idea of "merely happening to exist" has any meaning, continues to use the latter category, and, what is more, to use it as a term of reproach! This is a very advanced form of the method of having it both ways.

Our conclusion must be that Findlay has only disproved the existence of God if we mean by God a being whose existence is a matter of logical necessity. Since, however, we do not mean this, we may take Findlay's argument instead as emphasising that we must either abandon the traditional phrase "necessary being" or else be very clear that the necessary being of God is not to be construed as *logically* necessary being.

III

We have arrived thus far at an identification of the necessary being of the Godhead with incorruptible and indestructible being without beginning or end. These characteristics, however, can properly be regarded as different aspects of the more fundamental characteristic which the Scholastics termed aseity, or being *a se*. The usual English translation, "self-existence," is strictly a meaningless phrase, but for the lack of a better we must continue to use it. The core of the notion of aseity is independent being. That God exists *a se* means that He is not dependent upon anything for His existence. In contrast to this, the created universe and everything in it exist *ab alio*. For it is true of each distinguishable item composing the universe that its existence depends upon some factor or factors beyond itself. Only God exists in total non-dependence; He alone exists absolutely as sheer unconditioned, self-existent being.

From God's aseity, or ontic independence, His eternity, indestructibility, and incorruptibility can be seen to follow. A self-existent being must be eternal, i.e. without temporal limitation. For if He had begun to exist, or should cease to exist, He must have been caused to exist, or to cease to exist, by some power other than Himself; and this would be inconsistent with His aseity. By the same token He must be indestructible, for to say that He exists in total ontic independence is to say that there is and could be no reality with the capacity to constitute or to destroy Him; and likewise He must be incorruptible, for otherwise His aseity would be qualified as regards its duration. The question might, however, be asked at this point: "Although it is incompatible with the idea of a self-existent being that He should ever be destroyed from without, yet is there any contradiction in the thought of such a being destroying Himself?" Is it not possible in principle that God might "commit suicide"? The question perhaps deserves more than the brief discussion which is possible within the limits of this paper. I am inclined, however, to think that the query itself is as logically improper as it is obviously religiously improper; and this for three reasons. First, the expression "commit suicide" is highly misleading in this context. The "suicide" of the absolutely self-existent being would not be like a human suicide though on a much grander scale. For the concept of divine death is not analogous to that of human death. The death of a human being means the destruction or the cessation of function of his physical body; but God has no physical body to be destroyed, whether by Himself or by another. We have to try to think instead of a purely "mental suicide"; but as far as I can see this is a completely empty phrase, to which we are able to attach no positive meaning. Second, an absolute end is as inconceivable as is an absolute beginning. Third, there is an additional contradiction in the notion of sheer, unqualified *being* ceasing to exist. Specific modifications of being may alter or cease, but to speak of being itself ceasing to exist is apparently to speak without meaning. I cannot then accept the question as to whether God might commit suicide as a genuine question posing intelligible alternatives.

Finally, to refer back to Findlay's discussion, it is meaningless to say of the self-existent being that He might not have existed or that He merely happens to exist. For what could it mean to say of the eternal, uncreated Creator of everything other than Himself that He "merely happens to exist"? When we assert of a dependent and temporally finite being, such as myself, that I only happen to exist, we mean that if such-and-such an event had occurred in the past, or if such-and-such another event had failed to occur, I should not now exist. But no such meaning can be given to the statement "A self-existent being only happens to exist" or "might not have existed." There is no conceivable event such that if it had occurred, or failed to occur, a self-existent being would not have existed; for the concept of aseity is precisely the exclusion of such dependence. There is and could be nothing which would have prevented a self-existent being from coming to exist, for it is meaningless even to speak of a self-existent being as *coming to* exist.

What may properly be meant, then, by the statement that God is, or has, necessary as distinguished from contingent being is that God *is,* without beginning or end, and without origin, cause, or ground of any kind whatsoever. He *is,* as the ultimate, unconditioned, absolute, unlimited being.

On the one hand, the fact that God is, is not a logically necessary truth; for no matter of fact can be logically necessary. The reality of God is a sheer datum. But on the other hand this is an utterly unique datum. That God is, is not one fact amongst others, but is related asymmetrically to all other facts as that which determines them. This is the ultimate given circumstance behind which it is not possible to go with either question or explanation. For to explain something means either to assign a cause to it or to show its place within some wider context in relation to which it is no longer puzzling to us. But the idea of the self-existent Creator of everything other than Himself is the idea of a reality which is beyond the scope of these explanatory procedures. As self-existent, such a being is uncaused, and is therefore not susceptible to the causal type of explanation; and as the Creator of all things other than Himself He stands in no wider context—on the contrary, His creative action constitutes the context in which all else stands. He is the ultimate reality, about which it is no longer meaningful to ask the questions which can be asked concerning other realities. For this reason God cannot but be mysterious to us. He is mysterious, not merely because there are questions about Him to which we do not know the answers, but because we frame questions about Him to which there are no answers since the questions themselves can have meaning only in relation to that which is not ultimate. As the final unconditioned, all-conditioning reality, God cannot be included within any system of explanation. This is to say not that we cannot know any truths about Him, but that such truths are not logically deduced conclusions but sheer incorrigible facts disclosed within human experience. We may express this by saying that God has no characterising name; He is not of any kind, or for any reason, or from any cause; He just *is,* and is what He is. When He reveals His nature to man He says to Moses "I shall be what I shall be";[15] and the fulfilment of that prolepsis is in the fact, the given historical fact, of Jesus Christ.

IV

A further step remains to be taken. For there are two respects in which the concept of aseity is less than adequate to the Christian understanding of God, or at least there are two dangers to be guarded against in speaking of God's aseity. One is the danger of understanding aseity in a purely static sense; and the other is the readiness of aseity to be construed in merely negative terms, simply as independence. The next major original treatment of the subject since Aquinas, that of Karl Barth in our own time, would appear to have been undertaken with these two dangers in mind; and it is accordingly to Barth that we now turn.

In his great dogmatic work, Barth has a section on the *aseitas Dei* under the heading "The Being of God in Freedom."[16] As against any tendency to think of God as static, self-existent substance, the term "freedom" reminds us that God is the living God, the Life which is the source of all life, and that He is Life not only as an Agent in human time, but also in His own hidden being, apart from and prior to that which is other than Himself. This is an important aspect of the Christian concept of God. The Scholastic *actus purus* and the more Biblical term "life" both point to it; and Paul Tillich, in his own theological system, seeks to introduce the same dynamic note when he refers to God as "the power of Being." All these terms—pure act, divine life, freedom, and power—are of course symbolic in Tillich's sense of being expressions whose ordinary meaning is partially negated by that to which they point. That is to say (speaking more prosaically), even as we use them we are conscious of certain respects in which they would be misleading if taken literally. However, granting the symbolic character of all these words, the term "freedom" as Barth uses it does appear to have special appositeness as supplementing the notion of aseity.

Barth draws a distinction between what he calls the primary, or ontic, and the secondary, or neotic, absoluteness or freedom of God. The former refers to God's absoluteness in Himself, the latter to His absoluteness or Lordship in relation to His creation. This secondary absoluteness is characterised by Barth as total independence; God does not depend for His existence upon any factor external to Himself. From this point of view, He is "the One who is free from all origination, conditioning or determination from without, by that which is not Himself." [17] But, Barth insists, we must not think of God's unique mode of being only or even primarily in negative terms, as the absence of dependence upon His creation. God's absoluteness in relation to the world is secondary and derivative. Behind it there lies the primary absoluteness or freedom which is prior to and outside of all relations. God is free, says Barth, "quite apart from His relation to another from whom He is free." [18] God, in His own inner being, entirely apart from His creative action, is intrinsically free, and "the freedom to exist which He exercises in His revelation is the same which He has in the depths of His eternal being, and which is proper to Him quite apart from His exercise of it ad extra." [19] This insight of Barth's provides an important balancing note to the traditional discussion of aseity. Instead of being thought of primarily in His relation to the world, even though that relation be one of unqualified independence, God is to be conceived in the first instance as positive self-existence in infinite richness and plenitude. The ultimate Being should not be defined negatively as the One who does not depend upon other beings; on the contrary, His independence of the world is a corollary of His own sheer unique Godness, His infinite and absolute uncreated self-sustaining life.

Barth's doctrine of the primary absoluteness or freedom of God also provides the resources for his response to the question "How can we think of the absolute, self-existent Being as creating a universe and bestowing upon it a relative autonomy over against Himself, and yet remaining unimpaired in His own absolute self-sufficiency and freedom?" [20] This, however, is a distinct, though adjacent, topic which cannot be taken up in the present article.

Finally, a brief summary of conclusions. If we continue (as I think we properly may) to use the expression "necessary being," we must explicitly interpret it in terms of the concept of factual, as distinguished from logical, necessity.[21] So interpreted, the necessary being of the Godhead is His aseity, understood primarily, however, not as non-dependence upon His creation, but positively, as absolute and unlimited being in infinite plenitude and freedom.

NOTES

1. B.184.
2. B.279–80.
3. *Introduction to Mathematical Philosophy*, 2nd edn. (1920), ch. 16.
4. Whether or not this notion occurs prominently in Christian thought, it does apparently have a place in Muslim theology. Apparently the *pons asinorum* which the theological novice must cross is the distinction between the necessary, the possible, and the impossible; and the necessary is defined as that the non-existence of which cannot be thought. (D. B. Macdonald, *Aspects of Islam* [London, 1911], p. 121.)
5. *Meditations*, V.
6. *Responsio editoris*, ch. IV. Cf. *Proslogion*, ch. XXII.
7. Ch. VI.
8. *Summa Theologica*, I, q. 2, a. 3.
9. Cf. Norman Malcolm, "Anselm's Ontological Arguments," *Philosophical Review*, 69 (1960).
10. "Necessity and Contingency" in *Essays in Thomism*, ed. Robert E. Brennan (New York, 1942).
11. *Mind*, 57 (1948). Reprinted in *New Essays in Philosophical Theology*, edd. Flew and MacIntyre (London, 1955).
12. *New Essays*, p. 49.
13. *Ibid.*, p. 55.
14. *Ibid.*, p. 52.
15. Exodus 3:14.
16. *Church Dogmatics*, Vol. II, pt. I, ch. VI, § 28, 3.
17. *Ibid.*, p. 307.
18. *Ibid.*
19. *Ibid.*, p. 305.
20. It should be noted that Barth has developed his position further, in IV/1, ch. XIV, § 59, 1, in the direction of holding that the self–other relationship is already present within the triune Godhead, so that creation does not involve the problem of the inherently unrelated entering into relations.
21. Cf. Terrence Penelhum, "Divine Necessity," *Mind*, 69 (1960).

8

A New Theory of Analogy

James F. Ross

University of Pennsylvania

THE RELATIONSHIP OF THF FIRST ANALOGY THEORY
TO THE SECOND

THE BASIC EVIDENCE THAT THERE IS SOMETHING within the
structure of natural language which affects meaning derivation
for its terms was remarked by the ancients. It was adroitly in-
corporated by Aristotle into his partial account of meaning and
was applied by him to the solution of metaphysical problems.
Aristotle's doctrine was considerably expanded by Aquinas,
and it is to Aquinas that I attribute the first Analogy Theory,
the first organized account of the basic evidence, its philosophical implications, and its application to the solution of a family
of philosophical problems. It is only by having appropriated
his insights and observations that one can pretend to set about
the construction of a new Theory of Analogy.[1]

The basic evidence consists of three things: (*a*) that many
terms have varying meanings in different contexts and that the

Reprinted from the *Proceedings* of the American Catholic Philosophical Association, 44 (1970), 70–85, with the permission of the author and the publishers.

meanings of some pairs of same-terms may be regarded as being derivative either from one another (*unius ad alterum*) or from some "prior" use (or set of uses) of the same term (*multorum ad unum*) ; (*b*) that there are sets of same-term-occurrences which are, taken pair by pair, equivocal but which can be ordered as "meaning derivates" with respect to certain weak generalizations ("rules of meaning derivation" or "analogy rules") ;[2] and (*c*) that a person competent in the use of his native language (and this includes even small children) will have no more difficulty understanding a derivative use of a term which he already knows how to use in another sense, than he will in understanding simple syntactical transformations of common expression forms.

Sets of same-term-occurrences which are in pairs equivocal with one another are not all equivocal in the same way: within some sets the equivocation is "regularity-controlled"; and, persons competent in the language have apparently internalized these regularities because derivative meanings of terms are employed with the same facility as are the various grammatical transformations.

There is, of course, a great deal to be said about the historical details of the first Analogy Theory,[3] especially about St. Thomas' sensitive location (with the help of Aristotle) of some of the regularities of meaning derivation; about his appreciation of the relativity to speaker, subject matter, kind of thing, etc., of "priority" of meaning, and about his application of his results to the solution of theological and metaphysical problems (and the subsequent history of misinterpretation, misapplication, and misunderstanding of his results).

But there were certain defects and incompletenesses in the first Analogy Theory, some of which stem from the fact that the philosophy of language was not being investigated systematically but only as far as was needed to resolve problems in metaphysics, theology, ethics, etc. Some of the defects are "formal," located in the principles upon which the theory is based.

For example, the first Analogy Theory was not general enough; it did not account for the fact that *most* words in the language (and that includes Latin and Greek as well as English) admit of derivative uses, and that when we compare sets of same-term-occurrences, analogy of meaning or "regularity conforming meaning derivation" is the rule rather than the exception.

Charles Fries observed: "It became clear from more than seventy-five years of work upon the great historical dictionaries, that multiple meaning for words is normal, not 'queer.' . . . The number of different meanings for each of the commonly used words of English, as recorded and illustrated by verifiable quotations in *The Oxford Dictionary,* is just unbelievable." [4] Reflecting even briefly upon whether those multitudinous meanings for same terms may be without any discernible order, one will be struck by how unlikely that hypothesis would be. Rather, analogy as meaning derivation for sets of same terms is practically omnipresent within human discourse.[5] A convincing but simple illustration of this is a typical vocabulary-controlled second-grade linguistic reader (like the Fries–Wilson–Rudolph *Merrill Linguistic Readers,* numbers four and five[6]). Terms like "fix," "can," "but," "pick," "fit," "make," "had," "see," "sit" occur in a multitude of meanings which, even on simple inspection, we can see must be interrelated not by historical principles alone but by forms of meaning derivation. And a child has no difficulty whatever understanding them; in fact, he has difficulty in realizing that the meanings are diverse because the uses of the words are familiar from spoken language and the tokens look the same; his automatic and intuitive grasp of their meanings inhibits distinction: "fix dinner," "fix a date," "fix a car," "fix a hook to a wall," "fix a dispute."

Analogy, considered as a semantical feature of natural language, is part of the expansion structure of the language; it belongs to those structural features by which the language is adaptable to new kinds of thoughts and transformable to express new kinds of experience. Therefore the analogy rules will be described as rules which partly control the generation of new uses for terms. And yet the regularities from which we extrapolate the analogy rules are actual relationships among already existent sets of same-term-occurrences (especially in recorded and written discourses); and it is to those regularities that one attends in attempting to formulate analogy rules, and to those regularities that one appeals for the verification of the rules.[7] Because this is to be an analogy theory for English (though I venture to claim that the basic principles hold for every natural language and that it will be only the particular rules which will differ), the analogy rules must not only allow us to derive new uses for terms in English but must in an illuminating way order the sets of meaning-differentiated same-term-occurrences within the corpus of available actual discourse in English. For it is only by appeal to meaning regularities within the corpus of actual discourse that one could ever show that analogy, rule-governed-meaning-derivation, is a feature of the semantics of natural language.

Falsification of the particular analogy rules I shall mention will not falsify the claim that meaning derivation is "rule governed" in our language; for I may not have grasped correctly the way in which the derivations are regularized. To falsify the analogy hypothesis for our language, I think one would have to show that there is *no* feature of the semantics which accounts for the derivation of meaning within sets of meaning-differentiated same-term-occurrences (which seems apparent to us in literally thousands of examples) and which will also provide an explanation of cognitivity preservation, despite equivocation across utterances.

A NEW THEORY OF ANALOGY

A new Theory of Analogy will differ from the first theory primarily in its formality, in its explicit formulation of its assumptions and hypotheses, and in its attempt to provide reasons for each part of the theory; secondly, the second Analogy Theory will be more explicit about the fact that it is an empirical theory, depending upon investigation of the analogy regularities.

In this brief summary, I present seven of the hypotheses upon which the theory is based, arguing in some detail for four of them, and, in the process, presenting some of the basic distinctions and assumptions of the theory.

I shall argue as follows:

1. Every pair of same-term occurrences within discourse contexts each of which is in a discourse environment is either univocal or equivocal

2. Any pair which is equivocal is either simply equivocal or analogous.

3. A pair of equivocal same-term-occurrences is analogous: if and only if there is an analogy rule (which may be a conjunction of, or other logical concatenation of, "atomic" analogy rules—analogy rules which contain no analogy rules as logical parts) with respect to which one member of the pair of same-term-occurrences is meaning generable from the other. *And* a pair of same-term-occurrences is such that one element is meaning generable from the other with respect to an analogy rule R if and only if: a native speaker of L who understands the use of t^1 in its context (1), and also understands R (either explicitly or through experience), can generate a discourse context with a same-term-occurrence T^3, which is univocal with t^2. (Two other accounts of "derivation" are presented in what follows.)

4. Analogues ordering within sets of same-term-occurrences may be either direct or indirect; family resembling terms occur in sets which are, overall, indirectly analogous.

5. The analogy structure of English may be at least partially formulated in specific rules of analogy (and the "output" of the application of an analogy rule may be used as "input" for other rules).

6. Any term in the language may be used analogously with respect to some pairs of its same-term-occurrences.

7. There is a set of analogy regularities which involve meaning-derivations which parallel what St. Thomas called "analogy of proportionality" where the *modus significandi* of a term is altered by the presence of a countervailing term in its environment.

Let us consider these theses and the distinctions needed to understand them.

Same Term

Since "is analogous with," "is equivocal with," and "is univocal with" are metalanguage relationships which obtain primarily between distinct occurrences in utterance or writing of the same term, we need an account of the sameness of terms.[8]

It is particularly important that our criterion of whether two phoneme sequences or two grapheme sequences are tokens of the same term be independent of the meaning relationships which may obtain between the sequences and be applicable to both written and uttered speech. This is indicated by the fact that any pair of same-term-tokens may be either univocal or equivocal; and hence, the particular meaning relationships which hold between the same-term-tokens must be irrelevant to their classification as tokens of the same word.

While there are some disputes among linguists about how best to carry out the identification of words in English,[9] I think that we can take the following as well enough established for our purposes: (1) that distributional analysis of the sounds of uttered speech will result in the identification of the set of phonemes in English;[10] (2) that the morphs (the minimum meaningful units) of the language can be identified by the distributional (especially contrastive) study of the phonemes, and that such study will also identify the morphemes, the minimal free variant meaningful units in English.[11] "It may be noted here that the morphemes are not distinguished directly on the basis of their meanings or meaning differences, but by the result of distributional operations upon the data of linguistics (these data including the meaning-like distinction between utterances which are not repetitions of each other)."[12] By common practice, "morpheme" means "minimum unity of grammatical analysis," and "morph" means "minimal unit of meaning,"[13] so that both "boy" and "-s" are morphs but "boys" is the morpheme.[14]

With the medieval-sounding expression "term" we are talking about something which is more like a morpheme than like a word; for one thing, a term does not have to be a spatially continuous expression; and we will regard "back up" as an expression type which has equivocal and analogous uses; and the same holds for some expressions of the form "with the———," "of a———," "in the———," etc.

Resolution of the disputes about the relationships of morphemes to words is not crucial since it is simply my claim that for two parts of two uttered expressions it is possible on distributional analysis to determine whether or not they are same-term-utterances.[15] The same holds for inscriptions.[16]

Discourse Context

In order to make our claims clear and conceptually manageable we introduce certain stipulations, some of which are more restrictive than is ideally desirable; but they can be relaxed later. For instance, we are concerned only with term occurrences (term tokens) which are within a discourse context and are used in it (rather than mentioned).

A discourse context for a term, T, is a complete uttered or inscribed sentential expression used by a speaker or writer within a discourse environment to make an assertion. A term occurs in a discourse context when and only when a token of that term is used in a sentential expression (uttered or inscribed) which is employed by some speaker or writer to make a statement within an environment of discourse.

Wherever a token for a term, T, occurs in a discourse context, we have a distinct occurrence of T, a distinct T-token; there are as many T-tokens or "same-term-occurrences of T" as there are numerically distinct tokens of T within discourse contexts, and there are as many discourse contexts as there are numerically distinct sentential expressions used assertively. Thus repetition of one's statement in exactly the same words constitutes a distinct discourse context for its terms as compared with the first expression.

Discourse Environment

A discourse environment for a given discourse context is specified by its subject matter and by the class of utterances and inscriptions which would be appropriate within an environment of thought for the speaker or writer who uses a sentential expression assertively. Every discourse context has at least one discourse environment. By insisting that all discourse contexts occur within discourse environments, I call attention to the fact that differential meanings for whole expressions are frequently derived from their different environments and that the meaning of a sentential expression may differ from speaker to hearer just because their discourse environments differ. So we consider all our examples as speaker-oriented and as having environments which are available to us in as much detail as we want them to be.

For instance in an environment of "baseball discourse," "It's a run!" has quite a different meaning from the same form of utterance in a discourse environment when a woman is putting on her stockings, even if the intonations happen to be the same. We therefore stipulate that for each example we can complete an environment to roughly the same degree that we can do so in our own speaking and writing, and can determine authoritatively when pairs of same-term-occurrences have the same meaning. We count the discussion of "force" in a political, a physical, and a police discussion as belonging to distinct environments: "Castro used force"; "Newton used force"; "The cat burglar used force." So too, religious discourse, historical discourse, philosophical discourse, etc., are considered as distinct discourse environments.

We can now state generally that the only term-occurence sets we are concerned with are term-occurrences in distinct discourse contexts each of which is within some discourse environment. Whenever we use expressions of the form "t^1" and "t^2" we are referring to same-term-occurrences in distinct discourse contexts (which are indexed by the superscripts), each of which is within some discourse environment.

Thesis I: *Every pair of same-term occurrences is either univocal or equivocal.* Every pair t^1 and t^2 either has the same meaning or differs in meaning, since those two predicates are contradictory opposites, and, since "is univocal with" and "is equivocal with" are the corresponding metalanguage predicates, *Thesis I* is analytically true.

Formal properties of "is univocal with": where "is univocal with" is a metalanguage predicate applicable to a pair of term tokens t^1 and t^2, the relation is reflexive, symmetrical, and transitive. Every term token is univocal with itself.

Thesis II: *Every pair of same-term-occurrences which is equivocal is either simply equivocal or is analogous.*

Formal properties of "is equivocal with": Where "is equivocal with" is a metalanguage predicate applicable to a pair of same-term-tokens, t^1 and t^2, the relation is irreflexive, symmetrical, and aliorelative. In general "is equivocal with" is *non*-transitive because in the set t^1-t^2-t^3, t^3 may be equivocal with t^2 just *because* t^3 is univocal with t^1 which is already equivocal with t^2.

Simply Equivocal: t^1 and t^2 are simply equivocal if t^1 and t^2 differ in meaning and there is no synchronic regularity of the language by which t^1 and t^2 are semantically ordered in such a way that one is rendered prior and the other "derived in meaning." Thus "fast" in "He ran fast"; "He observed the fast," "He stood fast" and "He considered her fast," is, pair by pair of same-term-occurrences, simply equivocal.

It is possible that the members of some equivocal pair may be *diachronically derived* with respect to general principles of linguistic evolution from one another. But if that principle is not also a *synchronic*[17] semantic regularity of the language, the terms are simply equivocal despite their historical derivation, etymology, etc.

Since the disjunction of "simply equivocal with" and "is analogous with" will be exclusive, *Thesis II* is analytically true.

Thesis III: T^1 is analogous with t^2 if there is a set of synchronic semantic REGULARITIES (R) which hold for L with respect to which (or with respect to some sub-set of which) one member of the pair is prior in meaning and the other derived.

We now have to explain "being ordered with respect to a semantic regularity of L" and "being derived in meaning." T^1 and t^2 are *ordered* with respect to R (some subset of [R]) if R has initial conditions or conditions of applicability to one element of a pair of same-term-occurrences which either t^1 or t^2 (but not both) satisfies and "derivation conditions" which are satisfied by the other member of the pair. The term-occurrence which satisfies the initial conditions of R is "prior" in meaning with respect to R. While t^1 may be prior to t^2 with respect to R, nothing precludes that t^2 may be prior (with respect to that same R) to t^3, which is equivocal with t^1. And it may happen that t^1 is prior to t^2 on R and that the order is reversed on R^1; for there is nothing which *a priori* rules it out that a pair of terms may have distinct analogy orderings with respect to two different semantical regularities. Moreover, as will be explained, not all analogous orderings will be *direct* (*unius ad alterum*).

The heart of the notion of semantic analogy lies in the requirement that the meaning or use of t^2 be derived from that of t^1 with respect to the Analogy Regularities. Naturally we do not mean "historically" derived but descriptive or theoretical derivation. There are several ways of explaining "derivation."

(1) We can treat "being derived" as an operational relation. T^2 is meaning generable from t^1 with respect to R if : a native speaker of L who understands the use of t^1 in its discourse context and who understands R (either explicitly or by experience) can generate a discourse context which contains t^2 (or an occurrence t^3 which is univocal with t^2) and which satisfies the "derivation conditions" of R.

(2) We can treat "being derived" as somewhat similar to the relationship of conclusion to premises in logic. When we say that the conclusion of a valid argument is, with respect to the applicable rules of logic, derived from the premises, we mean that by applying those rules of logic to legitimize transformations of the premises we can eventually *generate* the conclusion. Similarly, we can say that if t^2 is derived from t^1 with respect to R, then, taking t^1 as given and as satisfying the initial conditions of R, and applying R, we can generate t^2.

The function served by the analogy rules is to provide a *legitimizing parentage* within the established usage of terms for new, occasional, infrequent, or common but derived uses of terms, and to allow a speaker to shift without notice from one use to another.

(3) There is a third account of "meaning derivation," in terms of the paradigmatic and syntagmatic relations of term tokens within contexts and context environments.

The meaning of a given linguistic unit is a dependent function of that unit's (*a*) possible paradigmatic and syntagmatic relations with other units and (*b*) actual selection of such relationships which is brought about within a given context and environment. This principle is simply a specification of broader structural principles stated by Lyons,[18] that "linguistic units have no validity independently of their paradigmatic and syntagmatic relations with other units"; "every linguistic unit has a certain place in a system of relationships." Thus a term which may occur in "he Ψ-s" has relations of free variation and of contrast with other expressions which can occur in that frame. And a term token placed in that frame enters into syntagmatic (combinatorial) relations with the other term tokens in the frame and may have its paradigmatic relations affected by them. Thus, as Lyons points out, since "pint" can enter the frame "a . . . of milk," it contrasts paradigmatically with "bottle," "cup," "gallon," and even with "drink," "sip," and "taste." The syntagmatic relationships are combinatorial relationships in sentential expressions which are not necessarily sequential. It is through the syntagmatic relations that paradigmatic alterations in meaning for same-term-occurrences are contracted. Thus the reason t^1 differs in meaning from t^2 in (1) "The physical force was calculated (t^1)" and in (2) "The physical force was calculated (t^2)" is that the categorical difference in "physical force," which in (1) occurs in a discourse environment of "political persecution" and in (2) occurs in the environment of an engineering report, is communicated to "was calculated" through the syntagmatic relations within the expressions. This is exactly what happens in those cases in which same predicates are applied to categorically different things, a phenomenon St. Thomas described in terms of sameness of *res significata* and difference of *modus significandi*. The account of analogy as derivation comes to this: t^2 is derived in meaning with respect to t^1 if there is a regularity of L such that, given that t^1 satisfies certain paradigmatic and syntagmatic relations within (1), which are partially determined by some factor Ψ, then t^2 *differs* in (2), which occurs within an environment in which Φ occurs in *contrast* to Ψ, by paradigmatic relations which are communicated to t^2 by its syntagmatic relations to Φ. This suggests that derivation of meaning for T is accomplished by a pre-existent ordering of those other elements (Ψ and Φ) in the term-token environments which, by imposing different paradigmatic relationships upon t^1 and t^2, make t^2 derivative from t^1. E.g., in the frame (1) "Plato knows philosophy," "knows^1" is affected by the "category" of "Plato"; so too, in (2) "The Internal Revenue Service knows that 10 per cent of taxpayers lie about something," "knows^2" is paradigmatically affected by the category of "The Internal Revenue Service" and is appropriately altered in signification by the differences in the subjects (e.g., it would be inappropriate to ask "Is IRS conscious?").[19]

Thesis IV: Analogous ordering within sets of same-term-occurrences may be either direct or indirect.

So far we have been talking only about *direct* derivation with respect to analogy rules. But there are pairs of equivocal same-term-occurrences which, while they cannot be ordered into "prior-derived" by a simple-analogy rule, have common or at least overlapping derivations. And it would be misleading to say that they are simply equivocal. Sets of "family-resembling terms" are a good illustration.

The predicate "is analogous with" has direct and indirect applications. In one case t^2 can be analogous with t^1 because one term has its meaning generated from the other according to some analogy rule of the language; in another case t^3 will be said to be analogous to t^4, not because the meaning of t^3 was actually generated from t^4, but because there is an analogy rule according to which this could have happened, whether or not it did. In both cases the analogy is direct. In a third sense, t^5 will be said to be analogous to t^6 if there is a set of discourse contexts (7, 8, 9 involving t^7, t^8, t^9, etc.) such that there is an analogy rule R or a set of analogy rules (R), by which t^6 is generable from t^7, t^7 is generable from t^8, etc., and t^5 is generable from the last in that series. That is, t^5 and t^6 will be said to be analogous to one another if, regardless of the number of intermediate instances of the same terms which are analogous, there is an ordered application of the analogy rules of the language by which one use may be generated from the other. This is still direct, though intermediate, analogy-ordering. But there is also the possibility of analogy *duorum ad tertium* or *multorum ad unum*. We can suppose a tree which has at its summit the occurrence of t^1:

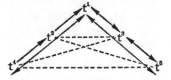

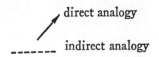

direct analogy

indirect analogy

You can imagine that the tree goes on indefinitely and has other second line branches than t^2 and t^3. The analogy down each side (t^1 to t^2 and t^2 to t^4, as well as t^1 to t^3) is already covered by the claim that these are analogous if there is an analogy rule by which the one could be directly generated from the other. But what of the relationships of the terms on opposite sides of the tree? Can t^2 be considered analogous to t^3 and to t^5? In the Aristotelian context this would be like asking whether, given that the "to be" of qualities and of relations is analogous to the "to be" of substances, the "to be" of qualities is analogous to the "to be" of relations? This is the same as our asking where the predicate "is analogous with" is transitive. "Is analogous with" is transitive only for direct analogy. We shall therefore have to acknowledge that the metalanguage predicate "is analogous with" is itself equivocal; whether it is simply equivocal or analogous, I do not as yet know.

The sense in which t^4 is analogous with t^1 in our tree may not be the sense in which t^4 is analogous with t^5. Thus the pair t^4-t^1 satisfies the condition that, with respect to the set of analogy rules, one may be generated from the other; but t^4 and t^5 may be said to be analogous because they belong to a set of same-term-occurrences constituted by *pairs* of same-term-occurrences which are ordered by analogy rules which apply in such a way that every term-occurrence is a member of some directly analogous pair but not such that every pair is directly analogous. Those term-pairs which are not directly analogous (t^4-t^5, t^4-t^3, t^2-t^3, t^2-t^4), but which belong to a set of term occurrences every member of which belongs to some directly ordered analogous pair, are indirectly analogous. But this is an equivocal and secondary use of "is analogous" and does not imply that such pairs of same-term-occurrences are "meaning-derivative" with respect to one another; rather each is part of an ordered set of meaning derivations.

So while the meta-language predicate "is analogous with" is applicable to paired same-term-occurrences, a pair of same-term-occurrences is analogous only (a) if there are analogy rules according to which the use in the one case is generable from the use in the other or (b) if the two occurrences occupy places in a set of ordered paired sets every member of which is related to some other member by an analogy rule such that its meaning in that use is generable from the use of some others within the set, except for the first, if there is a first. There is nothing that we know so far which precludes an analogous set from being circular; for there may be some rules of analogy by which one can generate from t^5 (for instance) a term-occurrence t^6 which is univocal with t^1.

Thus it is a reasonably likely hypothesis that all members of a set of family-resembling terms (like "to think," "to see," "to recognize," "to compare," "to judge," "to expect") are analogous with respect to one another; that is, either any pair of those same-term-occurrences will be derived one from the other (according to an analogy rule) and thus be directly analogous, or each of the members will belong to some other pair which satisfies that condition and such that the other member of the pair will belong to still other pairs each of which satisfies the conditions for direct analogy. Because there are a fairly large number of analogy rules for English, some of which may be applied to their own outputs, there is not a unique path from one set of same-term-uses to another.

Thesis V: The analogy structure for our natural language (English) may be formulated in specific rules of analogy, and the "output" of application of an analogy rule may be further employed as "input" for other rules.
The proof of this is primarily an empirical matter. It is something which I have not attempted but which can be illustrated by one or two analogy rules and by some further categories of analogy. For instance: An adjectival modifier (t^1) in a noun phrase of the form (art., adj., noun) completed by a verb phrase of the form (aux., verb-passive, no modifier), where it is used category-determinatively in (1), may be used category-partitively (t^2) in (2) of the same form, provided that the noun in (2) is already category-determinate. Example: (1) "The *physical* parts of the house were destroyed." (2) "The *physical* theories of the Arabs were destroyed." "Physical" is category-determining for "parts" and category-partitive for "theories."

(3) Adverbial modifiers which can be applied to a third-person-singular, active verb from the point of view of an observer may without sentential change be applied from the

point of view of the agent. (1) "Unhappily, he did it"; (2) "He did it unhappily." Or: (1) "Clumsily, he did it"; (2) "He did it clumsily."

There seems to be analogy of natural attribution (as Aquinas indicated), the use of same-terms for a quality and for the cause, sign, symptom, propensity-for, disposition-for, ability to, etc., related to that quality. (Able performance; able performer. Agile leap; agile person.) Also, attribution includes analogy of representation: whatever is considered to be related to something else as a representation of it may be denominated with its common or proper name: a unicorn-picture—"That's a unicorn."

There seems to be analogy of ascriptive attribution: where one or more uses of a term involve ascription of certain kinds of mental or internal states to an agent—scheming deed, scheming man; thoughtful deed, thoughtful man; deliberate act, deliberate decision; wary gesture, wary man; careless step, careless man, and so forth.

There are various kinds of proportionality derivations of meaning. Consider the generation of meanings for "freight": (1) "compensation paid for the transport of goods"; (2) "the stuff to be transported"; (3) "the transporting agency (freight line)"; and, by generalization, (4) "to load" or "to burden," in general. And "friction": (1) "the rubbing of one body against another"; (2) "clashing between parties in opinion or work"; (3) "*result* of (1) or (2)." (3) is a case of attribution after proportionality. The same things apply to "to correct," "to transport," "to execute," "to use," "to purchase," and so on, and so on. Is there an active verb which is not used both in "analogy by simulation" and in analogy of proportionality?

These examples must not be considered adequate substitutes for specific analogy rules; but they should be indicative of the presence of the rules which have yet to be formulated and verified.

Thesis VI: *Any predicative term within the language can be used analogously.* We will count anything which can occur in the F-place in a sentential frame of the form "x is (a/an) F" as a predicative term.

Any word in the language can occur as part of (or all of) a predicative expression used analogously with respect to the same predicative expression in a distinct discourse context, with cognitivity preservation from the one to the other discourse context.

Thesis VII: *There is in English a set of analogy regularities which relate meaning derivations in ways which parallel what St. Thomas called "analogy of proper proportionality" where the* modus significandi *is partly altered derivatively by the* modus essendi *of the* significata *of other terms in the environment.* The derivations are controlled through syntagmatic contraction of the paradigmatic relationships which derive from the distinct semantic categories of terms in the context. A general rule of this sort seems to hold: If t^1 attributes an activity to s^1, and t^2 to s^2, then t^1 differs in meaning from t^2 in exactly the ways in which the semantical categories of s^2 differ from those of s^1. Thus in "Children count when taught to" and "Computers count when programmed to," the meaning of "$count^2$" is derivative from "$count^1$" but is altered with respect to "computers" in just the way that the semantic categories of that term differ from those of "children." Needless to say, we must explain what difference of semantic category consists in and what the initial conditions for this sort of analogy rule may be. For it is this general form of difference-of-meaning by combinatorial contraction which corresponds to proportionality, and characterizes the shift of terms from one discourse environment to another, and is particularly appropriate to religious discourse.

CONCLUSION: A NEW THEORY OF ANALOGY

The point of this investigation is to display the way certain structural regularities affect meaning-derivations for sets of same-term-occurrences in our natural language, and thereby to explain the family resemblance of certain sets of terms and actually to make a reality of the answer to problems about the cognitivity of religious and metaphysical discourse which were addressed by the first Analogy Theory but which have since changed somewhat in form.[20] As we seek to provide an account of the preservation of intelligibility or cognitive meaning over the use of terms in new senses, we are also applying the "regularity" hypothesis, which has been so successful and predictively rich for the study of word-formation and of grammar, to the area of linguistic meaning.

The theological implications of these arguments will be that, since within environments of religious or metaphysical or theological discourse nothing semantically different happens from what happens within the discourse which is common to human life in general, then either there is no reason at all to attack the cognitive significance of religious assertions or there is the very same reason to attack the cognitive significance of those sorts of meaning changes which are part of every person's ordinary speech and would, linguistically, be considered indisputably meaningful.

NOTES

1. I shall not try here to distribute the credit for various elements of the theory among Aquinas' predecessors or to parcel out responsibility for defects in the theory, but shall regard attributing the theory to Aquinas as a matter of primacy of authorship rather than exclusive authorship.

2. Here we are ignoring morphemic changes like "smokes" to "smoker," and "heal thy" to "healthful" since these are morphemic-derivations which are variant from language to language and in English are a consequence of principles other than those of analogy of meaning. Some words change form with change of use, others do not. That fact is irrelevant to analogy.

3. I have already discussed this in "A Critical Analysis of the Theory of Analogy of St. Thomas Aquinas," Ph.D. thesis, Brown University, 1958; available from University Microfilms, Inc. There are many distinguished interpretive works in print.

4. Charles C. Fries, "Advances in Linguistics," *College English*, 25 (1961), 30–37; *Readings in Applied English Linguistics,* ed. H. B. Allen (New York: Appleton-Century-Crofts, 1964), p. 41.

5. The very ubiquity of analogy in discourse makes it difficult to isolate and explain. As Benjamin Lee Whoft said in "Science and Linguistics" (reprinted in Allen, *Readings in Applied Linguistics,* p. 59) : ". . . if a rule has absolutely no exceptions, it is not recognized as a rule or an anything else; it is then part of the background of experience of which we tend to remain unconscious. Never having experienced anything to contrast with it, we cannot isolate it and formulate it until we so enlarge our experiences and expand our base of reference, that we encounter an interruption of its regularity. The situation is somewhat analogous to that of not missing the water until the well runs dry, or not realizing that we need air till we are choking." Analogy in natural language is like gravity in nature, a fundamental and ubiquitous force which it takes the genius of Aristotle and Aquinas to describe.

6. Fries, Wilson, and Rudolph, *Merrill Linguistic Readers* (Columbus, Ohio: Merrill, 1966).

7. It is historically interesting that the analogists, as distinguished from the anomalists in the history of linguistics, were the proponents of regularity within language; the sort of semantic theory I am proposing is merely an extension to the domain of meaning of the principle of regularity which has been found so successful for the study of sound patterns, word forms, grammatical structure, and even the historical development of languages.

8. This is not to suggest that these metalanguage predicates are applicable *only* to pairs of term tokens; but rather to indicate that, even though the most common uses of such predicates may be to contrast a same-term token with its type used in an established sense, we can and will explain all the other uses of "is equivocal with," "is univocal with," and "is analogous with" as being derivative from the relationships between same-term tokens.

9. Cf. John Lyons, *Introduction to Theoretical Linguistics* (New York: Cambridge University Press, 1969), Chapter v, section 5.4, "The Word."

10. Cf. Zellig S. Harris, *Structural Linguistics* (Chicago: University of Chicago Press, 1961; originally titled *Methods in Structural Linguistics*), p. 361.

11. Harris, pp. 362–363: "The sequences (not necessarily contiguous) of phonemes or of components which represent the flow of speech are now divided into new segments each of which is uniquely identifiable in terms of phonemes (or components). . . . Each morpheme is composed directly of a sequence of morphophonemes each of which in turn is a class consisting of one or more complementary phonemes or components. . . . Morphemes are not distinguished directly on the basis of their meanings or meaning differences, but by the result of distributional operations upon the data of linguistics (these data including the meaning-like distinction between utterances which are not repetitions of each other)."

12. *Ibid.*

13. Cf. Lyons, p. 181.

14. Lyons, p. 183, says that "The distribution of a word is the product of the distributions of the morphemes of which it is composed."

15. This is somewhat more complex than I have indicated, because harmonyms are phonemically equivalent. But distributional linguists have found ways around this difficulty.

16. Sometimes we say of two term tokens which are spelled exactly the same way or are pronounced in the same way that they are tokens of two different words or of two different terms. But here the use of "different terms" or "different words" supposes as part of its conditions of application a comparison of the meanings of the term tokens in the particular context. Thus the tokens of "fast" in "red is a fast color" and "Good Friday is a fast day" are said to be different words. The criterion we need for "same term," while it need not suppose that we do not know the meaning of the terms, is independent of a *comparison* of the meanings of the term. And the distinction of "fast" in (*a*) from "fast" in (*b*) may finally be made on grounds of intonation or stress patterns for the whole expressions. It will not affect our overall theory a bit that our "intuitions" may occasionally conflict with the results of distributional analysis. Naturally if the two tokens are not of the same term, there is no question of their being analogous, although it is quite possible that there are other "meaning derivation" regularities which are not restricted to "same terms."

17. This distinction between *diachronic* and *synchronic* regularities was formulated by de Saussure and is explained in Lyons, pp. 45–46. It is of the very greatest importance for the theory we are constructing.

18. This distinction between paradigmatic and syntagmatic relations of various "levels" of language is explained by Lyons, pp. 70ff., and is applied to semantics pp. 428f.

19. In linguists' terminology (see Lyons, p. 73), analogous terms are the same in meaning because tokens of those types are in free variation with one another for all contexts of occurrence, since substitution of a token t^1 for another t^2, in a given context c, leaves the sentence entirely unchanged in meaning and structure. That tells us something important about analogy of meaning: meaning derivation is mediated by the meaning context.

20. Wittgenstein's notion that many terms form families of uses, especially those terms we want to consider paradigms of analogous terms, combined with my hypothesis that analogy rules may be something like transformation rules, permitting you, once you have certain kinds of things, to derive others, suggests that the analogy rules may establish a semantic parentage for uses of terms; they legitimize the occurrence of new uses by providing a traceable semantic chain; what they guarantee is an inheritance of cognitive content, of intelligibility for the utterance.

9

Hume on Evil

Nelson Pike
University of California

In parts x and xi of the *Dialogues Concerning Natural Religion,* Hume sets forth his views on the traditional theological problem of evil. Hume's remarks on this topic seem to me to contain a rich mixture of insight and oversight. It will be my purpose in this paper to disentangle these contrasting elements of his discussion.[1]

Philo's first position

A. God, according to the traditional Christian view put forward by Cleanthes in the *Dialogues,* is all-powerful, all-knowing, and perfectly good. And it is clear that for Cleanthes, the terms "powerful," "knowing," and "good" apply to God in exactly the same sense in which these terms apply to men. Philo argues as follows (pp. 61–69) : if God is to be all-powerful, all-knowing, and perfectly good (using all key terms in their ordinary sense), then to claim that God exists is to preclude

Reprinted from *The Philosophical Review,* 72 (1963), 180–197, with the permission of the author and the publishers.

the possibility of admitting that there occur instances of evil; that is, to preclude the possibility of admitting that there occur instances of suffering, pain, superstition, wickedness, and so forth.[2] The statements "God exists" and "There occur instances of suffering" are logically incompatible. Of course, no one could deny that there occur instances of suffering. Such a denial would plainly conflict with common experience.[3] Thus it follows from obvious fact that God (having the attributes assigned to him by Cleanthes) does not exist.

This argument against the existence of God has enjoyed considerable popularity since Hume wrote the *Dialogues*. Concerning the traditional theological problem of evil, F. H. Bradley comments as follows:

> The trouble has come from the idea that the Absolute is a moral person. If you start from that basis, then the relation of evil to the Absolute presents at once an irreducible dilemma. The problem then becomes insoluble, but not because it is obscure or in any way mysterious. To any one who has the sense and courage to see things as they are, and is resolved not to mystify others or himself, *there is really no question to discuss. The dilemma is plainly insoluble because it is based on a clear self-contradiction.*[4]

John Stuart Mill,[5] J. E. McTaggart,[6] Antony Flew,[7] H. D. Aiken,[8] J. L. Mackie,[9] C. J. Ducasse,[10] and H. J. McCloskey[11] are but a very few of the many others who have echoed Philo's finalistic dismissal of traditional theism after making reference to the logical incompatibility of "God exists" and "There occur instances of suffering." W. T. Stace refers to Hume's discussion of the matter as follows:

> [Assuming that "good" and "powerful" are used in theology as they are used in ordinary discourse], we have to say that Hume was right. The charge has never been answered and never will be. The simultaneous attribution of all-power and all-goodness to the Creator of the whole world is logically incompatible with the existence of evil and pain in the world, for which reason the conception of a finite God, who is not all-powerful . . . has become popular in some quarters.[12]

In the first and second sections of this paper, I shall argue that the argument against the existence of God presented in

Part X of the *Dialogues* is quite unconvincing. It is not at all
clear that "God exists" and "There occur instances of suffering" are logically incompatible statements.

B. Moving now to the details of the matter, we may, I think,
formulate Philo's first challenge to Cleanthes as follows:

(1) The world contains instances of suffering.
(2) God exists—and is omnipotent and omniscient.
(3) God exists—and is perfectly good.

According to the view advanced by Philo, these three statements constitute an "inconsistent triad" (p. 66). Any two of
them might be held together. But if any two of them are en-
dorsed, the third must be denied. Philo argues that to say of
God that he is omnipotent and omniscient is to say that he
could prevent suffering if he wanted to. Unless God could
prevent suffering, he would not qualify as both omnipotent
and omniscient. But, Philo continues, to say of God that he is
perfectly good is to say that God *would* prevent suffering if
he could. A being who would not prevent suffering when it
was within his power to do so would not qualify as perfectly
good. Thus, to affirm propositions (2) and (3) is to affirm
the existence of a being who both could prevent suffering if
he wanted to and would prevent suffering if he could. This, of
course, is to deny the truth of proposition (1). By similar
reasoning, Philo would insist, to affirm (1) and (2) is to deny
the truth of (3). And to affirm (1) and (3) is to deny the
truth of (2). But, as conceived by Cleanthes, God is both
omnipotent-omniscient and perfectly good. Thus, as understood by Cleanthes, "God exists" and "There occur instances
of suffering" are logically incompatible statements. Since the
latter of these statements is obviously true, the former must be
false. Philo reflects: "Nothing can shake the solidarity of this
reasoning, so short, so clear, [and] so decisive" (p. 69).

It seems to me that this argument is deficient. I do not think
it follows from the claim that a being is perfectly good that he
would prevent suffering if he could.

Consider this case. A parent forces a child to take a spoon-
ful of bitter medicine. The parent thus brings about an instance
of discomfort—suffering. The parent could have refrained

from administering the medicine; and he knew that the child would suffer discomfort if he did administer it. Yet, when we are assured that the parent acted in the interest of the child's health and happiness, the fact that he knowingly caused discomfort is not sufficient to remove the parent from the class of perfectly good beings. If the parent fails to fit into this class, it is not because he caused *this* instance of suffering.

Given only that the parent knowingly caused an instance of discomfort, we are tempted to *blame* him for his action—that is, to exclude him from the class of perfectly good beings. But when the full circumstances are known, blame becomes inappropriate. In this case, there is what I shall call a "morally sufficient reason" for the parent's action. To say that there is a morally sufficient reason for his action is simply to say that there is a circumstance or condition which, when known, renders *blame* (though, of course, not *responsibility*) for the action inappropriate. As a general statement, a being who permits (or brings about) an instance of suffering might be perfectly good providing only that there is a morally sufficient reason for his action. Thus, it does not follow from the claim that God is perfectly good that he would prevent suffering if he could. God might fail to prevent suffering, or himself bring about suffering, while remaining perfectly good. It is required only that there be a morally sufficient reason for his action.

c. In the light of these reflections, let us now attempt to put Philo's challenge to Cleanthes in sharper form.

(4) The world contains instances of suffering.
(5) God exists—and is omnipotent, omniscient, and perfectly good.
(6) An omnipotent and omniscient being would have no morally sufficient reason for allowing instances of suffering.

Unlike the first, this sequence is logically tight. Suppose (6) and (4) true. If an omnipotent and omniscient being would have no morally sufficient reason for allowing instances of suffering, then, in a world containing such instances, either there would be no omnipotent and omniscient being or that being would be blameworthy. On either of these last alternatives, proposition (5) would be false. Thus, if (6) and (4) are true, (5) must be false. In similar fashion, suppose (6) and

(5) true. If an omnipotent and omniscient being would have no morally sufficient reason for allowing suffering, then, if there existed an omnipotent and omniscient being who was also perfectly good, there would occur no suffering. Thus, if (6) and (5) are true, (4) must be false. Lastly, suppose (5) and (4) true. If there existed an omnipotent and omniscient being who was also perfectly good, then if there occurred suffering, the omnipotent and omniscient being (being also perfectly good) would have to have a morally sufficient reason for permitting it. Thus, if (5) and (4) are true, (6) must be false.

Now, according to Philo (and all others concerned), proposition (4) is surely true. And proposition (6)—well, what about proposition (6)? At this point, two observations are needed.

First, it would not serve Philo's purpose were he to argue the truth of proposition (6) by enumerating a number of reasons for permitting suffering (which might be assigned to an omnipotent and omniscient being) and then by showing that in each case the reason offered is not a morally sufficient reason (when assigned to an omnipotent and omniscient being). Philo could never claim to have examined all the possibilities. And at any given point in the argument, Cleanthes could always claim that God's reason for permitting suffering is one which Philo has not yet considered. A retreat to unexamined reasons would remain open to Cleanthes regardless of how complete the list of examined reasons seemed to be.

Second, the position held by Philo in Part x of the *Dialogues* demands that he affirm proposition (6) as a *necessary truth*. If this is not already clear, consider the following inconsistent triad.

(7) All swans are white.
(8) Some swans are not large.
(9) All white things are large.

Suppose (9) true, but not necessarily true. Either (7) or (8) must be false. But the conjunction of (7) and (8) is not contradictory. If the conjunction of (7) and (8) were contradictory, then (9) would be a necessary truth. Thus, unless (9) is a necessary truth, the conjunction of (7) and (8) is not contradictory. Note what happens to this antilogism when "colored" is substituted for "large." Now (9) becomes a necessary truth and, correspondingly, (7) and (8) become logically incompatible. The same holds for the inconsistent triad we are now considering. As already discovered, Philo holds that "There are instances of suffering" (proposition 4) and "God exists" (proposition 5) are logically incompatible. But (4) and (5) will be logically incompatible only if (6) is a necessary truth. Thus, if Philo is to argue that (4) and (5) are logically incompatible, he must be prepared to affirm (6) as a necessary truth.

We may now reconstitute Philo's challenge to the position held by Cleanthes.

Proposition (4) is obviously true. No one could deny that there occur instances of suffering. But proposition (6) is a necessary truth. An omnipotent and omniscient being would have no morally sufficient reason for allowing instances of suffering—just as a bachelor would have no wife. Thus, there exists no being who is, at once, omnipotent, omniscient, and perfectly good. Proposition (5) must be false.

D. This is a formidable challenge to Cleanthes' position. Its strength can best be exposed by reflecting on some of the circumstances or conditions which, in ordinary life, and with respect to ordinary agents, are usually counted as morally sufficient reasons for failing to prevent (or relieve) some given instance of suffering. Let me list five such reasons.

First, consider an agent who lacked physical ability to prevent some instance of suffering. Such an agent could claim to have had a morally sufficient reason for not preventing the instance in question.

Second, consider an agent who lacked knowledge of (or the means of knowing about) a given instance of suffering. Such an agent could claim to have had a morally sufficient reason for not preventing the suffering, even if (on all other counts) he had the ability to prevent it.

Third, consider an agent who knew of an instance of suffering and had the physical ability to prevent it, but did not *realize* that he had this ability. Such an agent could usually claim to have had a morally sufficient reason for not preventing the suffering. Example: if I push the button on the wall, the torment of the man in the next room will cease. I have the physical ability to push the button. I know that the man in the next room is in pain. But I do not know that pushing the button will relieve the torment. I do not push the button and thus do not relieve the suffering.

Fourth, consider an agent who had the ability to prevent an instance of suffering, knew of the suffering, knew that he had the ability to prevent it, but did not prevent it because he believed (rightly or wrongly) that to do so would be to fail to effect some future good which would outweigh the negative value of the suffering. Such an agent might well claim to have had a morally sufficient reason for not preventing the suffering. Example: go back to the case of the parent causing discomfort by administering bitter medicine to the child.

Fifth, consider an agent who had the ability to prevent an instance of suffering, knew of the suffering, knew that he had the ability to prevent it, but failed to prevent it because to do so would have involved his preventing a prior good which outweighed the negative value of the suffering. Such an agent might claim to have had a morally sufficient reason for not preventing the suffering. Example: a parent permits a child to eat some birthday cake knowing that his eating the cake will result in the child's feeling slightly ill later in the day. The parent estimates that the child's pleasure of the moment outweighs the discomfort which will result.

Up to this point, Philo would insist, we have not hit on a circumstance or condition which could be used by Cleanthes when constructing a "theodicy," that is, when attempting to identify the morally sufficient reason God has for permitting instances of suffering.

The first three entries on the list are obviously not available. Each makes explicit mention of some lack of knowledge or power on the part of the agent. Nothing more need be said about them.

A theologian might, however, be tempted to use a reason for the fourth type when constructing a theodicy. He might propose that suffering *results in goods* which outweigh the negative value of the suffering. Famine (hunger) leads man to industry and progress. Disease (pain) leads man to knowledge and understanding. Philo suggests that no theodicy of this kind can be successful (pp. 73–74 and 76). An omnipotent and omniscient being could find other means of bringing about the same results. The mere fact that evils give rise to goods cannot serve as a morally sufficient reason for an omnipotent and omniscient being to permit suffering.

A theologian might also be tempted to use reasons of the fifth type when constructing a theodicy. He might propose that instances of suffering *result from goods* which outweigh the negative value of the suffering. That the world is run in accordance with natural law is good. But any such regular operation will result in suffering. That men have the ability to make free choices is good. But free choice will sometimes result in wrong choice and suffering. Philo argues that it is not at all clear that a world run in accordance with natural law is better than one not so regulated (p. 74). And one might issue a similar challenge with respect to free will. But a more general argument has been offered in the contemporary literature on evil which is exactly analogous to the one suggested by Philo above. According to H. J. McCloskey, an omnipotent and omniscient being could devise a law-governed world which would not include suffering.[13] And according to J. L. Mackie, an omnipotent and omniscient being could create a world containing free agents which would include no suffering or wrong-doing.[14] The import of both these suggestions is that an omnipotent and omniscient being could create a world containing whatever is good (regularity, free will, and so on) without allowing the suffering which (only factually) results from these goods. The mere fact that suffering results from good cannot serve as a morally sufficient reason for an omnipotent and omniscient being to allow suffering.

Though the above reflections may be far from conclusive, let us grant that, of the morally sufficient reasons so far considered, none could be assigned to an omnipotent and omniscient being. This, of course, is not to say that proposition (6) is true—let alone necessarily true. As mentioned earlier, proposition (6) will not be shown true by an enumerative procedure of the above kind. But consider the matter less rigorously. If none of the reasons so far considered could be assigned to an omnipotent and omniscient being, ought this not to raise a sus-

picion? Might there not be a principle operating in each of
these reasons which guarantees that *no* morally sufficient reason for permitting suffering *could* be assigned to an omnipotent
and omniscient being? Such a principle immediately suggests itself. Men are sometimes excused for allowing suffering. But in
these cases, men are excused only because they lack the knowledge or power to prevent suffering, or because they lack the
knowledge or power to bring about goods (which are causally
related to suffering) without also bringing about suffering. In
other words, men are excusable only because they are limited.
Having a morally sufficient reason for permitting suffering
entails having some lack of knowledge or power. If this principle is sound (and, indeed, it is initially plausible), then proposition (6) must surely be listed as a necessary truth.

DEMEA'S THEODICY

But the issue is not yet decided. Demea has offered a theodicy
which does not fit any of the forms outlined above. And Philo
must be willing to consider all proposals if he is to claim "de-
cisiveness" for his argument against Cleanthes.

Demea reasons as follows:

> This world is but a point in comparison of the universe; this life but
> a moment in comparison of eternity. The present evil phenomena,
> therefore, are rectified in other regions, and in some future period of
> existence. And the eyes of men, being then opened to larger views of
> things, see the whole connection of general laws, and trace, with adora-
> tion, the benevolence and rectitude of the Deity through all mazes
> and intricacies of his providence [p. 67].

It might be useful if we had a second statement of this theodicy,
one taken from a traditional theological source. In Chapter
LXXI of the *Summa contra Gentiles,* St. Thomas argues as
follows:

> The good of the whole is of more account than the good of the part.
> Therefore, it belongs to a prudent governor to overlook a lack of
> goodness in a part, that there may be an increase of goodness in the
> whole. Thus, the builder hides the foundation of a house under-
> ground, that the whole house may stand firm. Now, if evil were taken

away from certain parts of the universe, the perfection of the universe would be much diminished, since its beauty results from the ordered unity of good and evil things, seeing that evil arises from the failure of good, and yet certain goods are occasioned from those very evils through the providence of the governor, even as the silent pause gives sweetness to the chant. Therefore, evil should not be excluded from things by the divine providence.

Neither of these statements seems entirely satisfactory. Demea might be suggesting that the world is good on the whole—that the suffering we discover in our world is, as it were, made up for in other regions of creation. God here appears as the husband who beats his wife on occasion but makes up for it with favors at other times. In St. Thomas' statement, there are unmistakable hints of causal reasoning. Certain goods are "occasioned" by evils, as the foundation of the house permits the house to stand firm. But in both of these statements another theme occurs. Let me state it in my own way without pretense of historical accuracy.

I have a set of ten wooden blocks. There is a T-shaped block, an L-shaped block, an F-shaped block, and so on. No two blocks have the same shape. Let us assign each block a value—say, an aesthetic value—making the T-shaped block most valuable and the L-shaped block least valuable. Now the blocks may be fitted together into formations. And let us suppose that the blocks are so shaped that there is one and only one subset of the blocks which will fit together into a square. The L-shaped block is a member of that subset. Further, let us stipulate that any formation of blocks (consisting of two or more blocks fitted together) will have more aesthetic value than any of the blocks taken individually or any subset of the blocks taken as a mere collection. And, as a last assumption, let us say that the square formation has greater aesthetic value than any other logically possible block formation. The L-shaped block is a necessary component of the square formation; that is, the L-shaped block is logically indispensable to the square formation. Thus the L-shaped block is a necessary component of the best of all possible block formations. Hence, the block with the least aesthetic value is logically indispensable to the best of all possible block formations. Without this very block, it would be logically impossible to create the best of all possible block formations.

Working from this model, let us understand Demea's theodicy as follows. Put aside the claim that instances of suffering are *de facto* causes or consequences of greater goods. God, being a perfectly good, omniscient, and omnipotent being, would create the best of all possible worlds. But the best of all possible worlds must contain instances of suffering: they are logically indispensable components. This is why there are instances of suffering in the world which God created.

What shall we say about this theodicy? Philo expresses no opinion on the subject.

Consider this reply to Demea's reasonings. A world containing instances of suffering as necessary components might be the best of all possible worlds. And if a world containing instances of suffering as necessary components were the best of all possible worlds, an omniponent and omniscient being would have a morally sufficient reason for permitting instances of suffering. But how are we to know that, in fact, instances of suffering are logically indispensable components of the best of all possible worlds? There would appear to be no way of establishing this claim short of assuming that God does in fact exist, and then concluding (as did Leibniz) that the world (containing suffering) which he did in fact create is the best of all possible worlds. But, this procedure assumes that God exists. And this latter is precisely the question now at issue.

It seems to me that this reply to Demea's theodicy has considerable merit. First, my hypothetical objector is probably right in suggesting that the only way one could show that the best of all possible worlds must contain instances of suffering would be via the above argument in which the existence of God is assumed. Second, I think that my objector is right in allowing that, if instances of suffering were logically indispensable components of the best of all possible worlds, this would provide a morally sufficient reason for an omnipotent and omniscient being to permit instances of suffering. And, third, I think that my objector exhibits considerable discretion in not challenging the claim that the best of all possible worlds *might* contain instances of suffering as necessary components. I know of no argument which will show this claim to be true. But on the other hand, I know of no argument which will show this claim to be false. (I shall elaborate this last point directly.)

Thus, as I have said, the above evaluation of the theodicy advanced by Demea seems to have considerable merit. But this evaluation, *if correct,* seems to be sufficient to refute Philo's claim that "God exists" and "There occur instances of suffering" are logically incompatible statements. If instances of suffering were necessary components of the best of all possible worlds, then an omnipotent and omniscient being would have a morally sufficient reason for permitting instances of suffering. Thus, if it is *possible* that instances of suffering are necessary components of the best of all possible worlds, then there *might be* a morally sufficient reason for an omnipotent and omniscient being to permit instances of suffering. Thus if the statement "Instances of suffering are necessary components of the best of all possible worlds" is not contradictory, then proposition (6) is not a necessary truth. And, as we have seen, if proposition (6) is not a necessary truth, then "God exists" and "There occur instances of suffering" are not logically incompatible statements.

What shall we say? Is the statement "Instances of suffering are logically indispensable components of the best of all possible worlds" contradictory? That it is, is simply assumed in Philo's first position. But, surely, this is not a trivial assumption. If it is correct, it must be shown to be so; it is not *obviously* correct. And how shall we argue that it is correct? Shall we, for example, assume that any case of suffering contained in any complex of events detracts from the value of the complex? If this principle were analytic, then a world containing an instance of suffering could not be the best of all possible worlds. But G. E. Moore has taught us to be suspicious of any such principle.[15] And John Wisdom has provided a series of counterexamples which tend to show that this very principle is, in fact, not analytic. Example: I believe (rightly or wrongly) that you are in pain, and become unhappy as a result of that belief. The resulting complex would appear to be better by virtue of my unhappiness (suffering) than it would have been had I believed you to be in pain but had not become unhappy (or had become happy) as a result.[16] Philo's argument against the existence of God is not finished. And it is not at all obvious that it is *capable* of effective completion. It is, I submit, far from clear that God and evil could not exist together in the same universe.

PHILO'S SECOND POSITION

At the end of Part X, Philo agrees to "retire" from his first position. He now concedes that "God exists" and "There occur instances of suffering" are not logically incompatible statements (p. 69). (It is clear from the context that this adjustment in Philo's thinking is made only for purposes of argument and not because Hume senses any inadequacy in Philo's first position.) Most contemporary philosophers think that Hume's major contribution to the literature on evil was made in Part X of the *Dialogues*. But it seems to me that what is of really lasting value in Hume's reflections on this subject is to be found, not in Part X, but in the discussion in Part XI which follows Philo's "retirement" from his first position.

A. Consider, first of all, a theology in which the existence of God is accepted on the basis of what is taken to be a conclusive (*a priori*) demonstration. (A theology in which the existence of God is taken as an item of faith can be considered here as well.) On this view, that God exists is a settled matter, not subject to review or challenge. It is, as it were, axiomatic to further theological debate. According to Philo, evil in the world presents no special problem for a theology of this sort:

> Let us allow that, if the goodness of the Deity (I mean a goodness like the human) could be established on any tolerable reasons *a priori,* these (evil) phenomena, however untoward, would not be sufficient to subvert that principle, but might easily, in some unknown manner, be reconcilable to it [p. 78].

This point, I think, is essentially correct, but it must be put more firmly.

Recalling the remarks advanced when discussing the inconsistent nature of propositions (4) through (6) above, a theologian who accepts the existence of God (either as an item of faith or on the basis of an *a priori* argument) must conclude either that there is some morally sufficient reason for God's allowing suffering in the world, or that there are no instances of suffering in the world. He will, of course, choose the first alternative. Thus, in a theology of the sort now under consideration, the theologian begins by affirming the existence of God and by acknowledging the occurrence of suffering. It follows *logically* that God has some morally sufficient reason for allowing instances of suffering. The conclusion is not, as Philo suggests, that there *might be* a morally sufficient reason for evil. The conclusion is, rather, that there *must be* such a reason. It *could* not be otherwise.

What, then, of the traditional theological problem of evil? Within a theology of the above type, the problem of evil can only be the problem of discovering a *specific* theodicy which is adequate—that is, of discovering which, if any, of the specific proposals which might be advanced really describes God's morally sufficient reason for allowing instances of suffering. This problem, of course, is not a major one for the theologian. If the problem of evil is simply the problem of uncovering the specific reason for evil—given assurance that there is (and must be) some such reason—it can hardly be counted as a critical problem. Once it is granted that there is some specific reason for evil, there is a sense in which it is no longer vital to find it. A theologian of the type we are now considering might never arrive at a satisfactory theodicy. (Philo's "unknown" reason might remain forever unknown.) He might condemn as erroneous all existing theodicies and might despair of ever discovering the morally sufficient reason in question. A charge of incompleteness would be the worst that could be leveled at his world view.

B. Cleanthes is not, of course, a theologian of the sort just described. He does not accept the existence of God as an item of faith, nor on the basis of an *a priori* argument. In the *Dialogues*, Cleanthes supports his theological position with an *a posteriori* argument from design. He argues that "order" in the universe provides sufficient evidence that the world was created by an omnipotent, omniscient, and perfectly good being.[17] He proposes the existence of God as a quasi-scientific explanatory hypothesis, arguing its truth via the claim that it provides an adequate explanation for observed facts.

Philo has two comments to make regarding the relevance of suffering in the world for a theology of this kind.

The first is a comment with which Philo is obviously well pleased. It is offered at the end of Part x and is repeated no fewer than three times in Part xi. It is this: even if the existence of God and the occurrence of suffering in the world are logically compatible, one cannot argue from a world containing suffering to the existence of an omnipotent, omniscient, and perfectly good creator. This observation, I think all would agree, is correct. Given only a painting containing vast areas of green, one could not effectively argue that its creator disliked using green. There would be no *logical* conflict in holding that a painter who disliked using green painted a picture containing vast areas of green. But given *only* the picture (and no further information), the hypothesis that its creator disliked using green would be poorly supported indeed.

It is clear that in this first comment Philo has offered a criticism of Cleanthes' *argument* for the existence of God. He explicitly says that this complaint is against Cleanthes' *inference* from a world containing instances of suffering to the existence of an omnipotent, omniscient, and perfectly good creator (p. 73). Philo's second comment, however, is more forceful than this. It is a challenge of the *truth* of Cleanthes' *hypothesis.*

Philo argues as follows:

Look round this universe. What an immense profusion of beings, animated and organized, sensible and active! You admire this prodigious variety and fecundity. But inspect a little more narrowly these living existences, the only beings worth regarding. How hostile and destructive to each other! How insufficient all of them for their own happiness! . . . There is indeed an opposition of pains and pleasures in the feelings of sensible creatures; but are not all the operations of nature carried on by an opposition of principles, of hot and cold, moist and dry, light and heavy! The true conclusion is that the original Source of all things is entirely indifferent to all these principles, and has no more regard to good above ill than to heat above cold, or to drought above moisture, or to light above heavy [p. 79].

Philo claims that *there is* an "original Source of all things" and that this source is indifferent with respect to matters of good and evil. He pretends to be inferring this conclusion from observed data. This represents a departure from Philo's much professed skepticism in the *Dialogues*. And, no doubt, many of the criticisms of Cleanthes' position which Philo advanced earlier in the *Dialogues* would apply with equal force to the inference Philo has just offered. But I shall not dwell on this last point. I think that the center of Philo's remarks in this passage must be located in their skeptical rather than their metaphysical import. Philo has proposed a hypothesis which is counter to the one offered by Cleanthes. And he claims that his hypothesis is the "true conclusion" to be drawn from the observed data. But the point is not, I think, that Philo's new hypothesis is true, or even probable. The conclusion is, rather, that the hypothesis advanced by Cleanthes is false, or very improbable. When claiming that evil in the world *supports* a hypothesis which is counter to the one offered by Cleanthes, I think Philo simply means to be calling attention to the fact that evil in the world provides *evidence against* Cleanthes' theological position.

Consider the following analogy which, I think, will help expose this point. I am given certain astronomical data. In order to explain the data, I introduce the hypothesis that there exists a planet which has not yet been observed but which will be observable at such and such a place in the sky at such and such a time. No other hypothesis seems as good. The anticipated hour arrives and the telescopes are trained on the designated area. No planet appears. Now, either one of two conclusions may be drawn. First, I might conclude that there is no planet there to be seen. This requires either that I reject the original astronomical data or that I admit that what seemed the best explanation of the data is not, in fact, the true explanation. Second, I might conclude that there is a planet there to be seen, but that something in the observational set-up went amiss. Perhaps the equipment was faulty, perhaps there were clouds, and so on. Which conclusion is correct? The answer is not straightforward. I must check both possibilities.

Suppose I find nothing in the observational set-up which is in the least out of order. My equipment is in good working condition, I find no clouds, and so on. To decide to retain the planet hypothesis in the face of the recalcitrant datum (my failure to observe the planet) is, in part, to decide that there is some circumstance (as yet unknown) which explains the datum *other* than the nonexistence of the planet in question. But a decision to retain the planet hypothesis (in the face of my failure to observe the planet and in the absence of an explicit explanation which "squares" this failure with the planet hypothesis) is made correctly *only* when the *evidence for* the planet hypothesis is such as to render its negation less plausible than would be the assumption of a (as yet unknown) circumstance which explains the observation failure. This, I think, is part of the very notion of dealing reasonably with an explanatory hypothesis.

Now Cleanthes has introduced the claim that there exists an omnipotent, omniscient, and perfectly good being as a way of explaining "order" in the world. And Philo, throughout the *Dialogues* (up to and including most of Part XI), has been concerned to show that this procedure provides very little (if any) solid evidence for the existence of God. The inference from the data to the hypothesis is extremely tenuous. Philo is now set for his final thrust at Cleanthes' position. Granting that God and evil are not logically incompatible, the existence of human suffering in the world must still be taken as a recalcitrant datum with respect to Cleanthes' hypothesis. Suffering, as Philo says, is not what we should antecedently expect in a world created by an omnipotent, omniscient, and perfectly good being (pp. 71–72). Since Cleanthes has offered nothing in the way of an explicit theodicy (that is, an explanation of the recalcitrant datum which would "square" it with his hypothesis) and since the *evidence for* his hypothesis is extremely weak and generally ineffective, there is pretty good reason for thinking that Cleanthes' hypothesis is false.

This, I think, is the skeptical import of Philo's closing remarks in Part XI. On this reading, nothing is said about an "original Source of all things" which is indifferent with respect to matters of good and evil. Philo is simply making clear the negative force of the fact of evil in the world for a hypothesis such as the one offered by Cleanthes.

It ought not to go unnoticed that Philo's closing attack on

Cleanthes' position has extremely limited application. Evil in the world has central negative importance for theology only when theology is approached as a quasi-scientific subject, as by Cleanthes. That it is seldom approached in this way will be evident to anyone who has studied the history of theology. Within most theological positions, the existence of God is taken as an item of faith or embraced on the basis of an *a priori* argument. Under these circumstances, where there is nothing to qualify as a "hypothesis" capable of having either negative or positive "evidence," the fact of evil in the world presents no special problem for theology. As Philo himself has suggested, when the existence of God is accepted prior to any rational consideration of the status of evil in the world, the traditional problem of evil reduces to a noncrucial perplexity of relatively minor importance.

NOTES

1. All references to Hume's *Dialogues Concerning Natural Religion* will be to the Hafner Library of Classics edition, ed. H. D. Aiken (New York, 1955).

2. It is clear that, for Philo, the term "evil" is used simply as a tag for the class containing all instances of suffering, pain, and so on. Philo offers no analysis of "evil" nor does his challenge to Cleanthes rest in the least on the particularities of the logic of his term. On p. 69, e.g., Philo formulates his challenge to Cleanthes without using "evil." Here he speaks only of *misery*. In what is to follow, I shall (following Hume) make little use of "evil." Also, I shall use "suffering" as short for "suffering, pain, superstition, wickedness, and so on."

3. Had Philo been dealing with "evil" (defined in some special way) instead of "suffering," this move in the argument might not have been open to him.

4. *Appearance and Reality* (Oxford, 1930), p. 174. Italics mine.

5. *Theism* (New York, 1957), p. 40. See also *The Utility of Religion* (New York, 1957), pp. 73ff.

6. *Some Dogmas of Religion* (London, 1906), pp. 212–213.

7. "Theology and Falsification," in Flew and MacIntyre (eds.), *New Essays in Philosophical Theology* (New York, 1955), p. 108.

8. "God and Evil: Some Relations between Faith and Morals," *Ethics*, 68 (1958), 77–97.

9. "Evil and Omnipotence," *Mind*, 64 (1955), 201.

10. *A Philosophical Scrutiny of Religion* (New York, 1953), ch. 16.

11. "God and Evil," *Philosophical Quarterly*, 10 (1960), 97–114.

12. *Time and Eternity* (Princeton, 1951), p. 56.

13. "God and Evil," pp. 103–104.

14. "Evil and Omnipotence," pp. 208–210.

15. I refer here to Moore's discussion of "organic unities" in *Principia Ethica* (Cambridge, 1903), pp. 28ff.

16. "God and Evil," *Mind*, 44 (1935), 13–14. I have modified Wisdom's example slightly.

17. It is interesting to notice that, in many cases, theologians who have used an argument from design have not attempted to argue that "order" in the world proves the existence of a perfectly moral being. For example, in St. Thomas' "fifth way" and in William Paley's *Natural Theology*, "order" is used to show only that the creator of the world was *intelligent*. There are, however, historical instances of the argument from design's being used to prove the goodness as well as the intelligence of a creator. For example, Bishop Berkeley argues this way in the second of the *Dialogues Between Hylas and Philonous*.

10

The Perfect Goodness
of God

ALVIN PLANTINGA
Calvin College

In *Religious Belief,* C. B. MARTIN taxes Christian theologians
with a contradiction:

> All seems to be well as long as the goodness of Christ is not really
> called in question. Theologians admit freely enough that if the good-
> ness of Christ is in doubt then his divinity must be in doubt, and, of
> course, if the goodness of Christ is denied then it must also be denied
> that he is God. However they think that there is nothing contradic-
> tory remaining if the goodness of Christ is asserted without qualifica-
> tion and he is called God, the Perfect Good. I have been at pains to
> point out that a contradiction of an irresoluble sort remains still. The
> contradiction is: Christ can be conceived to have been other (that is,
> not good) than he was, yet as God it should be not just false but
> *inconceivable* that he should have been not good.[1]

Reprinted from *Australasian Journal of Philosophy,* 40 (1962), 70–75, with the
permission of the author and the publishers.

Martin's argument apparently runs like this: theologians hold that (a) it is inconceivable that God be non-good and (b) Christ is God. Now, (a) and (b) entail (c) it is inconceivable that Christ be non-good. But, (d) it is conceivable that Christ be non-good. Hence the theologian is involved in a contradiction.

Now, an obvious point is that more must be said to convict the theologian of inconsistency. For it must be added, obviously, that theologians *believe* or *accept* (d) as well as (a) and (b). And Martin offers no evidence, as far as I can see, for the supposition that theologians ever accept that proposition. Indeed, on page 63 he offers an argument for it; this leads one to suspect that Martin's view is that theologians *ought* to accept (d) (whether they do or not) and *if* they did [and continued to accept (a) and (b)] they would be involved in contradiction. He apparently holds that (d) is obviously and demonstrably true; so his complaint against the theologians is presumably not that they hold self-contradictory beliefs, but that *either* they hold self-contradictory beliefs or one of their beliefs is demonstrably false in that it conflicts with a demonstrably true proposition, namely, (d).

Very many Christian theologians do, of course, accept (b). And doubtless many also accept (a); any theologian, for example, who regards "God" as short for a definite description such as "the all-powerful, all-good creator of the universe" would certainly agree that (a) is true. And it is clear that if (d) *is* true and the deduction of (c) from (a) and (b) is acceptable, then either (a) or (b) is false. But *is* that deduction valid? What Martin says elsewhere (e.g., pp. 41, 43) suggests that the intended use of "inconceivable" is such that "it is inconceivable that p" is equivalent to "it is necessarily false that p" and hence to "it is necessarily true that not-p." Accordingly, the argument in question may be rewritten as follows:

(a1) N∼(God is non-good)
(b)   Christ is God

therefore

(c1) N ∼ (Christ is non-good).[2]

And as it stands the argument is *not* valid. That it is not may be seen by comparing it with the following manifestly fallacious inference:

(1) N∼(the bachelor in my office is married)
(2) Jones is the bachelor in my office
therefore
(3) N∼(Jones is married).

Martin's argument could be rehabilitated, obviously, if it could be shown either that the proposition "Christ is God" is necessarily true or that at any rate theologians believed that it is. At first glance, however, one would think that to hold that (b) is necessarily true is to hold that the most important tenet of Christianity can be seen to be true from an analysis of meanings alone; next to this claim the Ontological Argument pales into insignificance. Now, of course, Martin does not accept that claim; but neither does he give any evidence for the supposition that Christian theologians are inclined to accept it. Indeed, one might think that belief quite out of keeping with the whole tenor of Christianity; for if it were true, the New Testament ought to have been an exercise in logical analysis rather than a Gospel. Hence it is far from clear that Martin has successfully unearthed a difficulty in the beliefs of those theologians who accept both (a) and (b). But perhaps appearances are deceiving, and perhaps it could be shown that the proposition "Christ is God" is in fact necessarily true. I propose to argue that there is indeed a respectable use of "Christ" in which a sentence like "Christ is God" expresses a necessarily true proposition; but I shall argue further that any interpretation of "Christ" which secures its necessity will be such as to render (d)—"It is conceivable that Christ was non-good"—false.

How could it be argued that "Christ is God" is necessarily true? Martin points out that proper names (or what appear to be proper names) sometimes function "descriptively" (p. 40) —i.e., as abbreviations for definite descriptions. "Christ," for example, might, in the theologians' use, be short for something like "The Second Person of the Divine Trinity"; [3] then "Christ is God" would be another way of saying "The Second Person of the Divine Trinity is God." Is that proposition necessarily true? Martin gives a reason for thinking so:

> If the term "God" is used descriptively and means something like "the eternal, all-good, all-knowing, all-powerful creator of all things,"

then the statement "God is good" is true by logical necessity. The statement "God is good" where "God" is used descriptively in the way indicated would come to: "The eternal, *all-good,* all-knowing, all-powerful creator of all things is good." [p. 41.]

And, of course, the same reasoning could be employed to show that "The Second Person of the Divine Trinity is God" is necessarily true. But this reasoning is questionable, to say the least. Presumably the proposition "The infinite, all-good . . . creator of all things is good" either entails (on Russell's account of definite descriptions) or presupposes (on Strawson's account) that there *is* an infinite all-good . . . creator of all things. But if a necessary proposition *p* entails a proposition *q*, then *q*, of course, is also necessary; and the same principle holds, presumably, with respect to presupposition in Strawson's sense. So, even if "God" is used descriptively in "God is good," it looks as if that proposition could be necessary only if some form of the Ontological Argument were sound. And, of course, the suggestion that "Christ is God" is necessary is open to precisely the same objection.

In a summary directly following the passage just quoted, however, Martin makes a significantly different claim: "It is inconceivable that a being truly described as 'God' (good, powerful and so on) should be truly described as 'not-good' " (p. 43).

Presumably a being truly described as God really *is* God; hence Martin is holding that if "God" is used descriptively, then "It is not true that God is non-good" expresses a necessarily true proposition. And this contention is not open to the objection raised against the previous claim. For "It is not true that God is non-good" is not equivalent to "God is good" if "God" is used descriptively; the former, but not the latter, would be true even if there were no infinite, all-powerful, all-good Creator of the universe. Indeed, "It is not true that God is non-good" is equivalent to "Anyone who is God is good"; and that proposition obviously does not entail that God exists. Hence Martin seems to me to be correct in holding that if "God" is used descriptively, "It is not true that God is non-good" is necessarily true. And by the same token, then, it might be argued that

(b1) It is not true that Christ is non-God

is necessarily true if "Christ" is used descriptively. (On this interpretation the burden of the New Testament becomes the proclamation, not that Christ is God, but that Jesus of Nazareth was the Christ.) But if Martin interprets (b) as (b1), then, if he is to avoid equivocation in his argument against the theologians, he must interpret (d) as (d1):

(d1) N(Christ is non-good)

where "Christ" is again short for "The Second Person of the Divine Trinity." Taking "it is not necessary that not-p" as equivalent to "it is possible that p" we see that (d1) is equivalent to the assertion that it is possible that the Second Person of the Divine Trinity is non-good. And now it is far from clear that (d1) is true. For (a1) and (b1) are clearly *true* (as Martin admits) if "God" and "Christ" are used descriptively; but their conjunction entails the negation of (d1); hence (d1) is false. It is, of course, possible that *Jesus of Nazareth* was non-good; but it is a necessary truth that if he *was* non-good, then he was not the Second Person of the Divine Trinity. Any interpretation of "Christ" under which (b) is necessary is an interpretation under which (d) is false.

There is a further complication which must be mentioned here. Martin holds the view that certain subject-predicate statements with proper names as subject are necessarily true. This is the case, roughly, when a property forming part of the "naming instruction" (p. 44) connected with a given name is predicated of the individual to which that name applies. If, for example, part of the "naming instructions" associated with the name "Napoleon" (or one of the names "Napoleon"—see pp. 52–54) enjoins that the name in question is to refer to someone who was an Emperor of France, then "Napoleon was an Emperor of France" is necessarily true.[4]

Now I am not at all sure that I understand this doctrine. How does it differ from the point that a proper name (or what appears to be a proper name) may sometimes function as an abbreviation for a description? But I am not here interested in discussing this doctrine in its own right; what is important for my purposes is the fact that it cannot be used to rescue Martin's argument against the theologians. For, with respect to that argument, this proper-name doctrine has the same consequences as the point that such words as "God" and "Christ" can sometimes serve as abbreviations for descriptions. Suppose, for example, that part of the "naming instructions" associated with the name "Christ" is the injunction to apply that name only to someone who is in fact God. Then on Martin's view, presumably, "it is not the case that Christ is non-God" will be necessarily true. And, accordingly, if the word "God" is used in such a way that "God is non-good" is necessarily false, "Christ is non-good" is also necessarily false. But, of course, if it is necessarily false that Christ is non-good, it is *not* conceivable that Christ be non-good—i.e., (*d*) is false. It is indeed conceivable that the son of Mary and Joseph who was born in a stable in Bethlehem in 4 B.C. (and who on the Christian view is identical with Christ) should have been non-good; for it is conceivable that he should have been other than Christ. It is, of course, conceivable that no one at all has ever met the condition laid down by the naming instruction hypothetically associated with the name "Christ." But that *Christ* should have been non-good will now be inconceivable in that the assertion that he was is inconsistent with a necessarily true statement.

The fundamental difficulty with Martin's argument is this: (*a*) and (*b*) must both be necessary if (*c*) is to follow from them. But any interpretation of "Christ" and "God" on which they *are* necessary renders (*d*) false. And to develop the difficulty for the theologian, Martin must hold both that (*c*) follows from (*a*) and (*b*) and that (*d*) is true. Martin's argument therefore has not the slightest tendency to show either that theologians are guilty of holding contradictory beliefs or that they hold beliefs from which an obviously false proposition follows.

NOTES

1. C. B. Martin, *Religious Belief* (Ithaca: Cornell University Press, 1959), p. 40 (page references in the text are all to this book). The same charge is repeated in exactly the same words on page 62. Martin makes the same charge in almost the same words in his article "The Perfect Good," *Australasian Journal of Philosophy*, 33 (1955), 31, reprinted in *New Essays in Philosophical Theology*, edd. A. Flew and A. MacIntyre (London: SCM Press, 1955), p. 225.

2. I use the letter "N" to abbreviate "it is necessarily true that. . . ."

3. I am assuming that the proposition "Anyone who is the Second Person of the Divine Trinity is God" is necessarily true.

4. Martin's view must again be amended here; "Napoleon was an Emperor of France" presumably entails that there was at least one Emperor of France; since any proposition entailed by a necessary proposition is itself necessary, "There was at least one Emperor of France" would, on Martin's view, be necessary. But surely it is not. The proposition for which Martin ought to have claimed necessity is this one: "It is not the case that Napoleon was not an Emperor of France." This proposition, of course, is not equivalent to Martin's candidate, since it does not entail that France ever had an Emperor.

11

C. B. Martin's
Contradiction in Theology

William L. Rowe

Purdue University

In an essay entitled "The Perfect Good," [1] C. B. Martin argues that there is an inconsistency between the doctrine of God and the doctrine of Christ in orthodox Christian theology. The contradiction, so Martin claims, is contained in the three statements: (i) Christ is God, (ii) It is conceivable that Christ should have been not good, and (iii) It is inconceivable that God should have been not good. The crucial paragraph in his essay is:

> Theologians admit freely enough that if the goodness of Christ is in doubt then his divinity must be in doubt and, of course, if the goodness of Christ is denied then it must also be denied that he is God. However, they think that there is nothing contradictory remaining if the goodness of Christ is asserted without qualification and he is

Reprinted from *Australasian Journal of Philosophy*, 40 (1962), 75–79, with the permission of the author and the publishers.

called God, the "perfect good." I have been at pains to point out that a contradiction of an irresoluble sort remains still. The contradiction is that Christ can be conceived to have been other than he was, that is, not good, yet as God it is inconceivable that he should have been not good.[2]

In this passage Martin begins by crediting the theologian with seeing that his theology would contain a contradiction if he admitted that Christ did evil. For, since Christ is God, it would follow that God did evil. But it is a contradiction in terms to say that God did evil. As Martin says, "we have so defined the concept 'God' and 'God's nature' that evil action should not be predicable of God." [3] To say "God is evil" is as senseless as saying "good is evil." Seeing what follows from allowing the statement "Christ did evil," the theologian, of course, will hold that statement to be false. It is crucial to Martin's argument that the theologian regard the statement "Christ did evil" as merely false, rather than as *contradictory*. It is crucial because one of the premises of Martin's argument is that it is *conceivable* that Christ did evil. As he puts it, "Though highly imaginary, it is conceivable that manuscripts should be discovered that proved beyond reasonable doubt that Christ was some sort of mad villain. This is not a self-contradiction." [4] Thus Martin is suggesting that the theologian treats differently the two statements: (1) Christ did evil, and (2) God did evil—(1) is taken to be false but not necessarily false, (2) is taken to be necessarily false. It is this difference in treatment which Martin seems to build upon in his argument. Having claimed that (1) is in fact false, whereas (2) is necessarily false, the theologian, as Martin notes, thinks that there is nothing contradictory remaining. On the contrary, argues Martin, "a contradiction of an irresoluble sort remains still. The contradiction is that Christ can be conceived to have been other than he was, that is, not good, yet as God it is inconceivable that he should have been not good." [5] Earlier in his essay, after noting that Christ might (logically) have been some sort of mad villain, Martin argues: "As long as these frightful imaginings did not become fact, Christ the good man would be safe from censure. But Christ is God—the Father, *the Son,* and the Holy Ghost! Imaginings that never happen do not upset the reputation of men, but it must be inconceivable that God should err." [6] Martin's point in both of these passages seems to be that a *contradiction* results if the theologian asserts, as he does, that (i) Christ is God, (ii) It is conceivable (logically possible) that Christ did evil, and (iii) it is inconceivable (logically impossible) that God did evil. Unfortunately, Martin does not derive an explicit contradiction from (i)–(iii). Perhaps he thinks it obvious that they are incompatible. But what may be obvious to Martin is not likely to be obvious to the theologian. Hence, it is important that (i)–(iii) be shown to be contradictory, rather than simply asserted to be so. One way (I suspect *the* way) in which Martin might think that the contradiction can be derived is as follows:

(1) It is not logically possible that God did evil.

(2) Christ is God.

(3) It is logically possible that Christ did evil. (Martin does not quote the theologians on this point, but he seems to regard it as expressing their view.)

(4) It is logically possible that God did evil. [I take it that Martin regards this as a logical consequence of (2) and (3). If he does not, I fail to see how he could claim that (1) contradicts (2) and (3). If (4) is not implied by (2) and (3), it would seem that (2) and (3) are compatible with (1).]

(5) But (4) contradicts (1). Hence, (1), (2), and (3) cannot be asserted without contradiction because (2) and (3) imply (4) and (4) is the denial of (1).[7]

The argument stated above is persuasive but invalid. It is persuasive because there are valid arguments to which it is similar. For example,

(6) Lewis Carroll is Charles Dodgson.

(7) Lewis Carroll wrote *Alice in Wonderland*.

therefore,

(8) Charles Dodgson wrote *Alice in Wonderland*.

(6) is a statement of identity. (8) is obtained by substituting in (7) one term of the identity statement for the other. Similarly, (2) is a statement of identity, and (4) is obtained by substituting in (3) one term of the identity statement ("God")

for the other ("Christ"). Thus the argument from (2) and (3) to (4) is quite similar to the valid argument from (6) and (7) to (8). But there is a crucial difference. One of the premisses of the first argument contains the modal concept of possibility. That this difference affects the *validity* of the argument can be shown by the following examples.

(9) The number of planets = 9.
(10) It is possible that the number of planets is less than 7.
therefore,
(11) It is possible that 9 is less than 7.[8]
(12) Napoleon was the losing general at the battle of Waterloo.
(13) It is possible that Napoleon was not a general at Waterloo.
therefore,
(14) It is possible that the losing general at Waterloo was not a general at Waterloo.

(9) and (12), like (2), are statements of identity. (10) and (13), *like* (3) and *unlike* (7), are statements of possibility involving one of the terms in the identity statements (9) and (12). (11) and (14), like (4), are obtained by substituting [in (10) and (13)] one term of the identity statements for the other. But the premisses of each of these arguments are true; whereas, their conclusions are false. Hence, the two arguments are *invalid*. By parity of reasoning, the argument from (2) and (3) to (4) must also be *invalid*. If this is so, then the original statements (i), (ii), and (iii) are *not* incompatible. For, since (i) and (ii) do not imply the denial of (iii), there is no way in which (i), (ii), and (iii) can involve a contradiction.[9]

The argument from (12) and (13) to (14) is not to be discounted because it employs the definite description "the losing general at Waterloo." "God," Martin suggests, means "the perfect good." It is because "God" functions as a description that Martin and the theologians assert that it is inconceivable that God should not have been good. The point Martin overlooks is that a given individual who never did evil can be uniquely determined in different ways, some of which have "never did evil" as a necessary consequence, and some do not.[10] The uniquely referring expression "Christ" (as used by Martin) does not have this consequence, whereas "God" (i.e., "the perfect good") does. This fact must not be forgotten when we try to substitute identities within modal statements.

Although he does not say so in his essay, Martin might claim that the statement of identity "Christ is God" is *logically necessary*. Of course, if this were so, then (i), (ii), and (iii) would contain a contradiction. But we must remember that in his essay Martin is using "Christ" to name an historical figure, namely, Jesus of Nazareth. Given this use of the expression "Christ," it would be incorrect (theologically) to say that it is *necessary* that Christ (i.e., Jesus) is God. For this is a matter of decision concerning an historical fact, not a logical truth. Hence, given Martin's use of the expression "Christ" he could not say that (i) is itself *necessary*. If "Christ" is used as a descriptive term or title—and this is the proper theological use of the expression—then one might reasonably claim that "Christ is God" is necessary. But the theologians Martin refers to would not then admit that it is possible that the Christ did evil. However, it would be possible that Jesus did evil. But, Martin might argue, Jesus is the Christ and it is impossible that Christ did evil. Clearly, to argue in this fashion would be to make the same mistake we noted in the argument from (2) and (3) to (4). (iv) Jesus is the Christ, (v) It is possible that Jesus did evil, and (vi) It is impossible that the Christ did evil, are no more incompatible than (i), (ii), and (iii). And, as we have seen, (i), (ii), and (iii) may be asserted without contradiction. Thus we must reject Martin's claim to have found an inconsistency between the doctrine of God and the doctrine of Christ in orthodox Christian theology.

NOTES

1. Martin's essay was originally published in the *Australasian Journal of Philosophy*, 33 (1955). The essay was again published in *New Essays in Philosophical Theology*, edd. Flew and MacIntyre (New York, 1955). The essay, in an expanded version, appears as chapters 3 and 4 in Martin's book *Religious Belief* (Ithaca, 1959). I shall refer to the essay as it occurs in *New Essays*.

2. *New Essays*, p. 225.

3. *Ibid.*, p. 220.

4. *Ibid.*, p. 220.

5. *Ibid.*, p. 225.

6. *Ibid.,* p. 220.

7. There are, of course, two other ways in which one might try to derive a contradiction; namely, using (1) and (2) to get the denial of (3), *or* using (1) and (3) to get the denial of (2).

8. I borrow this example from Professor W. V. O. Quine, *From a Logical Point of View* (New York, 1963), pp. 143–144.

9. I assume here that (i) is not itself contradictory. Martin apparently makes the same assumption. At any rate, he does not argue that one would be involved in a contradiction if he held (i) but not (ii) and (iii).

10. Cf. Quine, pp. 148–149.

12

Divine Foreknowledge
and Human Freedom

ANTHONY KENNY

Balliol College, Oxford

IN THIS PAPER* I intend to discuss whether belief in God's
foreknowledge of the future is compatible with belief in the
freedom of human actions. Before stating the problem in further detail, I must make clear which problems I do *not* intend
to consider. I shall not discuss whether there is a God, nor
whether it is the case that some human actions are free. I shall
not try to show that an action which is causally determined is
not free, nor that God knows the future free actions of men.
It might be thought, indeed, that this last at least needs no proving: surely, if there is a God at all, He knows all that is to
come; a God who did not know the future would not be a real
God. But this is not so. It is indeed the case that any God

From *Aquinas: A Collection of Critical Essays* by Anthony Kenny, copyright
© 1969 by Anthony Kenny. Reprinted by permission of Doubleday & Company, Inc., New York, and of Macmillan & Company, Ltd., London and Basing-
stoke.

worthy of the name knows everything that there is to be known; but it does not follow from this alone that He knows the future free actions of men. For many philosophers have maintained, and some do maintain, that statements about as-yet-undecided free actions, such as the statement "The United States will declare war on China," are as yet neither true nor false. Since only what is true can be known, then if it is not yet true either that the United States will declare war on China or that the United States will not declare war on China, then not even God can know whether the United States will do so or not. Again, as a matter of history there have been philosophers who have believed that God was omniscient without thereby believing that God knew the future free actions of men. Indeed, as we shall see, even a philosopher so orthodox as St. Thomas Aquinas denied, in one important sense, that God knows the future when the future is not already determined by causal necessity. Even to theists, therefore, it needs to be proved that God knows what is going to take place through the free action of his creature. As I have said, I do not intend to argue for this. I intend merely to investigate whether there is or is not compatibility between two statements—namely, "God knows beforehand everything that men will do" and "Some actions of men are free." Even in this restricted area I intend to examine only two arguments which have been brought up to show that the statements are incompatible. The question of incompatibility retains its interest for philosophers even if both statements are in fact false.

It is necessary, as a final preamble, to insist that the problem to be discussed concerns only foreknowledge and not foreordaining. Just as people have believed that God knows beforehand all that happens in the world, so also they have believed that He ordains beforehand all that happens in the world. Just as no human action escapes God's prescience, so no human action escapes His providence. Accordingly, just as there is a problem how God's foreknowledge may be reconciled with human freedom, so also there is a problem how human freedom may be reconciled with God's providence. In particular, since, according to traditional Christian belief, no-one is saved who is not predestined by God to be saved, those who accept that belief have a special problem in reconciling it with the belief that those who are damned are damned through their own fault. These further problems are interesting, complicated, and difficult; but they will not be our concern in this paper.

The problem may be stated as follows. God's foreknowledge appears to be incompatible with human freedom. It does not seem to be possible both that God should know what I shall do in the future and that I shall do freely whatever it is that I shall do. For in order for me to be able to do an action freely, it is necessary that it should be within my power not to do that action. But if God knows what my action is going to be before I do it, then it does not seem to be within my power not to do it. For it cannot be the case both that God knows that I shall do such and such an action and that I shall not in fact do it. For what God knows must be true: and indeed what anyone knows must be true, since it is impossible to know what is false. But if what God knows is true, and God knows that I will do such and such an action, then it must be true that I will do it. And if it is true that I will do it, then it seems that nothing I can do can prevent its coming true that I am doing it. And if nothing I can do can prevent its coming true that I am doing it, then I cannot prevent myself from doing it. And if I cannot prevent myself from doing a certain action, then that action cannot be free. Therefore, either God cannot know what I shall do tomorrow, or else whatever I shall do tomorrow will not be done freely.

For example: if God knows now that I will tell a lie this time tomorrow, then it seems that I cannot be free not to tell a lie this time tomorrow. For it cannot be the case both that God knows that I will tell a lie tomorrow and that I will not in fact tell a lie tomorrow. For what God knows must be true: so that if God knows that I will tell a lie tomorrow, it must be true that I will tell a lie tomorrow. But if it must be true that I will tell a lie tomorrow, then I cannot be free not to tell a lie tomorrow. But if I am not free not to tell a lie tomorrow, then when tomorrow I tell a lie, I shall not do so freely. A similar argument appears to hold, no matter what human action we consider instead of telling lies. Therefore it seems that if God foresees all human actions, no human action can be free.

This difficulty is a very old one. It is stated, for instance, in St. Thomas Aquinas' *Summa Theologiae,* Ia, 14, 3, 3. Aquinas' statement of the difficulty is as follows: "Whatever is known by God must be; for whatever is known by us must be, and God's knowledge is more certain than ours. But nothing which is future and contingent *must* be. Therefore, nothing which is future and contingent is known by God." This difficulty is recognizably the same as the one which I have just stated more verbosely. The only difference of importance is that while I spoke of future free actions, St. Thomas speaks of future contingent events. St. Thomas uses the word "contingent" as equivalent to "not causally determined." Assuming that no causally determined action is a free action, a free human action would be a contingent event within the meaning of St. Thomas' phrase. Indeed St. Thomas expressly states (ibid., *Sed contra*) that free human actions are contingent events. He thought also that there were other contingent events besides free human actions: the budding of a tree, for instance. Whether he was correct in thinking this is an interesting question, but not to our purpose.

To the difficulty which he has set, St. Thomas provides a long answer. Part of his answer runs as follows.

The proposition "whatever is known by God must be" can be analysed in two ways. It may be taken as a proposition *de dicto* or as a proposition *de re*; in others words, it may be taken either *in sensu composito* or *in sensu diviso*. As a *de re* proposition, it means:
Of everything which is known by God, it is true that that thing must be.
So understood the proposition is false. As a proposition *de dicto* it means:
The proposition "whatever God knows is the case" is necessarily true.
So understood, the proposition is true.

There is much more in St. Thomas' answer than this paragraph, but this argument, as it stands, seems to me an adequate answer to the difficulty. In order to understand it one must know something about the medieval distinction between propositions *de dicto* and propositions *de re*. Consider the following proposition.
(1) If there is a University at Oxford, then necessarily there is a University at Oxford.
Someone who asserts that proposition may be taken to assert

(2) "If there is a University at Oxford, then there is a University at Oxford" is a necessary truth.

Or he may be taken to assert

(3) If there is a University at Oxford, then "there is a University at Oxford" is a necessary truth.

The medievals would have called proposition (1), if interpreted in the sense of proposition (2), a proposition *de dicto*; if interpreted in the sense of proposition (3) they would call it a proposition *de re*. The difference between the two interpretations is obviously of crucial importance. For (2), which merely states that a certain conditional—whose consequent is a repetition of its antecedent—is necessarily true, is itself true. But (3) is false, since its antecedent is true (there is a University at Oxford), and its consequent is false (it is not a necessary truth that there is a University at Oxford, since there has not always been a University at Oxford).

It is not difficult to see how to apply this to the problem in hand. The proposition "Whatever is known by God is necessarily true" if taken *de dicto* means

(4) "Whatever is known by God is true" is a necessary truth.

Interpreted *de re*, however, it means

(5) Whatever is known by God is a necessary truth. Proposition (4) is true, but it has no tendency to show that acts foreseen by God are not free. For, it is equally a necessary truth that if I will tell a lie this time tomorrow, then I will tell a lie this time tomorrow: but this necessary truth has no tendency to show that my telling of a lie tomorrow will not be free. On the other hand, (5) if true would rule out the possibility of free action. If it is a necessary truth that I will tell a lie tomorrow, then I have no choice in the matter. But this need not trouble us; for proposition (5) is simply false. If God knows everything, then God knows that I am now writing this paper; but "I am writing this paper" is not a necessary truth, since it was in fact false ten days ago. We might bring out the difference between the two interpretations of "whatever is known by God is necessarily true" by punctuation, as follows.

(4a) Whatever is known by God is, necessarily, true.

(5a) Whatever is known by God is necessarily-true.

It seems to me, therefore, that St. Thomas' answer to this particular difficulty is entirely satisfactory. But he puts to him-

self a further, and more persuasive, difficulty; and his answer
to this second difficulty does not appear satisfactory at all.

The further difficulty runs as follows. In any true conditional proposition whose antecedent is necessarily true, the
consequent is also necessarily true. That is to say, whatever is
implied by a necessary proposition is itself a necessary proposition. The following is clearly a true conditional proposition:
"If it has come to God's knowledge that such and such a thing
will happen, then such and such a thing will happen." The antecedent of the conditional, if it is true at all, appears to be
necessarily true: for it is in the past tense, and what is past
cannot be changed. What has been the case cannot now not
have been the case. Therefore, the consequent is also necessarily true. Therefore, whatever is known by God is a necessary truth.

This is a powerful argument: it appears, at least at first
sight, impossible to deny any of its premises. St. Thomas himself treated it with great respect: before putting forward his
own solution he considered and rejected three attempts to deny
one or other premise. In the end, he could find no alternative to
accepting the argument, while trying to show that the conclusion is not, as it appears to be, incompatible with the occurrence of contingent events.

His solution runs as follows. God, he says, is outside time:
God's life is measured not by time, but by eternity. Eternity,
which has no parts, overlaps the whole of time; consequently,
the things which happen at different times are all present together to God. An event is known *as future* only when there is
a relation of future to past between the knowledge of the
knower and the happening of the event. But there is no such
relation between God's knowledge and any contingent event:
the relation between God's knowledge and any event in time is
always one of simultaneity. Consequently, a contingent event,
as it comes to God's knowledge, is not future but present; and
as present it is necessary; for what is the case, is the case, and
is beyond anyone's power to alter. Hence, we can admit that
what is known to God is a necessary truth; for as known by
God it is no longer future but present. But this necessity does
not destroy contingency: for the fact that an event is necessary

when it happens does not mean that it was predetermined by its causes.

St. Thomas adds plausibility to his solution with a famous illustration.

> To us, because we know future contingent events as future, there can be no certainty about them; but only to God, whose knowing is in eternity, above time. A man who is walking along a road cannot see those who are coming after him; but a man who looks down from a hill upon the whole length of the road can see at the same time all those who are travelling along it. So it is with God. . . . Future events which are in themselves contingent cannot be known to us. What is known to God is necessary in the way in which it lies open to God's knowledge [namely, in its presentness]; it is not necessary in regard to its own causes.[1]

This explanation of St. Thomas' has become the classic solution of the problem raised by God's foreknowledge. It is still sometimes presented in popular expositions of Christian theology, for instance in *Theology and Sanity* by F. J. Sheed.

> If God knew last Tuesday what you were going to do next Tuesday, what becomes of your free will? . . . God did *not* know *last* Tuesday. Tuesday is a period of time and part of the duration in which I act. But God acts in eternity which has no Tuesdays. God acts in the spacelessness of his immensity and the timelessness of his eternity: we receive the effects of his acts in space and time [p. 117].

Despite the authority of St. Thomas, the solution seems fundamentally misconceived. In the first place, it forces one to deny that it is true, in any strict sense, that God knows future free actions. St. Thomas insists repeatedly that no-one, not even God, can know contingent events *qua* future: he says of such events that we should rather say "if God knows something, then it *is*" than "if God knows something, then it *will be*" (*De Veritate* 2, 12 ad 7). Strictly speaking, then, God has no *fore*knowledge of contingent events: as He knows them, they are not still future but already present. A defender of St. Thomas might reply that this does not matter: when we say that God knows future events we mean merely that (*a*) God knows all events; (*b*) some events are future *to us*. Of any event which is future to us it will be true to say that God knows it, though He will not know *qua* future. Thus, let us suppose that at some future date a man will land on Mars. The event which is the landing on Mars is, as far as we are concerned, in the future; but to God it is already present. Thus, although we cannot say that God knows that a man *will* land on Mars (for this would be to make God know it *qua* future), we can say that God knows, timelessly, the event which is the landing on Mars. And this event is future to us—that is to say, it comes later in the time series than, e.g., your reading this.

But this reply does not meet the objection. If "to know the future" means to know more than "to know a fact which comes later in the time series than some other fact" then we, no less than God, can know the future. For we know about the Wars of the Roses which *were* future when Cleopatra was a girl. If we were to take St. Thomas' suggestion seriously, we should have to say that God knows that a man *is landing* on Mars; but we cannot say this, since the statement that a man is landing on Mars, being false, cannot be known, even by God, to be true.

St. Thomas' solution, then, is not so much a defence as a denial of God's foreknowledge. But it forces us to deny not only God's foreknowledge, but also God's omniscience. For the statement that God's foreknowledge is outside time must mean, if anything, that no temporal qualifications can be attached to God's knowledge. Where God is the subject, verbs of knowing cannot have adverbs of time affixed to them. We cannot, therefore, say that God knows now that Brutus killed Caesar; or that God will know tomorrow what time I went to bed tonight. But as A. N. Prior has remarked, it seems an extraordinary way of affirming God's omniscience if a person, when asked what God knows *now,* must say "Nothing," and when asked what He knew *yesterday,* must again say "Nothing," and must yet again say "Nothing" when asked what God will know *tomorrow.*

An argument *ad hominem* against St. Thomas' position may be drawn from the notion of prophecy. St. Thomas believed that God could foretell, and had foretold, future contingent events. He believed, for example, that God, as the principal

author of the Epistle to the Romans, had foretold the con-
version of the Jewish people to Christianity. On the view that
God's knowledge is timeless, such prediction becomes inexplicable. For, if God's knowledge is timeless, then we cannot
attach to statements about God's knowledge such adverbial
clauses as "at the time when the Epistle to the Romans was
written." We cannot, for example, say "At the time when the
Epistle to the Romans was written God already knew that
the Jews would finally be converted." But if God did not then
know it, how could He then foretell it? To put it bluntly: if
God did not then *know* that the Jews would be converted, He
had no right then to *say* that they would.

Indeed, the whole concept of a timeless eternity, the whole
of which is simultaneous with every part of time, seems to
be radically incoherent. For simultaneity as ordinarily understood is a transitive relation. If A happens at the same time
as B, and B happens at the same time as C, then A happens
at the same time as C. If the BBC programme and the ITV programme both start when Big Ben strikes ten, then they both
start at the same time. But, on St. Thomas' view, my typing
of this paper is simultaneous with the whole of eternity. Again,
on his view, the great fire of Rome is simultaneous with the
whole of eternity. Therefore, while I type these very words,
Nero fiddles heartlessly on.

If St. Thomas' solution to the difficulty is unacceptable, is
it possible to give a different one? The objection ran thus.
What is implied by a necessary proposition is itself necessarily
true. But from "it has come to God's knowledge that such and
such will be the case" it follows that "such and such will be
the case." But "it has come to God's knowledge that such and
such will be the case" is necessarily true; therefore "such and
such will be the case" is necessarily true. Therefore, if God
knows the future, the future is not contingent.[2]

The premises of the argument appear difficult to deny; yet
if its conclusion is true, there is no freedom or else no foreknowledge. For if it must be the case that I will murder my
grandfather, then I am not free not to murder my grandfather; and conversely, if I am free not to murder my grandfather, then God cannot know that I will murder him even
if in fact I will do so.

Let us examine each premise in turn. It appears incontrovertible that what follows from a necessary proposition is itself necessary.[3] Moreover, it cannot be denied that "it is the case that p" follows from "It has come to God's knowledge that p": this is true *ex vi termini* "know." So, for any substitution for "p," if "It has come to God's knowledge that p" is necessarily true, then "it is the case that p" is also necessarily true.

But is it true, for all substitutions for "p," that it must be the case that it has come to God's knowledge that p? St. Thomas accepted it without question. "It has come to God's knowledge that p" is a proposition in the past tense, and for St. Thomas as for Aristotle all propositions in the past tense are necessary. Now let us first notice that even if this doctrine were true, there has occurred a significant change in the sense of "necessary." Hitherto, "necessarily" has been used in such a way that in every case it could have been replaced by "it is a logical truth that. . . ." But if an Aristotelian claims that "Cesare Borgia was a bad man" is now necessarily true, he must be using "necessarily" in a different sense. For he cannot claim that it is a logical truth that Cesare Borgia was a bad man. Again, let us notice that the necessity of past propositions, if they are necessary, is not something that is *eo ipso* incompatible with freedom. If it is now necessary that Cesare Borgia was a bad man, it does not follow from this alone that it was, when he was born, necessary that he *would* be a bad man. For, according to Aristotle, necessity applies only to true past and present propositions, not to future propositions of contingent fact. But, when Cesare Borgia was born, the proposition "Cesare Borgia will be a bad man" was a future-tensed proposition of contingent fact—as indeed it still is.

It is clear, then, that if present- and past-tensed propositions are, as Aristotle thought, necessary in a way in which future-tensed propositions are not, they are not necessary in the way in which logical truths are necessary; and they are not necessary in a way which excludes the freedom of the action they report, if they report an action at all.

But is there any sense at all in which past- and present-tensed propositions have a necessity which is not shared by future-tensed propositions? The very least which seems to be demanded of a proposition if it is to be called "necessary" is that it is, always has been, and always will be, true. In this sense of "necessary" the proposition "there is a God" is necessarily true if it is true at all; but of course the proposition "there is a God" is not a logical truth, as critics of the ontological argument, from Gaunilo to Russell, have frequently pointed out. Now, the proposition "Queen Anne is dead," which is a true present-tensed proposition if ever there was one, is not a necessary truth in this sense at all, since before 1714 it was not true. The past-tensed proposition "Queen Anne has died" will indeed never cease to be true; but it *was* not true in King Alfred's day. So, even if "necessary" is given the weak interpretation of "true at all times," there seems no reason to believe the Aristotelian doctrine that past- and present-tensed propositions *in materia contingenti* are necessary.

Yet is it not true that what has happened cannot now not have happened, and that which is happening cannot now not be happening? We have a very strong inclination to think that there is some way in which we can change the future, in which we cannot change the past. But this inclination appears to be a delusion. There appears to be no sense in which we can change the future in which we cannot change the past. As A. N. Prior has pointed out, whatever changes of plan we may make, the future is whatever takes place after all the changes are made; what we alter is *not* the future, but our plans; the real future can no more be altered than the past. The sort of case which we have in mind when we are tempted to say that we can change the future is this: suppose that I have no intention of typing "elephant" backwards; then I decide I will do so; and finally I do so. Does not my decision change the future, since without my decision the word would never have been typed backwards? No, for even when I had no intention of doing so, e.g. ten years ago, it *was* true that I would, ten years later, type "elephant" backwards; and so my decision altered nothing except my own intentions. There is, indeed, a sense in which we can change the future: we can change the truth-value of a future-tensed proposition. Suppose that it is true that I will commit suicide: then the proposition "A. K. will commit suicide" now has the truth-value "true." I can change this truth-value by committing suicide; for, once I have committed suicide the proposition "A. K. will commit suicide" ceases to be true, and the quite different proposition "A. K. has committed suicide" becomes true instead. But if "to change the future" means merely "to change the truth-value of a future-tensed proposition" then in a corresponding sense I can change the past no less than the future. Nothing is easier. Tnahpele. The past-tensed proposition "A. K. has typed 'elephant' backwards" which *was* false, is now true; and so I have changed the past.

It seems, then, that there is no sense in which we can change the future in which we cannot change the past. Still, it does seem true that we can bring about the future, but cannot bring about the past; our present activity may have a causal effect on the future but cannot have a causal effect on the past. Consequently, deliberation about the future is sensible, deliberation about the past absurd; so if God's knowledge of what I will do tomorrow is already a thing of the past, deliberation about what I will do tomorrow appears already pointless, and once again there appears to be an incompatibility between foreknowledge and freedom.

However, in certain cases, it does seem that present actions can affect the past. By begetting a son, I make my grandfather, long dead, into a great-grandfather; by becoming Poet Laureate I make my late grandmother's belief that I would one day be Poet Laureate into a true belief. In such cases, of course, what we are doing is establishing new relations between past things and events and present or future things or events. But the truth of a belief, and the question of whether a certain belief does or does not constitute knowledge, involve relationships between those beliefs and the events they concern. So it is possible that it is precisely by telling a lie today that I bring it about that God knew yesterday that I would tell a lie today. Of course, I do not bring it about by today's lie that God yesterday *believed* that I would lie; but it is my current lie which makes His belief then true.

Even so, it might be retorted, this does not make it possible for God to have *known* yesterday without curtailment of my freedom; because knowledge is not true belief, but justified true belief; and the justification of a past belief would have to be past grounds for the belief; and nothing in the past could be adequate grounds for a belief about my current action unless it necessitated that action. To this the reply is open that even in non-theological contexts there seem to be cases in which true belief, without grounds, constitutes knowledge. One such case is our knowledge of our own actions. Commonly, we know what we are doing with our hands, and we do not know this on the basis of any evidence or grounds. Of course, we can be mistaken: I may think I am typing "piece" and in fact be typing "peice." But when I am not mistaken, my belief about what I am doing constitutes knowledge. It does not seem unreasonable to suggest that in this respect a Creator's knowledge of His creature's actions might resemble a human agent's knowledge of his own actions.

There seems, then, no reason to maintain that "It has come to God's knowledge that p" is a necessary truth, in any of the senses we have suggested, merely because it is past-tensed. Might it not be argued, however, that it is a necessary truth for a different reason: namely, that it is a truth about God's knowledge, which is the knowledge of a necessarily omniscient necessary being? If God is omniscient, it might be argued, then, whatever we substitute for "p," "it has come to God's knowledge that p" will be true. But "if it has come to God's knowledge that p" is true no matter what we substitute for "p," then it must be something like a logical truth, and so a necessary truth in the sense in which necessity is incompatible with freedom.

It does not take a moment to detect the fallacy in this argument. God's omniscience does not at all imply that whatever we substitute for "p" in "God knows that p" is true. For instance, if we substitute "$2 + 2 = 3$" we get not a necessary truth but the falsehood "God knows that $2 + 2 = 3$." It is indeed a logical truth that if p is true, then p is known by any omniscient being; but this is insufficient to provide the premise needed by St. Thomas' objector.[4] A sentence such as "God knows that I am sitting down" expresses not a necessary, but a contingent truth: it may be true now, but it was not true last night, and it will cease to be true as soon as I stand up. In fact, God's knowledge will only be necessary where what He knows is necessary: "$2 + 2 = 4$" is a necessary truth, so "God knows that 2 + 2 = 4" is a necessary truth.[5] But, by definition, a contingent proposition—such as a proposition reporting or predicting a free action—is never a necessary truth. Hence, the argument which we have been considering has no tendency to show that human freedom and divine foreknowledge are incompatible.

There are other arguments to prove this incompatibility: Aquinas alone gives thirteen of which we have considered only two. None, however, are as initially plausible, or as complicated to unravel, as the two we have considered.

NOTES

* Revised version of a paper read at Liverpool in 1960. In the original preparation of the paper I had the advantage of discussions with Miss G. E. M. Anscombe and Mr. A. N. Prior.

1. *Summa Theologiae,* Ia, 14, 13 ad 3 (words in brackets from the body of the article). The preceding paragraph is a mosaic of translations from *De Veritate* 2, 12.

2. Using "*Lp*" for "Necessarily *p*," "*Gp*" for "It has come to God's knowledge that *p*," and "*Cpq*" for "If *p*, then *q*," we could symbolise the argument thus: *LCLCGppLCLGpLp*; *LCGpp*; *LGp*; ergo, *Lp*.

3. *LCLCpqLCLpLq* is a law in every standard modal system.

4. We have not *LGp* but *LCpGp*.

5. We have not *LCpLGp*, but *LCLpLGp*.

13

Some Puzzles
Concerning Omnipotence

GEORGE I. MAVRODES
University of Michigan

THE DOCTRINE OF GOD'S OMNIPOTENCE appears to claim that God can do anything. Consequently, there have been attempts to refute the doctrine by giving examples of things which God cannot do; for example, He cannot draw a square circle.

Responding to objections of this type, St. Thomas pointed out that "anything" should be here construed to refer only to objects, actions, or states of affairs whose descriptions are not self-contradictory.[1] For it is only such things whose non-existence might plausibly be attributed to a lack of power in some agent. My failure to draw a circle on the exam may indicate my lack of geometrical skill, but my failure to draw a square circle does not indicate any such lack. Therefore, the fact that it is false (or perhaps meaningless) to say that God

Reprinted from *The Philosophical Review*, 72 (1963), 221–223, with the permission of the author and the publishers.

could draw one does no damage to the doctrine of His omnipotence.

A more involved problem, however, is posed by this type of question: can God create a stone too heavy for Him to lift? This appears to be stronger than the first problem, for it poses a dilemma. If we say that God can create such a stone, then it seems that there might be such a stone. And if there might be a stone too heavy for Him to lift, then He is evidently not omnipotent. But if we deny that God can create such a stone, we seem to have given up His omnipotence already. Both answers lead us to the same conclusion.

Further, this problem does not seem obviously open to St. Thomas' solution. The form "x is able to draw a square circle" seems plainly to involve a contradiction, while "x is able to make a thing too heavy for x to lift" does not. For it may easily be true that I am able to make a boat too heavy for me to lift. So why should it not be possible for God to make a stone too heavy for Him to lift?

Despite this apparent difference, this second puzzle *is* open to essentially the same answer as the first. The dilemma fails because it consists of asking whether God can do a self-contradictory thing. And the reply that He cannot does no damage to the doctrine of omnipotence.

The specious nature of the problem may be seen in this way. God is either omnipotent or not.[2] Let us assume first that He is not. In that case the phrase "a stone too heavy for God to lift" may not be self-contradictory. And then, of course, if we assert either that God is able or that He is not able to create such a stone, we may conclude that He is not omnipotent. But this is no more than the assumption with which we began, meeting us again after our roundabout journey. If this were all that the dilemma could establish it would be trivial. To be significant it must derive this same conclusion *from the assumption that God is omnipotent*; that is, it must show that the assumption of the omnipotence of God leads to a *reductio*. But does it?

On the assumption that God is omnipotent, the phrase "a stone too heavy for God to lift" becomes self-contradictory. For it becomes "a stone which cannot be lifted by Him whose power is sufficient for lifting anything." But the "thing" described by a self-contradictory phrase is absolutely impossible and hence has nothing to do with the doctrine of omnipotence. Not being an object of power at all, its failure to exist cannot be the result of some lack in the power of God. And, interestingly, it is the very omnipotence of God which makes the existence of such a stone absolutely impossible, while it is the fact that I am finite in power which makes it possible for me to make a boat too heavy for me to lift.

But suppose that some die-hard objector takes the bit in his teeth and denies that the phrase "a stone too heavy for God to lift" is self-contradictory, even on the assumption that God is omnipotent. In other words, he contends that the description "a stone too heavy for an omnipotent God to lift" is self-coherent and therefore describes an absolutely possible object. Must I then attempt to prove the contradiction which I assumed above as intuitively obvious? Not necessarily. Let me reply simply that if the objector is right in this contention, then the answer to the original question is "Yes, God can create such a stone." It may seem that this reply will force us into the original dilemma. But it does not. For now the objector can draw no damaging conclusion from this answer. And the reason is that he has just now contended that such a stone is compatible with the omnipotence of God. Therefore, from the possibility of God's creating such a stone it cannot be concluded that God is not omnipotent. The objector cannot have it both ways. The conclusion which he himself wishes to draw from an affirmative answer to the original question is itself the required proof that the descriptive phrase which appears there is self-contradictory. And "it is more appropriate to say that such things cannot be done, than that God cannot do them."[3]

The specious nature of this problem may also be seen in a somewhat different way.[4] Suppose that some theologian is convinced by this dilemma that he must give up the doctrine of omnipotence. But he resolves to give up as little as possible, just enough to meet the argument. One way he can do so is by retaining the infinite power of God with regard to lifting, while placing a restriction on the sort of stone He is able to create. The only restriction required here, however, is that God must not be able to create a stone too heavy for Him to lift. Beyond that the dilemma has not even suggested any necessary restriction. Our theologian has, in effect, answered the original question in the negative, and he now regretfully supposes that this has required him to give up the full doctrine of omnipotence. He is now retaining what he supposes to be the more modest remnants which he has salvaged from that doctrine.

We must ask, however, what it is which he has in fact given up. Is it the unlimited power of God to create stones? No doubt. But what stone is it which God is now precluded from creating? The stone too heavy for Him to lift, of course. But we must remember that nothing in the argument required the theologian to admit any limit on God's power with regard to the lifting of stones. He still holds that to be unlimited. And if God's power to lift is infinite, then His power to create may run to infinity also without outstripping that first power. The supposed limitation turns out to be no limitation at all, since it is specified only by reference to another power which is itself infinite. Our theologian need have no regrets, for he has given up nothing. The doctrine of the power of God remains just what it was before.

Nothing I have said above, of course, goes to prove that God is, in fact, omnipotent. All I have intended to show is that certain arguments intended to prove that He is not omnipotent fail. They fail because they propose, as tests of God's power, putative tasks whose descriptions are self-contradictory. Such pseudo-tasks, not falling within the realm of possibility, are not objects of power at all. Hence the fact that they cannot be performed implies no limit on the power of God, and hence no defect in the doctrine of omnipotence.

NOTES

1. St. Thomas Aquinas, *Summa Theologiae,* Ia, q. 25, a. 3.
2. I assume, of course, the existence of God, since that is not being brought in question here.
3. St. Thomas, *loc. cit.*
4. But this method rests finally on the same logical relations as the preceding one.

14

The Paradox of the Stone

C. WADE SAVAGE

University of Minnesota

A. (1) Either God can create a stone which He cannot lift, or He
cannot create a stone which He cannot lift.
   (2) If God can create a stone which He cannot lift, then He is
not omnipotent (since He cannot lift the stone in question).
   (3) If God cannot create a stone which He cannot lift, then He
is not omnipotent (since He cannot create the stone in question).
   (4) Therefore, God is not omnipotent.

Mr. Mavrodes has offered a solution to the familiar paradox
above;[1] but it is erroneous. Mavrodes states that he assumes
the existence of God,[2] and then reasons (in pseudo-dilemma
fashion) as follows. God is either omnipotent or He is not.
If we assume that He is not omnipotent, the task of creating
a stone which He cannot lift is not self-contradictory. And we
can conclude that God is not omnipotent on the grounds that
both His ability and His inability to perform this task imply
that He is not omnipotent. But to prove His non-omnipotence

Reprinted from *The Philosophical Review*, 76 (1967), 74–79, with the permission
of the author and the publishers.

193

in this way is trivial. "To be significant [the paradoxical argument] must derive this same conclusion *from the assumption that God is omnipotent*; that is, it must show that the assumption of the omnipotence of God leads to a *reductio*." However, on the assumption that God is omnipotent, the task of creating a stone which God cannot lift is self-contradictory. Since inability to perform a self-contradictory task does not imply a limitation on the agent, one of the premises of the paradoxical argument—premise A(3)—is false. The argument is, in consequence, either insignificant or unsound.

There are many objections to this solution. First, the paradoxical argument need not be represented as a *reductio*; in A it is a dilemma. Mavrodes' reasoning implies that the paradoxical argument must either assume that God is omnipotent or assume that He is not omnipotent. This is simply false: neither assumption need be made, and neither is made in A. Second, "a stone which God cannot lift" is self-contradictory—on the assumption that God is omnipotent—only if "God is omnipotent" is necessarily true. "Russell can lift any stone" is a contingent statement. Consequently, if we assume that Russell can lift any stone we are thereby committed only to saying that creating a stone which Russell cannot lift is a task which *in fact* cannot be performed by Russell or anyone else. Third, if "God is omnipotent" is necessarily true—as Mavrodes must claim for his solution to work—then his assumption that God exists begs the question of the paradoxical argument. For what the argument really tries to establish is that the existence of an omnipotent being is logically impossible. Fourth, the claim that inability to perform a self-contradictory task is no limitation on the agent is not entirely uncontroversial. Descartes suggested that an omnipotent God must be able to perform such self-contradictory tasks as making a mountain without a valley and arranging that the sum of one and two is not three.[3] No doubt Mavrodes and Descartes have different theories about the nature of contradictions; but that is part of the controversy.

Mavrodes has been led astray by version A of the paradox, which apparently seeks to prove that *God is not omnipotent*. Concentration on this version, together with the inclination to say that God is by definition omnipotent, leads straight to the conclusion that the paradox is specious. For if God is by definition omnipotent, then, obviously, creating a stone which God (an omnipotent being who can lift any stone) cannot lift is a task whose description is self-contradictory. What the paradox of the stone really seeks to prove is that the notion of an omnipotent being is logically inconsistent—that is, that *the existence of an omnipotent being, God or any other, is logically impossible.* It tries to do this by focusing on the perfectly consistent task of creating a stone which the creator cannot lift. The essence of the argument is that an omnipotent being must be able to perform this task and yet cannot perform the task.

Stated in its clearest form, the pardoxical argument of the stone is as follows. Where *x* is any being:

B. (1) Either *x* can create a stone which *x* cannot lift, or *x* cannot create a stone which *x* cannot lift.

(2) If *x* can create a stone which *x* cannot lift, then, necessarily, there is at least one task which *x* cannot perform (namely, lift the stone in question).

(3) If *x* cannot create a stone which *x* cannot lift, then, necessarily, there is at least one task which *x* cannot perform (namely, create the stone in question).

(4) Hence, there is at least one task which *x* cannot perform.

(5) If *x* is an omnipotent being, then *x* can perform any task.

(6) Therefore, *x* is not omnipotent.

Since *x* is any being, this argument proves that the existence of an omnipotent being, God or any other, is logically impossible.

It is immediately clear that Mavrodes' solution will not apply to this version of the paradox. B is obviously a significant, non-trivial argument. But since it does not contain the word "God," no critic can maintain that B assumes that God is omnipotent. For the same reason, the point that "a stone which God cannot lift" is self-contradictory is simply irrelevant. Notice also that B is neutral on the question of whether inability to perform a self-contradictory task is a limitation on the agent's power. We can, however, replace every occurrence of "task" with "task whose description is not self-contradictory" without damaging the argument in any way.

The paradox does have a correct solution, though a different one from that offered by Mavrodes. The two solutions are similar in that both consist in arguing that an agent's inability to create a stone which he cannot lift does not entail a limitation on his power. But here the similarity ends. For, as we shall see presently, the basis of the correct solution is not that creating a stone which the creator cannot lift is a self-contradictory task (which it is not). Consequently, the correct solution side-steps the question of whether an agent's inability to perform a self-contradictory task is a limitation on his power.

The fallacy in the paradox of the stone lies in the falsity of the second horn—B(3)—of its dilemma: "*x* can create a stone which *x* cannot lift" does indeed entail that there is a task which *x* cannot perform and, consequently, does entail that *x* is not omnipotent. However, "*x* cannot create a stone which *x* cannot lift" does not entail that there is a task which *x* cannot perform and, consequently, does not entail that *x* is not omnipotent. That the entailment *seems* to hold is explained by the misleading character of the statement "*x* cannot create a stone which *x* cannot lift." The phrase "cannot create a stone" seems to imply that there is a task which *x* cannot perform and, consequently, seems to imply that *x* is limited in power. But this illusion vanishes on analysis: "*x* cannot create a stone which *x* cannot lift" can only mean "If *x* can create a stone, then *x* can lift it." It is obvious that the latter statement does not entail that *x* is limited in power.

A schematic representation of B(1)–B(3) will bring our point into sharper focus. Let S = stone, C = can create, and L = can lift; let *x* be any being; and let the universe of discourse be conceivable entities. Then we obtain:

c. (1) $(\exists y)(Sy \cdot Cxy \cdot -Lxy) \text{ v} -(\exists y)(Sy \cdot Cxy \cdot -Lxy)$.
(2) $(\exists y)(Sy \cdot Cxy \cdot -Lxy) \supset (\exists y)(Sy \cdot -Lxy)$.
(3) $-(\exists y)(Sy \cdot Cxy \cdot -Lxy) \supset (\exists y)(Sy \cdot -Cxy)$.

That the second alternative in C(1) is equivalent to "$(y)[(Sy \cdot Cxy) \supset Lxy]$" schematically explains our interpretation "*x* cannot create a stone which *x* cannot lift" as meaning "If *x* can create a stone, then *x* can lift it." It is now quite clear where the fallacy in the paradoxical argument lies. Although

C(2) is logically true, C(3) is not. "(∃ y) (Sy · Cxy · −Lxy)"
logically implies "(∃ y) (Sy · −Lxy)." But "−(∃ y) (Sx ·
Cxy · −Lxy)" does not logically imply "(∃ y) (Sy · −Cxy)";
nor does it logically imply "(∃ y) (Sy · −Lxy)." In general,
"x cannot create a stone which x cannot lift" does not logically
imply "There is a task which x cannot perform."

For some reason the above analysis does not completely remove the inclination to think that an agent's inability to create
a stone which he himself cannot lift does entail his inability to
perform some task, does entail a limitation on his power. The
reason becomes clear when we consider the task of creating
a stone which someone *other than* the creator cannot lift. Suppose that y cannot lift any stone heavier than seventy pounds.
Now if x cannot create a stone which y cannot lift, then x cannot create a stone heavier than seventy pounds, and is indeed
limited in power. But suppose that y is omnipotent and can
lift stones of any poundage. Then x's inability to create a
stone which y cannot lift does not necessarily constitute a limitation on x's power. For x may be able to create stones of any
poundage, although y can lift any stone which x creates. If y
can lift stones of any poundage, and x cannot create a stone
heavier than seventy pounds, then x cannot create a stone
which y cannot lift, and x is limited in power. But if x can
create stones of any poundage, and y can lift stones of any
poundage, then x cannot create a stone which y cannot lift, and
yet x is not thereby limited in power. Now it is easy to see that
precisely parallel considerations obtain where x is both stone-
creator and stone-lifter.

The logical facts above may be summarized as follows.
Whether x = y or x ≠ y, x's inability to create a stone which
y cannot lift constitutes a limitation on x's power only if (i) x
is unable to create stones of any poundage, or (ii) y is unable
to lift stones of any poundage. And, since either (i) or (ii)
may be false, "x cannot create a stone which y cannot lift"
does not entail "x is limited in power." This logical point is
obscured, however, by the normal context of our discussions of
abilities and inabilities. Since such discussions are normally
restricted to beings who are limited in their stone-creating,
stone-lifting, and other abilities, the inability of a being to
create a stone which he himself or some other being cannot

lift *normally* constitutes a limitation on his power. And this produces the illusion that a being's inability to create a stone which he himself or some other being cannot lift *necessarily* constitutes a limitation on his power, the illusion that "*x* cannot create a stone which *y* cannot lift" (where either $x = y$ or $x \neq y$) entails "*x* is limited in power."

Since our discussions normally concern beings of limited power, the erroneous belief that "*x* cannot create a stone which *x* cannot lift" entails "*x* is limited in power" will normally cause no difficulty. But we must beware when the discussion turns to God—a being who is presumably unlimited in power. God's inability to create a stone which He cannot lift is a limitation on His power only if (i) He is unable to create stones of any poundage, or (ii) He is unable to lift stones of any poundage —that is, only if He is limited in His power of stone-creating or His power of stone-lifting. But until it has been proved otherwise—and it is difficult to see how this could be done— we are free to suppose that God suffers neither of these limitations. On this supposition, God's inability to create a stone which He cannot lift is nothing more or less than a necessary consequence of two facets of His omnipotence.[4] For if God is omnipotent, then He can create stones of any poundage and lift stones of any poundage. And "God can create stones of any poundage, and God can lift stones of any poundage" entails "God cannot create a stone which He cannot lift."

NOTES

1. See chapter 13. The heart of his solution is contained in paragraphs 6, 7, and 11.

2. See n. 2, p. 192.

3. Harry G. Frankfurt, "The Logic of Omnipotence," *Philosophical Review,* 73 (1964), 262–263. The relevant passage from Descartes is quoted by Frankfurt in a long footnote. Mavrodes assumes (on his "significant" interpretation of the paradox) that creating a stone which God cannot lift is a self-contradictory task, and contends that God therefore cannot perform it. This forces him onto the second horn of dilemma A, which he tries to break by arguing that inability to perform a self-contradictory task does not imply a limitation on the agent. Frankfurt also assumes that creating a stone which God cannot lift is a self-contradictory task, but contends with Descartes (for the sake of the argument) that God can nevertheless perform it. This forces him onto the first horn of the dilemma, which he tries to break with the following argument. If God can

perform the self-contradictory task of creating a stone which He cannot lift, then He can just as easily perform the additional self-contradictory task of lifting the stone which He (creates and) cannot lift. Frankfurt's fundamental error is the same as Mavrodes': both suppose that on any significant interpretation the paradox sets for God the self-contradictory task of creating a stone which God (an omnipotent being who can lift any stone) cannot lift.

4. Mavrodes apparently sees this point in the last three paragraphs of his article. But his insight is vitiated by his earlier mistaken attempt to solve the paradox.

15

Creation *ex nihilo*

JOHN DONNELLY

Fordham University

IS THERE A LOGIC OF CREATION? Can any sense be made of
the expression "God created the world *ex nihilo*"? To most
contemporary philosophers, the answer is indeed a negative
one. However, it is the intent of my paper to show that these
philosophers have been too quick to settle the issue, and that,
moreover, the creationist (a person who accepts the proposition "God created the world *ex nihilo*" and all which it entails) can present a defense, however preliminary in scope,
which amounts to more than theological pleading.

I

It is an indisputable empirical fact that there is an inherent
limitation in the causal activity of human agents. John Doe is
a human agent such that, when John Doe acts as the efficient
cause of event E, he can never cause E to exist *per se*. That is,
he cannot cause something previously non-existent to exist *ex*

A slightly different version of this paper appeared in the *Proceedings* of the
American Catholic Philosophical Association, 44 (1970), 172–184.

nihilo, but instead depends on something (*ex aliquo*) which already exists on which to demonstrate his causal efficacy. It was evidence from such empirical data which led realistically-minded Scholastics to draw a distinction between (1) the cause(s) of becoming (secondary causality), and (2) the cause of being itself (primary causality) which (*a*) both causes a previously non-existent entity y to be an F or a non-F, and/or (*b*) sustains or allows y to continue or remain in F-ness or non-F-ness.[1] This latter sense of causality—namely, primary causality—allows us to speak of X as the efficient cause of y, provided: (i) X causes y to be an F or a non-F; (ii) X sustains y in existence, allowing it to remain F or non-F; and (iii) there is no Z such that Z is not identical with X, and Z causes y to be an F or a non-F, and Z sustains y in existence.

It is instructive to recognize that the crux of the doctrine of creation is primarily concerned with accounting for the onto-logical dependence of the world upon God, and only second-arily is it concerned about the question of a literal beginning of the world. Accordingly, the primary cause of being (God) is to be viewed as an agent, power, or force which actively pro-duces certain entities, and without whose creative force such entities would not come-to-be. To speak of God as the creator of the universe is to imply that God caused, brought into being, and produced the universe.

The medievals distinguished three types of efficient causality (an efficient cause being what St. Thomas termed a *"causa quod,"* that by which an effect is produced and in terms of which the effect is explained). The following cases all qualify as immanent acts of causation, inasmuch as it is an agent and not an event which causes a particular event or state of affairs: (*a*) *Mere alteration*: where an agent causes an already exist-ing y to be an F. John Doe practices playing the violin very diligently, so that he actively causes himself who had the prop-erty of being non-musical at t_1 to be musical at t_2. Here it is to be noted that a new *ens per se* (e.g., a musician) does not come-into-being, but rather a modification or a new accidental characteristic (what Aquinas termed a "secondary determina-tion") of an already existing entity comes-into-being; (*b*) *sub-stantial change*: where an agent causes some already existent basic stuff w (prime matter)[2] to become F (take on a new substantial form), and in the causal process forfeit its non-F characteristic (the privation of F). Put schematically, an agent causes a w-not-F to become a w-F, so that a determinable becomes a determinant, or, as St. Thomas put it, not-F was "reduced" from w, while F was "educed" from w. The medieval theological doctrine of transubstantiation fits such a description in that the priest by his causal efficacy causes some stuff which was formerly bread and wine to be now the body and blood of Christ. Far less objectionable philosophically, the same phenomenon applies to the chemist who initiates the transference of a certain amount of hydrogen and oxygen into water; (c) *creatio ex nihilo*: God caused it to be the case that $(\exists\ x)$ (x is an atom). This might also be expressed as God caused it to be that $(\exists\ x)\ [\sim(x$ is F or non-F at $t_0)\ \cdot\ (x$ is F at $t_1)]$.[3] Sense (c) should not be confused with sense (d) which more properly relates to *divine providence*: $(\exists\ z)$ (God brought it about that z is an F). For an example of (d): there is a person such that this person is identical with Joan of Arc, and God brought it about that Joan of Arc would come to the defense of France. Clearly (c) is not equivalent in meaning to (d), for (d) presupposes an already existing entity *qua* patient, and emphasizes the sustaining power of God, whereas (c) emphasizes God's bringing (patientlessly) an entity-into-existence. Indeed the negation of (d) in conjunction with (c) better enables us to grasp the absolute nothingness which was before God's creative activity: God caused it to be the case that $(\exists x)$ (x is an atom), and for no z where z is a pre-existing entity, such that z is not identical with x, did God cause it to be the case that z became x-ish.

It seems manifestly clear that (a) and (b) are instances of what the medievals termed acts of "secondary causality," whereby an efficient cause does not cause the effect to *be* what it is, but rather to *become* what it is, and that (c) is an instance of "primary causality," with (d) helping to bring out some possible ramifications of (c).

II

An initial difficulty which confronts the creationist, and one his antagonists have long exploited, is what sense, if any, can

be made of the statement "God caused it to be *ex nihilo* that
$(\exists x)$ (x is an atom)." A corollary is, how can we meaningfully speak of something coming from nothing? Ironically
enough, the creationist can be buoyed in his investigation into
the linguistic proprieties of "nothing talk" by the Humean
possibility that there might be nothing, because such a non-
state of affairs, although perhaps not imaginable, is not inconceivable. The medieval antagonist Fredegisus was one of the
earliest philosophers to claim that, in denying that the term
"nothing" denotes something, the creationist commits himself
to maintaining that nothing is something.[4] If Fredegisus' remark were to hold, the doctrine of creation would be more
aptly described as an instance of secondary causality, inasmuch as there was always some "stuff" on which an agent exercised his creative action. I suspect that Fredegisus and his
modern allies would argue that the expression "nothing seems
to me to be nothing" logically entails that "nothing seems to be
something," on the presupposition that that which seems to
be cannot at the same time seem not to be. But, the creationist
wants to avoid such a muddle, and yet meaningfully claim that
the term "nothing" is significant, without committing himself
to the ontological claim that nothing is something. The creationist wants to maintain, then, that "nothing" is not a positive, concrete thing, nor is it the name of anything; rather, it
is a term which denotes "non-something." If there is to be a
possible solution to such metaphysical turmoil, then I would
suggest that an Anselmian distinction (cf. *De Casu diaboli,*
part 2) seems most instructive.[5] Anselm recognized that the
term "nothing" served a dual significative function, so that it
might be said that Fredegisus is partly correct and the creationist is partly correct. Consider the difference between the
following two senses of "nothing":

(1) Nothing$_1$, interpreted as a verbal utterance (*secundum formam
    loquendi*), which appears to signify not-something.
(2) Nothing$_2$, interpreted constitutively (*secundum rem*), which is
    the correct logical expression of the facts from the point of view
    of how things are, expressing the nought of complete annihilation.

This distinction may be further illustrated by the following
example. Consider the sentence often uttered by students:

"nothing went on in class today." Interpreting this sentence by Anselmian analysis, we might say, paralleling senses (1) and (2) above:

(1.1) "Nothing itself went on in class today," an interpretation which claims that not-something went on in class today, which seems blatantly false. For, assuming it to be the case that the professor lectured throughout the class period, so that something did go on, Fredegisus' criticism would here seem applicable. It further seems to me that Carnap would here also have grounds for his contention that if the metaphysician is to continue masquerading "nothing" as a noun-substantive, then it must designate some type of positive entity, however negatively qualified it might be. If so, then Carnap's suggestion that nothing means "not anything of the sort" is here pertinent, in that to the question "what happened in class today?" the answer "nothing" should be translated to read "not anything of importance happened." Nothing₁ might then be better translated as "nullity," meaning that what occurred was both insignificant and inconsequential.

(2.1) "Not (something went on in class today)," which could be construed as meaning "there was in fact no class today." Aristotle said ". . . to say of what is not that it is not, is true" (cf. *Metaphysics, IV, 7*), so that the sentence "Not (something went on in class today)" is true if and only if there was in fact no class today. Such an analysis, it seems to me, is to give whatever sense can be credited to Heidegger's claim that negation derives its logical force from the Not. Nothing₂ then designates the total absence of any determination or particularity (e.g., the utter nothingness of not-being).

Accordingly, the creationist might concede a fundamental equivocation in the use of the term "nothing," so that in the sense of nothing₁ it lends itself to the skeptic's criticism, in that some creationists have falsely assumed that a grammatical subject must necessarily be the name of some positive entity (e.g., the case is similar to St. Thomas' problem with the term "blindness" which grammatically seems to function as designating a positive feature of something, when in fact it denoted a privation). But the creationist need not concede nothing₂ to the skeptic, inasmuch as this constitutive sense eliminates any such abortive signification, as nothing₁ suggests. That is, the creationist can maintain that the use of nothing₁ in the expression "God made the world out of nothing," as used by some Scholastics, refers to a particular negative feature of experience, what Thomists such as Karl Rahner and Cornelio Fabro, in their phenomenological acquaintance with it, speak of as "experiential blanks," "voids," "absences," etc. Such a use of nothing₁ lends itself to the conceptualization or reification of the affective content in an emotional experience (Tillich calls this "the shock of non-being"), so that nothingness becomes recognized as a distinctive ontological entity. Although most Scholastics use the term "nothing" in the sense of nothing₁, because of their careless use of language, the medieval philosopher Fredegisus made the bolder assertion that, just as it was impossible for God to create a round square (Aquinas also held this view), so too it was impossible for God to create something out of nothing₂, though not out of nothing₁. Fredegisus views God much like Plato's Demiurge, as merely an arranger of pre-existing material. However, the creationist in his use of nothing₂ in the same expression is plainly not referring to some sort of tenuous material, some positive entity out of which the world was made, in the sense of "nothing is but what is not"; rather his use is akin to the use of nothing₂ in the expression "God was made out of nothing₂"—meaning that there was nothing He was made out of because He was not made at all. Putting this in terms of quantification theory, we might then speak of nothing₂ as

$$(x) \, [\, (x \text{ is nothing}_2) \equiv (x = x) \cdot - (x = x) \,].$$

A proper clarification of the term "nothing" in showing its fundamental equivocation allows us, then, to remove some perplexities of the expression "God brought it about *ex nihilo* that there is a world." Geach and Anscombe[6] would have us believe that the expression "something coming from nothing" need prove no more meddlesome than such empirical analogues as "Beethoven brought it about that ($\exists y$) (y is the Fifth Symphony)" or "The batsman brought it about that ($\exists z$) (z is a hit)." Just as it makes no sense to speak of the production of a "hit" or a "musical score" apart from batsmen and musicians, so too they would argue that it makes no sense to speak of *creatio ex nihilo* apart from a creator.

But are such examples really unqualified acts of creation,

as Geach and Anscombe would have us believe? Borrowing some terminology from Bishop Butler, we might make a distinction between (a) acts of creation in the loose and popular sense (LP) and (b) acts of creation in the strict and philosophical sense (SP).

> (a) X is a *qualified act of creation* in the LP sense provided: (i) there is an A such that A is an agent, and A is the efficient cause of x, and (ii) x results from either mere alteration or substantial change as a result of A's causal efficacy.
>
> (b) Y is an *unqualified act of creation* in the SP sense provided: (i)there is an A such that A is an agent, and A is the efficient cause of y, and (ii) A brings y into existence *ex nihilo* and/or (iii) A sustains y in existence.

It seems clear that the Geach and Anscombe variety of examples fails to capture the spirit of (b), although it fits the description of (a), which I have previously termed instances of "secondary causality." Musical composers in exercising their artistic talent work with such pre-existing "raw materials" as musical instrumentation, knowledge of cadence, etc., and their compositions endure *in toto,* although the composer may be long since deceased. Thus, the Beethoven case fails to satisfy either conditions (ii) or (iii) of (b).[7] But the same applies for "hits" as products of the batsman's creative activity; surely it would be difficult to make or bring about a hit without a bat and ball, so that criterion (ii) of (b) fails to be satisfied, although—to move from cricket to baseball—there is a sense in which Babe Ruth's actual home runs ceased upon withdrawal of his causal activity, so that criterion (iii) may be satisfied.

But what account can be given for unqualified creative acts in the strict and philosophical sense, as in (b)? Perhaps not a great deal, inasmuch as (b) being a description of "primary causality" applies *sui generis*—strictly speaking, to God. But suppose that there is a legitimacy to the program of Husserl's *epoché,* the phenomenological "bracketing" of existence-claims. Now, suppose further that the subject initiating such a procedure has a thought of an intentional object (e.g., the ideal woman); could he not be said to have created such an object in an unqualified manner? Such a thought of the ideal woman would by the doctrine of "intentional inexistence" be to create an ideal woman with a mode of being which falls short of actuality, yet is more than mere nothingness in its distinctive state of "immanent objectivity." The creation of the thought of such an ideal woman would then be said to bring an object into existence *ex nihilo*, inasmuch as the phenomenological *epoché* had been operative, and such an object would continue to exist as long as the subject thought of it, so that criteria (i), (ii), and (iii) of (*b*) are plainly satisfied. Borrowing some terminology from Bishop Berkeley we might say that the thought of the ideal woman has an "ectypal existence" in the human agent's mind, and an "archetypal existence" in God's mind. I assume that there would be no strong objection should an empiricist, like Hume, argue that we have no idea of x unless we have a sensation which constitutes the idea of x, for the *epoché* has ruled out any antecedent sensations, and clearly I can have an idea of the ideal woman, but yet no corresponding sensation of her.[8]

Some philosophers (e.g., H. J. McCloskey) claim that "A caused it to be that $(\exists x)$ (x is an assassination)" also qualifies as an unqualified act of creation. For "assassination" we might equally well substitute such terms as "war," "depression," etc. Consider the sentence "L. H. O. brought into being the event described as the death of J. F. K." Clearly, we can agree that this is a unique, non-recurring causal action, so that there is a sense in which, much like the batsman example, this event ceased to occur at t_n on November 22, 1963, in Dallas; so that condition (iii) of (*b*) may be satisfied. But surely, sense (ii) of (*b*) fails to be satisfied. This is so, because such necessary conditions for Oswald's action as the use of a rifle, suitable location in the Texas Book Depository Building, the direction of the motorcade, etc., along with such negative necessary factors as there being no hindrance to his firing the shots, no bullet-proof cover atop the limousine, no atmospheric obstacles, etc., all contributed to the complex event of "J. F. K.'s being assassinated in Dallas." Thus condition (ii) of (*b*) is clearly unsatisfied.

III

Another troublesome objection to the formulation of the creation thesis is the claim raised by certain linguistic purists that to talk of the "creation of the universe" is to commit a category mistake, inasmuch as the "universe" is not, as Kant put it, "an intelligible object in itself."

Three remarks might be made in the creationist's behalf here.

(A) The creationist might avoid such an objection by formulating the creation thesis in terms of ontological dependence, so that instead of speaking of the universe as a whole, he argues that for any x, if x were not created by God and/or sustained in existence by God, then x would not exist. That is, the creationist need not involve himself with the controversial issue of supposing that the world as a whole is an intelligible thing. Rather, in speaking of the world as contingent, he might be employing the term "world" distributively, meaning that of each of the things in the world it might be said that it is possible that it might not have existed, and that a complete causal explanation of this dependency leads us to affirmation of a God by the principle of sufficient reason.

(B) Secondly, certain philosophers (e.g., Russell, Ryle) claim that the creationist commits the fallacy of composition, in concluding falsely that a class term has a certain property because every member-term of that class has such a property. To this objection, the creationist might well reply that to talk of the universe as a class and of its constituents as members of that class is to violate the distinction between members and classes; yet it seems that there are cases in which such a distributive use does not violate a collective use of a term. Economists speak quite legitimately of individual incomes which comprise the national income; scientists speak of the class of all physical objects when considering their applicability to laws of gravitational force, and there seems to be a clear sense in which the universe in connoting all that there is, even in its collective sense, can entail cosmologically extended physical concepts, as in the statement "the universe is tending to states of increasing entropy." But, the critic might well ask, can philosophers speak in similar fashion as the economists and scientists do? It seems to me that the creationist *qua* philosopher can both recognize the logical force of the fallacy of composition whereby, from inferences of the form that all the parts of X (y, z, w, etc.) have the property G, it still does not follow that X itself has the property G, and yet also claim that there are cases in which such an inference is legitimate in virtue of the meanings of the arguments substituted for X and G. Consider: all the pickets in the fence are green, and suppose that there are only a limited number of fences in the world, from which we could conclude that all the fences themselves are green. However, the fallacy remains cogent should one argue that each and every picket in the fence weighs four pounds, to the obviously false conclusion that the entire fence weighs four pounds.[9]

(c) Thirdly, it seems, then, that it is not so *prima facie* obvious that the universe is not an intelligible object, in that it designates all that there is or may be, except God. But it does seem clear that the creationist must weaken his claim about the universe, as this term is understood in the ordinary sense. For example, scientists describe the universe on the basis of certain cosmological models, so that quite apart from the inductivistic truism that the universe is not observable in its entirety, one can nonetheless attempt an account of the universe by submitting a weaker claim now formulated in terms of a cosmological model to the verification process of the observational data.

Thus, the creationist can agree with his critics that the (observed) universe is not itself an intelligible whole, but that which is defined by the features of his cosmological model is an intelligible object, so that one can predicate the universe as a whole in this latter sense. However, the creationist must concede that in the case of his cosmological model, one cannot find any empirical warrant of its legitimacy which may be obtained by directly examining the object of which it may be thought to articulate the structure. That is, one cannot verify cosmological models as one can verify our ordinary scale models, with actual things already in existence. For example, I can have a scale model of the Rockefeller Library, and it is possible for me to examine independently the original edifice in order to note points of similarity between it and the scale model, but the creationist cannot so directly inspect the universe. The creationist is thus left with his only cognitive access to the universe via his cosmological model, and that, I submit, is an intelligible object.

IV

In causation, there is usually alleged to occur some relationship between the cause and the effect. Yet Aquinas wants to maintain that, whereas every creature has a relation to God, the converse does not obtain. This fosters the problem of "divine otherness," which seems to prohibit any intelligible account of the relationship between God and the world. The creationist maintains that if the converse were the case—if it were the case that God was related to creatures—then such a relation in God would either be identical with the divine substance, or it would be an accidental modification of God. But this cannot be the case for, if God were necessarily related to creatures, He would depend on them for His existence, and if God is so defined as absolutely simple, then He cannot receive or possess accidents.

Some Scholastics get into certain muddles by maintaining that no cause can be totally unlike the effect which it produces, for if *per impossibile* it were, the activity of the cause would be totally unrelated to its effect (*omne agens agit sibi simile*). But this principle seems absurd. C may be said to be a partial cause of E in conjunction with a set of events FGH, such that E results, and yet C is not the same object in kind as E. For example, the sun in combination with soil, rain, and other atmospheric conditions causes the grass to be green, but clearly these antecedent conjunctive states of affairs are not themselves green. I suspect that Aquinas may have wished to avoid such Scholastic blunders when he spoke of the non-necessity of the perfection of the effect to be found in its cause according to the same formality.

It is instructive, in order to understand the issue of "divine transcendence," to compare the relationship of God to creatures with the model of the relationship between the knower and the object known. There is a "real relation" between my concrete state of knowing and the object (sense data, impression, representation, etc.) which is grasped in sense perception, and which causes me to judge that "I am appeared to rosily"; but the rose itself is not so really related to my knowledge claim, since my awareness of the rose does not cause the rose itself to exist (*esse non est percipi*). So too, the creature is really related to the creator, in the sense that he is dependent upon him for his continuation in existence, much as the knower is dependent on certain sense impressions for his knowledge of the external world, but the creator is only by a "relation of reason" so related to the creature, in that just as there would be roses even if there were not perceivers, so too there would be a creator even if there were not any creatures. Put schematically:

(1) Creator ——— relation of reason ——→ creature
(2) Creator ←——— real relation ————————— creature[10]

Again, there seems to be a sense in which there is a "real relationship" between a son and a son inasmuch as they both share the common property of brotherhood [what John of St. Thomas in *Cursus philosophicus* calls a "transcendental relationship" $(\exists x)(\exists y)(Bxy \cdot Byx)$]; but there is only a "relation of reason" between a son and another son in that it might be the case that $(\exists x)(\exists y) \sim (Bxy \cdot Byx)$, yet it would be true to say that they are related by the relationship of sonhood.

Accordingly, I am suggesting that the relation of God to His creatures must be understood as asymmetrical; if x has a relationship to y, then y cannot have that same relationship to x (e.g., if x is older than y, then clearly y is not older than x, although they are related by certain units of time). But all asymmetrical relations share the further property of being ir-reflexive—that is, a relation which no individual has to itself, so that if x is older than y, it plainly makes no sense to suggest that x is older than x himself. Similarly, it may be the case that it makes no sense to speak of God as the creator of Him-self, for, as Aquinas noted, He is *ipsum esse subsistens*.[11]

v

Another objection confronting the creationist is how to handle the claim that, if God is spoken of as the sufficient causal condition for the existence of creatures, it then seems to follow quite unobjectionably that God's causal activity and the non-existence of creatures are an impossibility. But, while this may be acceptable for the creationist, it further follows that these creatures in turn are the necessary condition for God's causal activity, inasmuch as their non-existence and God's causal activity is a distinct impossibility. The puzzle is, then, as follows: (i) if God is described as the sufficient causal condition for the existence of creatures, then it follows (logically) that these creatures are the necessary causal conditions for God's causal activity, and (ii) conversely, if God is described as the necessary causal condition for the existence of creatures, then these creatures in turn are the sufficient causal condition for God's causal activity. On either account, the importance of the doctrine of ontological dependence seems to be greatly jeopardized.

However, the creationist might reply that this modern version of the Spinozistic fallacy "confuses causal conditionals with logical conditionals." The objection is best supported by a logical conditional; for example, if an object's being a triangle is sufficient for its having three sides, it follows that its having three sides is necessary for its being a triangle. But causal conditionals are not logical ones. The Spinozistic objection in claiming that, if any state of affairs is sufficient for the occurrence of some other state of affairs, in a causal sense, then the latter necessitates the former, even though the two may be logically disconnected plainly seems false. For instance, if Jones is beheaded, it follows by a law of nature that Jones will die within n-moments of time, so that if Jones's being beheaded is a sufficient causal condition of his dying within n-moments of time, then his dying within n-moments of time is in turn a necessary causal condition for his being beheaded. But there is something odd about such a conclusion. Surely, Jones's dying within n-moments of time is not a necessary condition for his being beheaded, for Jones may have died of quite natural causes as well, such as old age, cancer, etc.

Philosophers who so abrogate the distinction between causal and logical implication thus confuse the following two conditionals.

> (a) "If God is the creator of the universe, then creatures are onto-
> logically dependent upon Him," which asserts a causal connec-
> tion, the factual truth of the consequent being dependent on the
> antecedent.

(*b*) "If God is the creator of the universe, then creatures are ontologically dependent upon Him," which asserts a truth-functional
compound, in which there need be no causal relation of content
between antecedent and consequent.

Clearly (*a*) and (*b*) are connected if in both cases the antecedent is true and the consequent is true, in which case the
whole conditional is true; or in case the antecedent is true and
the consequent false, in which case the whole conditional is
false. But all similarity ends here. Suppose that it is granted
that God is not the creator of the universe; it would then seem
to follow that conditional (*a*) is pointless, but (*b*) would, far
from being pointless, be truth-functionally valid. Thus, the
Spinozistic objection which relies on the highly suspect paradox
of material implication seems confused, inasmuch as it equivo-
cates between the ordinary causal sense of "if—then" and the
technical sense of "follows logically from," whereby a true sentence follows logically from any sentence, and any sentence
follows logically from a false sentence. This use of logical implication to support statements of causal efficacy is no philo-
sophic-strawman case, as the following remarks of Richard
Taylor suggest:

> The statement that X is necessary for E, is logically equivalent to
> saying that E is sufficient for X, and similarly the statement that X
> is sufficient for E is logically equivalent to saying that E is necessary
> for X.[12]

However, in my claim that God as efficient cause makes a certain effect come-to-be, or remain-in-being, I wished to deny any
necessitation in a reverse direction, so that it makes no sense to
speak of creatures as necessary causal conditions for God's
causal efficacy. To cite an empirical analogue: a teacher might
be spoken of as the sufficient causal condition for the student's
failing a course, but it seems odd to suggest that the student is
the necessary causal condition of the teacher's causal efficacy
in making him fail, for the teacher might have accidentally
marked an F on a grade report where he intended an extra
scratch mark to show an E. Accordingly, the creationist con-
curs with Reid's remark that a correct analysis of God's causal

activity shows him to have the power or efficacy to produce certain effects, which property of power rather than strict logical implication allows us to distinguish properly a cause from an effect, and to avoid such muddles as the Spinozistic objection.

Putting aside the Spinozistic confusion between logical and causal conditionals, the creationist might well reply to the more sophisticated critique of Taylor's, that what the skeptic says is true in the loose and popular sense of creative activity—inasmuch as when we speak of agent A acting as efficient cause of event E, we do not ordinarily mean to imply that A did not have certain "materials" (operating as necessary and/or sufficient conditions) on which to exercise his causal efficacy. We merely wish to emphasize that ultimately the agent's action depended on his own causal power, not so much on previously existing antecedent conditions. But, in the strict and philosophical sense of creative activity, such a sophisticated argument fails, for before God's creative activity, nothing$_2$ was, so that it makes no sense to speak of necessary and/or sufficient conditions' determining God's action, if such conditions simply do not exist. This is not to say that God's action was uncaused, so that it is false that "every event has a cause"; it is merely to say that God's creative activity itself was caused by His own divine agency. That is, in God's creating *ex nihilo*, there are no sufficient or necessary causal conditions for His not undertaking to make a certain event come-to-be, so that if a certain event does come-to-be, then God may be said to have brought about such an event.

Thus, in the loose and popular sense, no agent, acting as efficient cause, can perform any given creative action if there is lacking some condition or state of affairs necessary for the occurrence of that action. It is a necessary condition for Jones's acting as efficient cause in any particular type of activity that there be present a requisite amount of oxygen in the atmosphere. So too, it makes no sense to speak of an agent bringing himself around to swimming a mile without his ever having been immersed in water. But from such a loose and popular sense of creative activity, it does not follow that God acting as efficient cause in a strict and philosophical sense cannot perform any given action *ex nihilo*, so that it makes no sense to speak of necessary and/or sufficient conditions as obtaining before the occurrence of His causal efficacy, because in fact nothing$_2$ was.[13]

NOTES

1. This use of "and/or" needs to be clarified. First of all, God's creative activity is not primarily concerned with the initial conjunct of the conjunctive state of affairs "bringing an entity into existence *ex nihilo* and sustaining that entity in existence." Accordingly, the creationist can grant the Darwinist his evolutionary theory, so that God is not constantly engaged in performing creative acts *ex nihilo,* as the Malebranchian occasionalist would claim, although He is engaged in sustaining already existing creatures in existence.

Secondly, if God's creative activity is analyzed as a disjunction—"either God creates an entity *ex nihilo* or sustains that entity in existence"—then such a disjunction should be interpreted again in what might be termed an "inclusive sense of 'or'," inasmuch as emphasis is to be placed on God's sustaining power, though by no means does the creationist wish to affirm an "exclusive 'or'," which would negate God's creating *ex nihilo,* at the expense of rescuing His conserving power.

St. Thomas stressed the sustaining power of God, when he remarked that "A thing which exists always is not exempted from needing another in order to exist" (III *De Potentia,* 13 ad 1; my translation). The Angel Gabriel cannot not exist in the sense that it is neither generable nor corruptible, but it can non-exist in the sense that it is ontologically dependent on God.

2. "'Matter,' in the best and controlling sense of the term, is to be identified with the substratum which is receptive of coming-to-be and passing-away" (Aristotle, *De Gen. et Cor.* I, 4, 319b). I realize that there may be inherent difficulties in Aquinas' claim that this basic stuff cannot exist by itself apart from any formal properties, since it is only logically distinguishable from form, yet also maintain that it is a real element (not a logical construct) in the entity, and the ultimate basis of change.

But two points seem clear: (i) even if the distinction between accidental and substantial change is denied, and the latter reduced to the former, it still would not follow that our now enlarged category of accidental change is not an instance of secondary causality; (ii) also, those who so deny the distinction run into many difficulties over proper handling of the case of the blastula-fetus—Mr. Smith type. The skeptic here reminds one of the misguided alumnus who upon witnessing a "fullback-draw play over left-guard" prove unsuccessful, and on the very next play produce a touchdown, remarks: "That's what I like about State's quarterback: he's always mixing up his plays." Somehow, one feels, he fails to see the continuity!

3. This formulation in terms of quantification theory allows us to speak of God's causing an atom to be not *in tempore* but *cum tempore.* That is, the creationist can agree with St. Augustine that time be recognized as the mode under which created beings exist, rather than, as Bergson suggests, as some pre-existent flux in which they are immersed. St. Thomas said: "God brought into being both the creature and time together" (*Summa contra Gentiles* II, 35).

4. ". . . nothing is a word that has signification. But every signification has reference to that which it signifies. From this it is proved that something cannot be non-existent. Likewise every signification is signification of what is. Nothing,

however, signifies something. Nothing, therefore, is the signification of what is, that is, something existing" ("*Epistola de Nihilo et Tenebris*," *Medieval Philosophy*, edd. J. F. Wippel and A. B. Wolter [New York: Free Press, 1969], pp. 133–134).

5. "For this one assertion, namely, that nothing existed before the Supreme Being, carries two meanings. For, one sense of this statement is that, before the Supreme Being, there was a time when nothing was. But another understanding of the same statement is that, before the Supreme Being, not anything existed. Just as supposing I should say 'Nothing has taught me to fly,' I could explain this assertion either in this way, that nothing, as an entity in itself, which signifies *not anything* has taught me actually to fly—which would be false; or in this way, that not anything has taught me to fly, which would be true" (St. Anselm, *Monologion*, Chap. XIX).

6. Geach (P. T. Geach, G. E. M. Anscombe, *Three Philosophers* [Oxford: Blackwell, 1963], p. 110) contrasts the following two cases of causal efficacy: (3) "the minstrel made music," and (4) "the blacksmith made a shoe." Geach maintains that (3) is an unqualified act of creation and that (4) is a qualified act of creation. To be sure, Geach is correct in realizing that (4) fails to approximate an unqualified act of creation. But the question remains, does (3) so approximate an unqualified act of creation? Granted, the minstrel did not make the music out of pre-existing sounds, and also that the music ceases upon the advent of his non-performance; nonetheless, surely the minstrel could not have created the particular musical score in question apart from his harp, etc. Accordingly, Geach's model of (3) fails to capture condition (ii) of (*b*).

7. If it were the case that Beethoven had composed the Fifth Symphony only within his own mind, so that it was never heard or made public in content, then sense (*b*) might be satisfied. R. G. Collingwood said: "A work of art may be completely created when it has been created as a thing whose only place is in the artist's mind" (cf. Vincent Tomas [ed.], *Creativity in the Arts*, p. 9).

8. In my example of (1) "A causes it to be the case that ($\exists$x) (x is the thought of the ideal woman)," I did not wish this sense to be confused with instances of "secondary causality," such as: (2) ($\exists$y) (y is an hallucinatory drug, and y causes A to have a thought of the ideal woman); or (3) ($\exists$w) ($\exists$z) (w = Sophia Loren, and z = Raquel Welch, and w and z cause A to have a thought of the ideal woman).

9. Incidentally, I am well aware that a fallacious argument may yield a true conclusion (i.e., If $\emptyset$ is other than a three-sided figure, then $\emptyset$ is not a triangle; $\emptyset$ is not a triangle; therefore, $\emptyset$ is other than a three-sided figure), as well as cognizant that logicians speak of fallacious arguments *qua* fallacious whenever the reasoning process in question fails to demonstrate the truth of the conclusion given the truth of the premises. My point is simply that the picket-fence example admits of a non-enthymemic expansion into the following sound argument: (1) If all the parts of fences (i.e., pickets) are green, the fences are green; (2) The pickets are green; (3) ∴ The fences are green.

Analogously, the creationist can argue: (1.1) If all the entities (i.e., parts) in the universe are contingent, the universe (i.e., whole) is contingent; (2.1) The entities in the universe are contingent; (3.1) ∴ The universe is contingent.

I realize that (2.1) is somewhat dubious, given the possibility of the truth of the law of conservation of mass-energy. However, to regard the above arguments as fallacious is surely to call fallacious a valid pattern of argumentation. But this is precisely what C. B. Martin, R. Hepburn, etc., disallow in claiming, against the creationist, that there can be a whole which was not caused to exist even though each of its parts was caused to exist. And, this skeptical rejoinder is indeed fallacious!

10. ". . . it is manifest that creatures are really related to God Himself; whereas in God there is no real relation to creatures, but a relation only in idea . . ." (*Sum. Theol.* I, 13, 7, c).

11. It seems to me that Geach ("God's Relation to the World," *Sophia*, 8 [July 1969], 1–9) has provided the creationist with the means to explain meaningfully his use of "real relation" and "relation of reason." Consider the relational proposition "A envies B." Here we have a state of envy as an actual condition of A, but not of B, inasmuch as the state of being envied is not the actual condition of B. Accordingly, A is "really related" to B by A's envy, and B is only "related by reason" to A.

Geach proceeds to distinguish between: (3) "real changes," namely, processes which actually occur in a given individual, and (4) "Cambridge changes," which are any changes whatsoever which are a matter of contradictory attributes holding good of individuals at different times.

Now, in light of the above distinction, there is no "real change" in B in B's becoming an object of envy to A, but there is nonetheless a "Cambridge change." Analogously, God does not undergo any "real change," but He does undergo "Cambridge changes." For instance, the creationist while asleep can be said not to think of God, so that God is not thought of by the creationist, although in most situations God is thought of by the creationist. Accordingly, the distinction drawn in (3) and (4) allows us to speak of a "changeless" God (albeit not in the trivial Cantabrigian manner) who is not just one more individual in the aggregate of changeable beings which comprise the world.

12. "Causation," *The Monist*, 47 (1963), p. 300. Taylor's view seems absurd when one considers cases of causes' necessitating their effects in a manner in which the converse is never the case (e.g., rain dampens the highway, such that it seems odd to suggest that the road in becoming wet makes the rain fall upon it). The purport of Taylor's remark is to obliterate any distinction between cause and effect.

13. "The word 'nothing' here does not refer to some kind of material, or even to some kind of cause of what exists. . . . Neither does it mean anything co-essential with God, or anything He might have made use of as a kind of material from which to fabricate the world. The name then indicates the total deprivation of anything essential . . ." (Joannes Scotus [Erigena], *De Divisione naturae*, IV, 1).

16

The Miraculous

R. F. HOLLAND

University of Leeds

MOST PEOPLE THINK OF A MIRACLE as a violation of natural
law; and a good many of those who regard the miraculous in
this way incline to the idea that miracles are impossible and
that "science" tells us this (the more sophisticated might say
that what tells us this is an unconfused *conception* of science).
I shall argue that the conception of the miraculous as a violation of natural law is an inadequate conception because it is unduly restrictive, though there is also a sense in which it is not
restrictive enough. To qualify for being accounted a miracle,
an occurrence does not have to be characterizable as a violation of natural law. However, though I do not take the conception of miracles as violations of natural law to be an adequate conception of the miraculous, I shall maintain that occurrences are conceivable in respect to which it could be said
that some law or laws of nature had been violated—or it could
be said equally that there was a contradiction in our experience: and if the surrounding circumstances were appropriate it

Reprinted from *American Philosophical Quarterly*, 2 (1965), 43–51, with the
permission of the author and the publishers. Revised by the author.

would be possible for such occurrences to have a kind of human significance and hence intelligible for them to be hailed as miracles. I see no philosophical reason against this.

But consider first the following example. A child riding his toy motor-car strays on to an unguarded railway crossing near his house and a wheel of his car gets stuck down the side of one of the rails. An express train is due to pass with the signals in its favor and a curve in the track makes it impossible for the driver to stop his train in time to avoid any obstruction he might encounter on the crossing. The mother coming out of the house to look for her child sees him on the crossing and hears the train approaching. She runs forward shouting and waving. The little boy remains seated in his car, looking downward, engrossed in the task of pedaling it free. The brakes of the train are applied and it comes to rest a few feet from the child. The mother thanks God for the miracle; which she never ceases to think of as such, although, as she in due course learns, there was nothing supernatural about the manner in which the brakes of the train came to be applied. The driver had fainted, for a reason which had nothing to do with the presence of the child on the line, and the brakes were applied automatically as his hand ceased to exert pressure on the control lever. He fainted on this particular afternoon because his blood pressure had risen after an exceptionally heavy lunch during which he had quarrelled with a colleague, and the change in blood pressure caused a clot of blood to be dislodged and circulate. He fainted at the time when he did on the afternoon in question because this was the time at which the coagulation in his blood stream reached the brain.

Thus the stopping of the train and the fact that it stopped when it did have a natural explanation. I do not say a *scientific* explanation, for it does not seem to me that the explanation here as a whole is of this kind (in order for something to be unsusceptible of scientific explanation it does not have to be anything so queer and grandiose as a miracle). The form of explanation in the present case, I would say, is *historical*; and the considerations which enter into it are various. They include medical factors, for instance, and had these constituted the whole extent of the matter the explanation could have been called scientific. But as it is, the medical considerations, though obviously important, are only one aspect of a complex story, alongside other considerations of a practical and social kind; and in addition there is a reference to mechanical considerations. All of these enter into the explanation of, or story behind, the stopping of the train. And just as there is an explanatory story behind the train's stopping when and where it did, so there is an explanatory story behind the presence of the child on the line at the time when, and in the place where, he was. But these two explanations or histories are independent of each other. They are about as disconnected as the history of the steam loom is from the history of the Ming dynasty. The spacio-temporal coincidence, I mean the fact that the child was on the line at the time when the train approached and the train stopped a few feet short of the place where he was, is exactly what I have just called it, a coincidence—something which a chronicle of events can merely record, like the fact that the Ming dynasty was in power at the same time as the house of Lancaster.

But unlike the coincidence between the rise of the Ming dynasty and the arrival of the dynasty of Lancaster, the coincidence of the child's presence on the line with the arrival and then the stopping of the train is impressive, significant; not because it is very unusual for trains to be halted in the way this one was, but because the life of a child was imperiled and then, against expectation, preserved. The significance of some coincidences as opposed to others arises from their relation to human needs and hopes and fears, their effects for good or ill upon our lives. So we speak of our luck (fortune, fate, etc.). And the kind of thing which, outside religion, we call luck is in religious parlance the grace of God or a miracle of God. But while the reference here is the same, the meaning is different. The meaning is different in that whatever happens by God's grace or by a miracle is something for which God is thanked or thankable, something which has been or could have been prayed for, something which can be regarded with awe and be taken as a sign or made the subject of a vow (e.g., to go on a pilgrimage), all of which can only take place against the background of a religious tradition. Whereas what happens by a stroke of luck is something in regard to which one just seizes one's opportunity or feels glad about or feels relieved about. something for which one may thank one's lucky stars. To say that one thanks one's lucky stars is simply to express one's relief or to emphasize the intensity of the relief: if it signifies anything more than this it signifies a superstition (*cf.* touching wood).

But although a coincidence can be taken religiously as a sign and called a miracle and made the subject of a vow, it cannot without confusion be taken as a sign of divine interference with the natural order. If someone protests that it is no part of the natural order that an express train should stop for a child on the line whom the driver cannot see, then in *protesting* this he misses the point. What he says has been agreed to be perfectly true in the sense that there is no natural order relating the train's motion to the child which could be either preserved or interfered with. The concept of the miraculous which we have so far been considering is distinct therefore from the concept exemplified in the Biblical stories of the turning of water into wine and the feeding of five thousand people on a very few loaves and fishes. Let us call the former the contingency concept and the latter the violation concept.

To establish the contingency concept of the miraculous as a possible concept it seems to me enough to point out (1) that *pace* Spinoza, Leibniz, and others, there are genuine contingencies in the world, and (2) that certain of these contingencies can be, and are in fact, regarded religiously in the manner I have indicated. If you assent to this and still express a doubt —"But are they really miracles?"—then you must now be questioning whether people are right to react to contingencies in this way, questioning whether you ought yourself to go along with them. Why not just stick to talking of luck? When you think this you are somewhat in the position of one who watches others fall in love and as an outsider thinks it unreasonable, hyperbolical, ridiculous (surely friendship should suffice).

To turn now to the concept of the miraculous as a violation of natural law: I am aware of two arguments which, if they were correct, would show that this concept were not a possible concept. The first can be found in chapter ten of Hume's *Enquiry Concerning Human Understanding*:

Nothing is esteemed a miracle, if it ever happen in the common course of nature. It is no miracle that a man, seemingly in good health, should die on a sudden: because such a kind of death, though more unusual than any other, has yet been frequently observed to happen. But it is a miracle, that a dead man should come to life; because that has never been observed in any age or country. There must, therefore, be a uniform experience against every miraculous event, otherwise the event would not merit that appellation. And as a uniform experience amounts to a proof, there is here a direct and full *proof,* from the nature of the fact, against the existence of any miracle; nor can such a proof be destroyed, or the miracle rendered credible, but by an opposite proof, which is superior.

The plain consequence is (and it is a general maxim worthy of our attention), "That no testimony is sufficient to establish a miracle, unless the testimony be of such a kind, that its falsehood would be more miraculous, than the fact, which it endeavours to establish; and even in that case there is a mutual destruction of arguments, and the superior only gives us an assurance suitable to that degree of force, which remains, after deducting the inferior." When anyone tells me, that he saw a dead man restored to life, I immediately consider with myself, whether it be more probable, that this person should either deceive or be deceived, or that the fact, which he relates, should really have happened. I weigh the one miracle against the other; and according to the superiority, which I discover, I pronounce my decision, and always reject the greater miracle. If the falsehood of his testimony would be more miraculous, than the event which he relates; then, and not till then, can he pretend to command my belief or opinion.

Hume's concern in the chapter from which I have just quoted is ostensibly with the problem of assessing the *testimony of others* in regard to the allegedly miraculous. This is not the same problem as that which arises for the man who has to decide whether or not he himself has witnessed a miracle. Hume gives an inadequate account of the considerations which would influence one's decision to accept or reject the insistence of another person that something has happened which one finds it extremely hard to believe could have happened. The character and temperament of the witness, the kind of person he is and the kind of understanding one has of him, the closeness or distance of one's personal relationship with him are obviously important here, whereas Hume suggests that if we give credence to some witnesses rather than others the reason must be simply that we are accustomed to find in their case a conformity between testimony and reality (§ 89). Maybe the weakness of Hume's account of the nature of our trust or lack of trust in witnesses is connected with the fact that in some way he intended his treatment of the problem of witness concerning the miraculous to have a more general application—as if he were trying to cut across the distinction between the case in which we are ourselves confronted with a miracle (or something we may be inclined to call one) and the case in which other people intervene, and wanting us to consider it all as fundamentally a single problem of evidence, a problem of witness in which it would make no difference whether what were doing the witnessing were a person other than oneself, or oneself in the role of a witness to oneself, or one's senses as witnesses to oneself. This, anyway, is the view I am going to take of his intention here.

I can imagine it being contended that, while Hume has produced a strong argument against the possibility of our ever having certitude or even very good evidence that a miracle has occurred, his thesis does not amount to an argument against the possibility of miracles as such. But I think that this would be a misunderstanding. For if Hume is right, the situation is not just that we do not happen as a matter of fact to have certitude or even good evidence for the occurrence of any miracle, but rather that *nothing can count* as good evidence: the logic of testimony precludes this. And in precluding this it must, as far as I can see, preclude equally our having *poor* evidence for the occurrence of any miracle, since a contrast between good evidence and poor evidence is necessary if there is to be sense in speaking of either. Equally it must follow that there can be no such thing as (because nothing is being allowed to count as) discovering, recognizing, becoming aware, etc., that a miracle has occurred; and if there be no such thing as finding out or being aware (etc.) that a miracle has occurred, there can be no such thing as failing to find out or failing to be aware that a miracle has occurred either; no such thing as a discovered or an undiscovered miracle . . . *en fin*, no such thing as a miracle. So Hume's argument is, after all, an argument against the very possibility of miracles. I do not think that his argument is cogent either on the interpretation I have just put upon it or on the interpretation according to which it would be an argument merely against the possibility of our having good evidence for a miracle. But before giving my reason I would like first to mention the only other line of argument which I can at present envisage against the conception of the miraculous as a violation of natural law.

Consider the proposition that a criminal is a violator of the laws of the state. With this proposition in mind you will start to wonder, when someone says that a miracle is a violation of the laws of nature, if he is not confusing a law of nature with a judicial law as laid down by some legal authority. A judicial law is obviously something which can be violated. The laws of the state prescribe and their prescriptions can be flouted. But are the laws of nature in any sense prescriptions? Maybe they are, in the sense that they prescribe to us what we are to expect; but since *we* formulated the laws, this is really a matter of our offering prescriptions or recipes to ourselves. And we can certainly fail to act on these prescriptions. But the occurrences which the laws are about are not prescribed to: they are simply *de*scribed. And if anything should happen of which we are inclined to say that it goes counter to a law of nature, what this must mean is that the description we have framed has been, not flouted or violated, but falsified. We have encountered something which the description does not fit, and we must therefore withdraw or modify our description. The law was wrong; we framed it wrongly: or rather what we framed has turned out not to have been a law. The relation between an occurrence and a law of nature is different, then, from a man's relation to a law of the state, for when the latter is deviated from, we do not, save in exceptional circumstances, say that the law is wrong but rather that the man is wrong—he is a criminal. To suggest that an occurrence which has falsified a law of nature is *wrong* would be an absurdity: and it would be just as absurd to suggest that the law has been violated. Nothing can be conceived to be a violation of natural law, and if that is how the miraculous is conceived, there can be no such thing as the miraculous. Laws of nature can be formulated or reformulated to cope with any eventuality, and would-be miracles are transformed automatically into natural occurrences the moment science gets on the track of them.

But there is an objection to this line of argument. If we say that a law of nature is a description, what exactly are we taking it to be a description of? A description of what has happened up to now or is actually happening now? Suppose that we have a law to the effect that all unsupported bodies fall. From this I can deduce that if the pen now in my hand were unsupported it *would* fall and that when in a moment I withdraw from it the support it now has it *will* fall. But if the law were simply a description of what has happened up to now or is happening now and no more, these deductions would be impossible. So it looks as if the law must somehow describe the future as well as the past and present. "A description of the future." But what on earth is that? For, until the future ceases to be the future and becomes actual, there are no events for the description to describe—over and above those which either have already taken place or are at this moment taking place.

It seems that if we are to continue to maintain that a natural law is nothing but a description, then we must say that the description covers not only the actual but also the possible and is every bit as much a description of the one as it is of the other. And this only amounts to a pleonastic way of saying that the law tells us, defines for us, what is and is not *possible* in regard to the behavior of unsupported bodies. At this point we might just as well drop the talk about describing altogether and admit that the law does not just describe—it stipulates: stipulates that it is impossible for an unsupported body to do anything other than fall. Laws of nature and legal laws, though they may not resemble each other in other respects, are at least alike in this: that they both stipulate something. Moreover the stipulations which we call laws of nature are in many cases so solidly founded and knitted together with other stipulations, other laws, that they come to be something in the nature of a framework through which we look at the world and which to a considerable degree dictates our ways of describing phenomena.

Notice, however, that insofar as we resist in this way the second of the two arguments for the impossibility of the violation concept of the miraculous, and insofar as we object to the suggestion that it is possible for our laws of nature to be dropped or reformulated in a sort of *ad hoc* manner to accommodate any would-be miracle, we seem to be making the first argument—the Humean argument against the miraculous—all the stronger. For, if we take a law of nature to be more than a generalized description of what has happened up to now, and if at the same time we upgrade the mere probability or belief to which Hume thought we were confined here into certainty and real knowledge, then surely it must seem that our reluctance to throw overboard a whole nexus of well-established, mutually-supporting laws and theories must be so great as to justify us in rejecting out of hand, and not being prepared to assign even a degree of probability to, any testimony to an occurrence which our system of natural law decisively rules out; and surely we shall be justified in classifying as illusory any experience which purports to be the experience of such an occurrence.

The truth is that this position is not at all justified, and we should only be landed in inconsistency if we adopted it. For if it were granted that there can be no certainty in regard to the individual case, if there can be no real knowledge that a particular event has occurred in exactly the way in which it has, how could our system of laws have been established in the first place?

On Hume's view, the empirical in general was synonymous with the probable. No law of nature could have more than a degree of probability, and neither for that matter could the occurrence of any particular event. This is what gave point to the idea of a balance of probabilities and hence to his thesis about the impossibility of ever establishing a miracle. But while in the one case, that of the general law, he was prepared (in the passage from which I quoted) to allow that the probability could have the status of a proof, in the other case he was curiously reluctant to allow this.

Now, if in the interest of good conceptual sense we upgrade the probability of natural laws into certainty, so as to be able to distinguish a well-established law from a more or less tenable hypothesis, it is equally in the interest of good conceptual sense that we should upgrade in a comparable fashion the probability attaching to particular events and states of affairs, so as to allow that some of these, as opposed to others, can be certain and really known to be what they are. Otherwise a distinction gets blurred which is at least as important as the distinction between a law and a hypothesis—namely the distinction between a hypothesis and a fact. The distinction between a hypothesis and a fact is, for instance, the distinction between my saying when I come upon an infant who is screaming and writhing and holding his ear "he's got an abscess" and my making this statement again after looking into the ear, whether by means of an instrument or without, and actually seeing, coming upon, the abscess. Or again it is the difference between the statement "it is snowing" when made by me now as I sit here and the same statement uttered as I go outside the building into the snow and get snowed on. The second statement, unlike the first, is uttered directly in the face of the circumstance which makes it true. I can be as certain in that situation that it is snowing as I can be of anything. And if there were not things of this kind of which we can be certain, we would not be able to be uncertain of anything either.

If it were remarked here that our senses are capable of deceiving us, I should reply that it does not follow from this that there are not occasions when we know perfectly well that we are not being deceived. And this is one of them. I submit that nothing would persuade you—or if it would it should not—that you are not at this moment in the familiar surroundings of your university and that in what you see as you look around this room you are subject to an illusion. And if something very strange were to happen, such as one of us bursting into flame, you would soon know it for what it was; and of course you would expect the natural cause to be duly discovered (the smoldering pipe which set fire to the matches or whatever it might be).

But then suppose that you failed to discover any cause. Or suppose that something happened which was truly bizarre, like my rising slowly and steadily three feet into the air and staying there. You could *know* that this happened if it did, and probably you would laugh and presume that there must be some natural explanation: a rod behind, a disguised support beneath, a thin wire above. Or could it even be done by air pressure in some way? Or by a tremendously powerful magnet on the next floor, attracting metal in my clothing? Or if not by magnetic attraction then by magnetic repulsion? I rise in the air, then, and since it is no magician's demonstration you can and do search under me, over me, and around me. But suppose that you find nothing, nothing on me and nothing in the room or above, below, or around it. You cannot think that it is the effect of an anti-gravity device (even if there be sense in that idea) because there just is no device. And you know that, excluding phenomena like tornadoes, it is impossible for a physical body in free air to behave thus in the absence of a special device. So does it not come to this: that if I were to rise in the air now, you could be completely certain of two incompatible things: (1) that it is impossible, and (2) that it has happened?

Now, against what I have just said I envisage two objections. The first is that my rising three feet into the air in the absence of some special cause can only be held to be an impossibility by someone who is ignorant of the statistical basis of modern physics. For example, the water in a kettle comprises a vast number of atoms in motion, and anything I do to the kettle, such as tilting it or heating it, will affect the movements of these atoms. But there is no way of determining what the effect will be in the case of any single atom. It is no more within the power of physicists to predict that a particular atom will change its position in such and such a way, or even at all, than it is within the power of insurance actuaries to predict that a certain man will die next week in a road accident, or die at all. However, reliable statistical statements can be made by actuaries about the life prospects of large numbers of people taken together, and, somewhat similarly, statistical laws are framed by physicists about the behavior of atoms in large numbers. Statistical laws are laws of probability, and it gets argued that, since this is the kind of law on which the behavior of water in a heated vessel ultimately rests, there can be no *certainty* that the kettle on the hob will boil however fierce the fire, no certainty that it will boil absolutely *every* time, because there is always the probability—infinitesimally small, admittedly, but still a definite probability—that enough of the constituent atoms in their molecules will move in a way which is incompatible with its doing so. Vessels of water and rubber balls seem to be the most frequently used examples when this argument is deployed, but the suggestion has been made to me that it (or some similar argument) could be applied to the behavior of an unsupported body near the surface of the earth, in respect of which it could be maintained that there is a certain probability, albeit a very low one, in favor of the body's having its state of rest three feet above the ground.

However, it seems to me that any such argument must rest on the kind of confusion which Eddington fell into when he said, mentioning facts about atoms as the reason, that his table was not solid but consisted largely of empty space. If you add to this that your table is in a continuous vibratory motion and that the laws governing its behavior are laws of probability only, you are continuing in the same vein. To make the confusion more symmetrical you might perhaps go on to say that the movements of tables in space are only predictable even with probability when tables get together in large numbers (which accounts for the existence of warehouses). Anyway, my point is that, using words in their ordinary senses, it is about as certain and as much a matter of common understanding that my kettle, when put on a fierce fire, will boil or that I shall not next moment float three feet in the air as it is certain and a matter of common understanding that my desk is solid and will continue for some time to be so. The validity of my statement about the desk is not impugned by any assertion about the behavior of atoms whether singly or in the aggregate; neither is the validity of the corresponding statements about the kettle and my inability to float in the air impugned by any assertion about the statistical basis of modern science.

The second objection grants the impossibility of a body's rising three feet into the air in the absence of a special cause and grants my certitude of this. But what I can never be certain of, the objection runs, is that all the special causes and devices which accomplish this are absent. So I am entirely unjustified in asserting the outright impossibility of the phenomenon—especially when I think to do so in the very teeth of its occurrence. My saying that it is impossible could only have the force here of an ejaculation like " 'struth!" *Ab esse ad posse valet consequentia.* Supposing the thing to have occurred, we as ungullible people should respond by maintaining confidence in the existence of a natural cause, by persisting indefinitely in searching for one, and by classifying the occurrence in the meantime as an unsolved problem. So runs the second objection.

However, the idea that one cannot establish the absence of a natural cause is not to my mind the unassailable piece of logic it might seem at first glance to be. Both our common understanding and our scientific understanding include conceptions of the sort of thing which can and cannot happen, and of the sort of thing which has to take place to bring about some other sort of thing. These conceptions are presupposed to our arguing in such patterns as "A will do such and such unless Y," or "If Z happens it can only be from this, that or the other (kind of) cause," or "If W cannot be done in this way or that way it cannot be done at all." An example of the first pattern is "The horse will die if it gets no food." My rising steadily three feet in the air is a subject for argument according to the second pattern. The second pattern presents the surface appearance of being more complicated than the first, but logically it is not. Let us turn our attention to the example of the first pattern.

Suppose that a horse, which has been normally born and reared, and is now deprived of all nourishment (we could be completely certain of this), instead of dying, goes on thriving (which again is something we could be completely certain about). A series of thorough examinations reveals no abnormality in the horse's condition: its digestive system is always found to be working and to be at every moment in more or less the state it would have been in if the horse had eaten a meal an hour or two before. This is utterly inconsistent with our whole conception of the needs and capacities of horses; and because it is an impossibility in the light of our prevailing conception, my objector, in the event of its happening, would expect us to abandon the conception—as though we had to have consistency at any price. Whereas the position I advocate is that the price is too high and that it would be better to be left with the inconsistency; and that in any event the prevailing conception has a logical status not altogether unlike that of a necessary truth and cannot be simply thrown away as a mistake —not when it rests on the experience of generations, not when all the other horses in the world are continuing to behave as horses have always done, and especially not when one considers the way our conception of the needs and capacities of horses interlocks with conceptions of the needs and capacities of other living things and with a conception of the difference between animate and inanimate behavior quite generally. These conceptions form part of a common understanding which is well-established and with us to stay. Any number of discoveries remain to be made by zoologists, and plenty of scope exists for conceptual revision in biological theory, but it is a confusion to think that it follows from this that we are less than well enough acquainted with, and might have serious misconceptions about, what is and is not possible in the behavior under familiar conditions of common objects with which we have a long history of practical dealings. Similarly with the relation between common understanding and physical discoveries, physical theories: what has been said about the self-sustaining horse seems to me applicable *mutatis mutandis* to the levitation example also. Not that my thesis about the miraculous rests on the acceptance of this particular example. The objector who thinks that there is a loophole in it for natural explanation strikes me as lacking a sense of the absurd but can keep his opinion for the moment, since he will (I hope) be shown the loophole being closed in a further example with which I shall conclude.

I did not in any case mean to suggest that if I rose in the air now in the absence of any device it would be at all proper for a religious person to hail this as a miracle. Far from it. From a religious point of view it would either signify nothing at all or else be regarded as a sign of devilry; and if the phenomenon persisted I should think that a religious person might well have recourse to exorcism, if that figured among the institutions of his religion. Suppose, however, that by rising into the air I were to avoid an otherwise certain death: then it would (against a religious background) become possible to speak of a miracle, just as it would in what I called the contingency case. Or the phenomenon could be a miracle although nothing at all were achieved by it, provided that I were a religiously significant figure, one of whom prophets had spoken, or at least an exceptionally holy man.

My thesis, then, in regard to the violation concept of the miraculous, by contrast with the contingency concept, which we have seen to be also a possible concept, is that a conflict of certainties is a necessary though not a sufficient condition of the miraculous. In other words, a miracle, though it cannot only be this, must at least be something the occurrence of which can be categorized at one and the same time as empirically certain and conceptually impossible. If it were less than conceptually impossible, it would reduce merely to a very unusual occurrence such as could be treated (because of the empirical certainty) in the manner of a decisive experiment and result in a modification to the prevailing conception of natural law; while if it were less than empirically certain, nothing more would be called for in regard to it than a suspension of judgment. So if there is to be a type of the miraculous other than the contingency kind, it must offend against the principle *ab esse ad posse valet consequentia.* And since the violation concept of the miraculous does seem to me to be a possible concept, I therefore reject that time-honored logical principle.

I know that my suggestion that something could be at one and the same time empirically certain and conceptually impossible will sound to many people ridiculous. Must not the actual occurrence of something show that it *was* conceptually possible after all? And if I contend, as I do, that the fact that something has occurred might *not* necessarily show that it was conceptually possible, or—to put it the other way round—if I contend, as I do, that the fact that something is conceptually impossible does not necessarily preclude its occurrence, then am I not opening the door to the instantiation of round squares, female fathers, and similar paradigms of senselessness? The answer is that the door is being opened only as far as is needed and no farther; certainly not to instantiations of the *self*-contradictory. There is more than one kind of conceptual impossibility.

Let me illustrate my meaning finally by reference to the New Testament story of the turning of water into wine. I am not assuming that this story is true, but I think that it logically could be. Hence if anyone chooses to maintain its truth as a matter of faith I see no philosophical objection to his doing so. A number of people could have been quite sure, could have had the fullest empirical certainty, that a vessel contained water at one moment and wine a moment later—good wine, as St. John

says—without any device having been applied to it in the inter-
vening time. Not that this last really needs to be added; for
that any device should have existed *then* at least is inconceivable, even if it might just be argued to be a conceptual possibility now. I have in mind the very remote possibility of a
liquid chemically indistinguishable from, say, mature claret being produced by means of atomic and molecular transformations. The device would have to be conceived as something
enormously complicated, requiring a large supply of power.
Anything less thorough-going would hardly meet the case, for
those who are alleged to have drunk the wine were practiced
wine-bibbers, capable of detecting at once the difference between a true wine and a concocted variety in the "British Wine,
Ruby Type" category. However, that water could conceivably
have been turned into wine in the first century A.D. by means of
a device is ruled out of court at once by common understanding; and though the verdict is supported by scientific knowledge, common understanding has no need of this support.

In the case of my previous example of a man, myself for instance, rising three feet into the air and remaining there unsupported, it was difficult to deal with the objection that we
could not be certain that there was not some special cause operating, *some* explanation even though we had searched to the
utmost of our ability and had found none. And I imagined the
objector trying to lay it down as axiomatic that, while there is
such a thing as not knowing what the cause or explanation of a
phenomenon might be, there can be no such thing as establishing the absence of a cause. The example of water being turned
into wine is stronger, and I would think decisive, here. At one
moment, let us suppose, there was water and at another moment wine, in the same vessel, although no one had emptied
out the water and poured in the wine. This is something which
could conceivably have been established with certainty. What
is not conceivable is that it could have been done by a device.
Nor is it conceivable that there could have been a natural cause
of it. For this would have had to be the natural cause of the
water's becoming wine. And water's becoming wine is not the
description of any conceivable natural process. It is conceptually impossible that the wine could have been gotten naturally
from water, save in the very strained sense that moisture is

needed to nourish the vines from which the grapes are taken, and this very strained sense is irrelevant here.

"But can we not still escape from the necessity to assert that one and the same thing is both empirically certain and conceptually impossible? For what has been said to be conceptually impossible is the turning of water into wine. However, when allusion is made to the alleged miracle, all the expression 'turned into' can signify is that at one moment there was water and at a moment later wine. This is what could have been empirically certain: whereas what is conceptually impossible is that water should have been turned into wine if one really *means* turned into. It is not conceptually impossible that at one moment water should have been found and at another moment wine in the same vessel, even though no one had emptied out the water and poured in the wine." So someone might try to argue. But I cannot see that it does any good. To the suggestion that the thing is conceivable so long as we refrain from saying that the water *turned into* the wine I would reply: either the water turns into the wine or else it disappears and wine springs into existence in its place. But water cannot *conceivably* disappear like that without going anywhere, and wine cannot *conceivably* spring into existence from nowhere. Look at it in terms of transformation, or look at it in terms of "coming into being and passing away"—or just look at it. Whatever you do, you cannot make sense of it: on all accounts it is inconceivable. So I keep to the position that the New Testament story of the turning of water into wine is the story of something which could have been known empirically to have occurred, and it is also the story of the occurrence of something which is conceptually impossible. It has to be both in order to be the miracle-story which, whether true or false, it is.

That expression "the occurrence of something which is conceptually impossible" was used deliberately just then. And it will be objected, no doubt, that to speak of something which is conceptually impossible is to speak of a nullity. To ask for an example of something which is conceptually impossible is not (I shall be told) like asking for a sample of a substance, and you cannot in order to comply with this request produce anything visible or tangible, you cannot point to an occurrence. Indeed you cannot, strictly speaking, offer a description either:

you can only utter a form of words. What I have been arguing in effect is that there is a contradiction in St. John's "description" of the water-into-wine episode. But if so, then nothing has really been described; or alternatively something has been —one should not say misdescribed but rather garbled—since a conceptual impossibility is *ex vi termini* one of which sense cannot be made.

I would reply to this that sense can certainly be made of a conceptual impossibility in the respect that one can see often enough that there *is* a conceptual impossibility there and also, often enough, what kind of a conceptual impossibility it is and how it arises. We can see that there is an inconsistency; and words, moreover, are not the only things in which we can see inconsistency. Human actions can be pointed to here quite obviously. And I am maintaining that there is also such a thing as making sense, and failing to make sense, of *events*. If the objector holds that in the case of events, unlike the case of human actions, sense must always be there although one perhaps fails to find it, I ask: how does he know? Why the *must*? It is not part of my case that to regard a sequence of events as senseless or miraculous is to construe it as if it were a sort of action, or to see the invisible hand of a super-person at work in it. I have contended that there are circumstances in respect to which the expression "occurrence of something which is conceptually impossible" would have a natural enough use, and I have offered three examples. I think that the expression "violation of a law of nature" could also be introduced quite naturally in this connection, or we could speak of a contradiction in our experience.

17

On Miracles

PAUL J. DIETL

Syracuse University

SOME OF THE MOST REMARKABLE TURNS in recent philosophical discussion have been the resurrection of issues original
readers of *Language, Truth, and Logic* would have thought
forever dead. "Freewill" is no longer considered a pseudo-
problem. There is serious controversy concerning the existence
of God. Ethics is considered cognitively significant in respectable circles. In fact the concept of a miracle is probably the only
concept left for resurrection. Here there is general agreement
—among sophisticated theologians as well as militant atheists
—that *a priori* rejection of claims is justified. Miracle claims,
it is generally believed, could not be true because of the very
nature of the concept of a miracle. Nonetheless I should like to
argue for its vindication. The crucial issue is whether conditions could ever obtain which would justify one in applying
"miracle" in any way resembling its standard historical use. I
shall argue that there could be such conditions, that we could

Reprinted from *American Philosophical Quarterly*, 5 (1968), 130–134, with the
permission of the author and the publishers.

very well recognize them, so that we do know what miracles are, and therefore that miracle claims are at worst false.

Here as elsewhere Hume anticipated much later opinion, so it is reasonable to begin with his contribution. The difficulty is that in much of what he wrote on the subject Hume seemed to be arguing that the event which is supposed to have been an exception to a law of nature could not happen. The laws themselves are based on "a firm and unalterable experience" and "as a uniform experience amounts to a proof, there is here a direct and full proof, from the nature of the fact, against the existence of any miracle. . . ." [1] In at least one place, though, Hume does admit that bizarre events could occur.

> Suppose all authors, in all languages, agree that from the first of January, 1600, there was total darkness over the whole earth for eight days; suppose that the tradition of this extraordinary event is still strong and lively among the people; that all travelers who return from foreign countries, bring us accounts of the same tradition without the least variation or contradiction—it is evident that our present philosophers, instead of doubting the fact, ought to receive it as certain and ought to search for the causes from whence it might be derived.[2]

Apparently the bizarre cannot be ruled out on the grounds that it is bizarre. Indeed, given the right circumstances, even the second-hand *reports* of bizarre events are immune to the criticism that the claim must be false on the grounds that it goes against laws of nature. Nevertheless, even though it is possible that exceptions to established laws should occur, apparently we are never justified in describing the events as miraculous. One looks in vain for Hume's reasons for this latter thesis.

P. H. Nowell-Smith has tried to defend this second view.[3] Nowell-Smith repudiates the view that miracle-claims can be refuted on the grounds that they are exceptions to laws of nature, but he cannot understand the difference between the natural and the supernatural upon which the interpretation or explanation of a bizarre event as miraculous depends.[4] Science, he reminds us, has come to explain things which at an earlier date were beyond its very concepts. He claims that no matter what happens, if it is explained at all, that explanation will take its place in some department of the university. Perhaps a new department will have to be created to accommodate it but that the new department will be among the natural-science faculties Nowell-Smith has no doubt. The point is that to describe an event as miraculous is to say that it could never be explained in any natural science whatsoever, and we can never say that. Not even science itself could show it.

> To say that it is inexplicable as a result of natural agents is already beyond the competence of any scientist as a scientist, and to say that it must be ascribed to supernatural agents is to say something that no one could possibly have the right to affirm on the evidence alone.[5]

Some would answer this charge by attempting to reconcile an event's being miraculous with its eventually being naturally explainable but, say, highly coincidental.[6] That there is such a usage for "miracle" I do not contest, but I am interested in defending the concept Nowell-Smith is attacking. That there is also a usage of "miracle" according to which to call an event a miracle is to attribute it to the will of a supernatural agent and to claim that if the supernatural agent had not intervened that event would not have taken place is, I think, equally clear. Indeed this latter usage is unquestionably more frequent in the history of religion.

It follows that in the way in which I am using "miracle" miracle-claims do have the implications Nowell-Smith envisages. "Supernatural" implies that the agent be able to bring about events which are exceptions to physical laws. Nothing else about the agent is at issue, however. For example, we are not concerned with questions of whether he is all-good or all-powerful or eternal or even with the question of whether there is more than one such being. But he must be a being who can control the laws of nature. The question is whether or not any event would ever be rationally described as a manifestation of power of such a being. It will only be such if all causes other than such a being can be ruled out—which is precisely what Nowell-Smith denied could be done.

Before I construct what I think is a counterexample to Nowell-Smith's thesis, I want to call attention to two features of miracles. The first is simply that there is nothing amiss in one person having several miracles he can perform. In the Book of Exodus, for example, Moses is given more than a dozen miracles with which he attempts to melt the Pharaoh's heart. He brings on several miraculous catastrophes and then stops them. The Pharaoh's heart remains hard, and so Moses brings about several more. The second feature of historical accounts to which I wish to call attention is the rather elaborate circumstances in which they may take place. The people who wrote the Old Testament quite obviously had some notion of how to tell the real thing from a fake. Take the story about Elijah at Carmel (I Kings 18). Controversy had arisen whether prayer should be directed to the Lord God of the Jews or to Baal. Elijah took the people to Mt. Carmel and said: "Let them . . . give us two bullocks; and let them choose one bullock for themselves, and cut it to pieces, and lay it on wood." The ministers of Baal took the meat from one animal and made a pile, and Elijah called upon the ministers of Baal to ask Baal to cook their meat. "But there was no voice, nor any that answered. And they leaped upon the altar which was made. And it came to pass at noon, that Elijah mocked them, and said, Cry aloud; for he is a god; either he is talking, or he is pursuing, or he is on a journey, or peradventure he sleepeth, and must be awakened. And they cried aloud, and cut themselves after their manner with knives and lances, till the blood gushed out upon them." But all this to no avail. Then Elijah stepped up and said: "Fill four barrels with water, and pour it on the burnt sacrifice, and on the wood." And he said, Do it the second time. And they did it the second time. And he said, Do it the third time. And they did it the third time. And the water ran round about the altar; and he filled the trench also with water. Then he called on God for fire and "Then the fire of the Lord fell, and consumed the burnt sacrifice, and the wood, and the stones, and the dust, and licked up the water that was in the trench."

We are given here, first of all, about as artificial a setting as any laboratory affords. The account also involves a random sampling of the material to be set on fire, a prediction that one pile will burn up and one will not, a prediction when the fire will start, and twelve barrels of precaution against earthly independent variables. There is obviously nothing wrong with applying somewhat sophisticated experimental design to miracles.

Now for the example. Its essential ingredients are simply a bundle of miracles no larger than Moses had and a randomizing technique just a little more complicated than Elijah's. Let us assume that a local prophet opens, or appears with the help of God to open, the mighty Schuylkill River. Two possibilities arise. The first is that the prophet does not figure causally in the natural explanation but that he notices a cue in the physical situation which indicates natural sufficient conditions. This is especially tempting because he might not be consciously aware of the cue and so might himself honestly believe in the miracle. This sort of explanation can be ruled out, however, if he is required to do miracles at random. Say he allows non-believers to pick twelve miracles and number them. Which one he will do will be determined by the roll of a pair of unloaded dice, and the hour of the day at which it will occur will be determined by a second roll. Rolling the dice without his prediction could establish that the dice had no efficacy and using the dice to randomize the predictions proves that the prophet does not predict on the basis of a natural cue.[7]

This randomizing also establishes that there is a cause at work other than would have operated if the prophet had not been there. But perhaps there is still some law covering the events. To see how vastly different this would be from an ordinary scientific law, however, one has only to realize that there would be no new scientific department on a par with, say, physics or chemistry, which included such laws. This would be a department which dealt with all the other sciences and had no laws of its own, except that when this prophet spoke, all laws, or any one of an indefinitely large number, are broken.

Odd, you might say, but not yet miraculous. Such a prophet might require a new metascientific department, but we still have not been forced to admit supernatural explanation. But this is so only because we have not yet looked at the *explanans* in these supposed scientific explanations. What could possibly be the natural conditions which this new department will ascertain to be necessary and sufficient for the unexpected events?

If the prophet prayed we might think that the prayer was connected in some curious way with the exceptions. But what if he does not pray? What if he just requests? Could it be the sounds of his words which have the extraordinary effect? Then let him predict in different languages. Might we mention language-independent brain processes as the sufficient conditions? Let him predict what will happen later when he is asleep—even drugged, or dead.

But surely it has become obvious that there is nothing which could be pinned down as the independent variable in a scientific explanation; for no conceivable candidate is necessary. The prophet asks God to do miracle No. 4 at midnight and then goes to sleep. Or he asks God to do whatever miracle turns up at whatever hour turns up and then dies. We are dealing with requests and answers—that is, thoughts, and thoughts not as psychological occurrences but as understood.

No natural law will do because only vehicles of thought could function as the natural *explanans* and no such vehicle is necessary. There would have to be one law connecting the acoustics of English with general law-breaking, another for French, and so on indefinitely—and when the prophet asks that whatever miracle turns upon the dice be performed and then goes to sleep before the dice are thrown, there just is not anything left except his request as understood.[8]

What is needed here is not a law but an understanding which can grasp the request and then bring it about that a physical law be broken. But an understanding physical-law breaker is a supernatural being, and that is why if a new department is set up it will not be with the science faculties at all. It will be a department of religion.

I should like here to attempt to forestall some foreseeable objections. The first one is that even if what I have said is all true, that still does not prove that there ever has been a miracle. Of course I agree with this objection. The sophistication of the experimental design of the Elijah account may be the progressive result of centuries of anxious parents' trying to convince doubting children of false stories. The point is that the concept of miracle allowed such sophistication. What they *meant* to say was ascertainable, or at least they meant to *say* that it was ascertainable, in principle. Whether or not their claims were actually true is another question.

A second criticism shows a hankering after a simple *a priori* disproof. Believing in miracles, it will be said, inevitably involves believing in the suspension of some physical law. We can always avoid this by doubting the data. Hallucinations do not rest on the suspension of such laws. The trouble with this sort of objection to the miraculous is that it can quickly be pushed to the point at which the very distinction between hallucinatory and veridical experiences breaks down. Faith, it has been said, can move mountains. Suppose that someone moved the Poconos to nothern Minnesota. Thousands saw them flying through the air. Old maps showed them in Pennsylvania where we all remembered them to have been, and a thriving ski industry grows up where there had only been the exhausted open mines of the Mesabi Range. If that is a hallucination then everything is.

A third criticism is that the account of physical laws in this paper is hopelessly over-simple and crude. I agree. One must show, however, that the crudity and simplicity make a difference to the general thesis about miracles. As far as I can see, the introduction of statistics and probability, or the ideal nature of some or all laws, or of accounts of laws as models or inference tickets or as the designation of patterns we find intelligible, makes no difference. Specifically, the account offered here does not rest on belief in metaphysical connections between causes and effects. Of course, physical laws are only descriptive. But I take it that they do serve as bases for predictions and also for contrary-to-fact conditionals. They are not ontological, but they must be nomological. As long as according to the natural laws operative (e.g., gravity) and the state of the world at one time (e.g., including a free body) another state can be predicted to occur (e.g., the body's fall), then, even though there may never have been an exactly true formulation of the law or a perfect instantiation of the initial conditions (no body ever quite free), as long as the denial of the predicted event is internally coherent, to speak of exceptions is meaningful.

A fourth rejoinder to my arguments might be that even if I have proved that there could be conditions which, if you experienced them, would justify your belief in a miracle, and even though we might have reason to believe second-hand reports of bizarre phenomena, we could still never have better reasons to believe a second-hand miracle claim than to doubt the veracity of the man reporting it; and surely this is really all that Hume, if not Nowell-Smith, set out to prove. In answer let me say first that if you had good reason to believe that what the report describes as happening really did happen—and happened as the reports describe, viz., with randomizing and predictions—then it seems to me that you have good reasons to believe in supernatural intervention as an explanation of the events. But in any case remember Exodus once more. Moses had brought several miraculous plagues, then called them off, then brought down a new batch. Now say that you happened into Egypt during the second batch of catastrophes. Could you rule out *a priori* the possibility that there had been an earlier set? I think not.

Fifthly, one might object that even if I have shown that there could be evidence for miracles and even in the sense in which "miracle" implies supernatural intervention, this is still of no religious significance unless "miracle" also implies *divine* intervention. Miracles, as defined here, in short, do not tend to prove the existence of God. My only answer is that to prove the existence of a being who deserves some of the predicates which "God" normally gets would be to go some way toward proving the existence of *God*. The question whether the comprehensibility of miracle claims strengthens the position of the theologians or whether the paucity of latter-day evidence has the opposite effect, I leave to the theologians and more militant atheists.

A final criticism might be that calling an event a miracle appears to be offering an explanation for it, but is really not an explanation at all since explanations must always rest on laws. In fact, it might be held, this is the real dilemma behind miracle hypotheses. Either there are laws covering miracles or not. If there are no laws then miracles cannot be explanations: they are not hypotheses at all. But if there are laws, then there is no difference between natural and supernatural explanations. Nowell-Smith's argument goes:

(A) Calling an event a miracle is apparently to explain it.
(B) Explanations must rest on laws.
(c) If one has laws one can predict the events they explain.

(D) We cannot predict miracles, therefore calling an event a miracle
has no (explanatory) meaning over and above a mere (descriptive) statement of the phenomena to be explained.[9]

Now, a prediction was involved in the Elijah story, and I do
not see how one could pin down God as the independent variable unless predictions like those were possible. These predictions, however, were not made possible by anything Nowell-
Smith would call a law. Indeed, that the prediction did not rest
on the knowledge of a regularity between initial conditions and
effect was the reason for looking to the supernatural. In other
words, it cannot be objected that miracles are not explanations
because miracles are not lawful until it has been proved that all
explanations are lawful. This is all the more pressing since part
of the point of interpreting an event as a miracle is to see it not
as a natural event but as an action, or the result of an action,
of an intelligent being.[10] That all intelligible *actions* are sub-
sumable under laws is even less credible than that all *events*
are. An action can be made intelligible by showing its *point*
(for example, to bring wayward children back to the truth, to
reward the holy, to save the chosen people, etc.), and showing
the good of an action is not automatically to subsume it under
a law.

I conclude that "miracle" is perfectly meaningful. To call
an event a miracle is to claim that it is the result of supernatural intervention into the natural course of events. We could
know that the supernatural agent was intelligent, but little else
(though when and for whom he did miracles would be evidence
about his character).[11]

NOTES

1. David Hume, *An Enquiry Concerning Human Understanding*, sect. 10, pt.
I, p. 115 (references are to the L. A. Selby-Bigge edition entitled *Enquiries*).
2. *Ibid.*, p. 128.
3. In "Miracles," reprinted in *New Essays in Philosophical Theology*, edd.
A. Flew and A. MacIntyre (London, 1955), pp. 243–253.
4. *Ibid.*, p. 244.
5. *Ibid.*, pp. 246–247.
6. For an interesting discussion of that concept of "miracle," see chapter 16.
7. One might object to "proves," but such procedures eliminate candidates
with as much certainty as any non-logical procedures ever could.

8. Since in this case the prophet does not know what miracle will be asked for, pre-cognition is also ruled out.

9. Nowell-Smith, p. 250.

10. This is the point of drawing an analogy between explanations in terms of miracles and human intervention into the course of nature. Whether or not such divine intervention would have to be in conformity to the laws of nature because human intervention apparently is would be a further question. Nowell-Smith seems to think that anyone who draws the analogy at all must admit that divine intervention would have to be in accordance with laws (p. 249).

11. This paper has profited from criticisms by Professors William Wisdom and Michael Scriven.

18

The Tacit Structure
of Religious Knowing

JERRY H. GILL
Florida Presbyterian College

THE FOLLOWING ESSAY IS PROGRAMMATIC IN CHARACTER.
That is to say, its primary purpose is to mark a new direction
in the development of religious epistemology. Thus it does not
include as much detailed analysis as is necessary to complete
the case for viewing religious knowledge as a form of tacit
knowing. I hope that it does include enough such analysis to
establish the fruitfulness of interpreting religious knowledge
as being essentially tacit in structure.

I. THE PROBLEM: EPISTEMOLOGICAL DUALISM

Contemporary philosophical and theological thought is characterized by an irresolvable stalemate. On the one side stand
those thinkers primarily influenced by the empiricist and posi-

Reprinted from *International Philosophical Quarterly,* 9 (1969), 533–559, with
the permission of the author.

tivist tradition: they emphasize the priority of cognitive (objective) experience over non-cognitive (subjective) experience. On the opposite side stand those thinkers primarily influenced by the existentialist tradition: they emphasize the priority of non-cognitive (valuational) experience over cognitive (factual) experience. These two groups of thinkers alternate between ignoring each other and dropping disparaging remarks about each other. Such a stalemate creates a great deal of frustration in the life of one who is at all concerned with both the cognitive and non-cognitive aspects of experience. At best he constructs a dichotomized, schizophrenic life-style, while at worst he succumbs to one of these emphases and negates the other—thereby becoming only half a man.

The philosophical aspect of this stalemate needs no documentation. Even the cursory student of our times is aware of the character and influence of contemporary empiricism. The theological aspect of this stalemate, however, may be in need of a word of explanation. While for a time it was common to classify nearly all contemporary theologians as being under the existentialist influence of Kierkegaard, it has now become apparent that there exists an essential difference between those thinkers who follow Barth and those who follow Bultmann. To my mind this difference parallels that which exists between empiricist and existentialist philosophers. Barthian theology is essentially similar to empiricist (or positivist) philosophy in that it emphasizes the objective (factual) character of revelation. Religious experience is cognitive in Barthianism. Bultmannian theology, on the other hand, is essentially similar to existentialist philosophy in that it emphasizes the subjective (valuational) character of revelation. Religious experience is non-cognitive in Bultmannianism. The former stresses the *"Word of God"* while the latter stresses the *faith of man.*

This split between the empiricist and existentialist approaches has thoroughly eliminated the possibility of an adequate form of religious knowledge. Either religious experience is to be equated with the factual realm, in which case it hardly does justice to the valuational depth of human existence, or religious experience is to be equated with the valuational realm, in which case it hardly does justice to the cognitive concern of human existence. The fact/value dichotomy which underlies contemporary thought thus leads necessarily to truncated views of religious knowledge as either "flat" or humanistic in nature.

It is my primary contention in this section that the dichotomy which characterizes contemporary philosophical and theological thought is the result, at bottom, of an essential agreement between the two main schools of thought. Although they differ with respect to which aspect of human experience and/or reality is more important, both empiricism and existentialism agree that human experience and/or reality is to be divided into two main aspects, those of fact and of value. Thus at the foundation of all contemporary thought lies the dichotomy between factual (cognitive) experience and language on the one side and valuation (non-cognitive) experience and language on the other. This unchallenged, dualistic epistemological foundation has led to the elimination of the possibility of an adequate view of religious knowledge. It is my purpose in this paper to challenge this epistemological dualism by replacing it with a view which is more in line with the knowing experience, and which is more favorable to the possibility of religious knowledge.

Before proceeding directly to this challenge, however, it will prove helpful to explicate further the fact/value dichotomy by providing a brief sketch of its historical development. To my mind the source of this dichotomy is to be found in philosophical distinctions developed in the seventeenth and eighteenth centuries by the likes of Descartes, Locke, Hume, and Kant. Moreover, it is in Kant's *Critique of Pure Reason* that the dichotomy between fact and value receives its most profound and influential statement. Indeed, all of modern philosophy and theology has been played out according to the ground rules set up by Kant's theory of knowledge. There are, to be sure, traces of the fact/value dichotomy in philosophers as far back as Plato, but in none of these is it presented as pointedly and thoroughly as it is in Kant. In large measure the gulf which separates contemporary empiricism and existentialism is traceable to their mutual dependence upon Kant's epistemological distinctions.[1]

The distinctions of Kant's which I have in mind are three in number. First, he distinguished between the phenomenal world and the noumenal world. The one can be known and corresponds to the factual realm, while the other cannot be known and corresponds to the valuation realm. Second, he distinguished between pure and practical reason. Pure reason is cognitive in nature and provides knowledge of the phenomenal world. Practical reason is non-cognitive in nature and provides direction for the ethical life—and "postulational knowledge" of the noumenal world. Third, Kant distinguished between the known object and knowing subject. Human knowledge was said to be the result of the organization of the former by the mental categories of the latter. Now, it is not just the fact that Kant made these distinctions which makes him the villain of my plot. The really insidious nature of his distinctions lies in the absolute way in which they were made. They are more than distinctions; they are dichotomies. Once the various aspects of human experience and/or reality are dichotomized into unrelated realms, the result is epistemological schizophrenia and the elimination of the possibility of religious knowledge. Witness the contemporary philosophical and theological scene.[2]

This particular interpretation of the historical source of the contemporary stalemate is corroborated by the fact that the various epistemological options developed in the nineteenth century are also best understood as responses to the dichotomies laid down by Kant. Hegel's thought can be understood as a total rejection of Kant's dichotomies in that he maintained the essential identity of the phenomenal world and the noumenal world, as well as the identity of the known object and the knowing subject. Hegel sought to vault over Kant's wall of separation by means of rational speculation.

Kierkegaard, on the other hand, accepted Kant's dichotomies and then maintained that the noumenal world made itself known to the man of faith by means of radical revelation. For Kierkegaard, God vaulted over the Kantian wall of separation. Schleiermacher also accepted Kant's dichotomies, but then he went ahead and maintained that they can be overcome by non-cognitive means. He sought to tunnel under Kant's wall of separation by identifying man's feelings with the noumenal world. Feuerbach, who was in some ways the most realistic of all, accepted Kant's dichotomies and then turned his back on the unattainable noumenal world, focusing his attention on man's aspirations alone. Feuerbach's way of negation has provided inspiration both for Marxism and for the "Death of God" movement. Thus Kant's dichotomies provide the key to the nineteenth century as well as to the twentieth.

II. A FUNCTIONAL VIEW OF LANGUAGE

In this section I will seek to delineate a point of departure for an epistemological position which is more adequate than the one which has been under attack in the foregoing pages. My point of departure is taken from the later work of Ludwig Wittgenstein and J. L. Austin. The spatial limitations of this paper render a thorough analysis of these thinkers quite impossible. I will simply outline those aspects of their work which provide a clue to a new epistemological beginning.

It is fairly common knowledge that the view of language which underlies contemporary empiricism, and against which Wittgenstein's later work was directed, is what has been termed "the picture theory of language and meaning." According to this theory, the purpose of language is to picture or represent reality. Language is made up of words which name objects, and when these words are combined in sentences they may be said to picture a state of affairs, or relations between objects. Thus only statements which picture a possible state of affairs can be said to be cognitively meaningful.[3]

It is my contention that it is the implicit acceptance (at times in spite of explicit denials) of this view of language which underlies modern epistemology and leads to the dualism of our day. Both empiricism and existentialism accept the picture theory of meaning. On the basis of it the former proceeds to eliminate metaphysics, theology, and ethics from the realm of meaningful discourse, while the latter proceeds to maintain that there are other kinds of meaning beyond the cognitive which lie outside the picturing function of language. Thus arises the fact/value dichotomy discussed in Section One. Even Descartes, Locke, Hume, and Kant can be shown ultimately to rely upon the picture theory.

The later Wittgenstein has successfully undermined the picture theory by making it quite clear that there is a vast and constantly changing variety of language functions in addition to those of naming objects and picturing states of affairs. Thus meaning can no longer be limited to those statements which perform this function. The meaning of a given statement can only be determined in terms of the function it is used to perform. Thus, meaning is a function of the use to which a statement is put within a specific context. Moreover, Wittgenstein maintained that, far from being isolated utterances, all uses of language are part of much broader sub-sets of human activity which he termed "language-games." In other words, there are certain overlapping human enterprises which provide the broader context within which any particular locution must be understood. Finally, Wittgenstein stressed that our language-games can only be understood against the backdrop of their place in our total way of being in the world. The structure of our language and language games reflects the structure of the various "forms of life" which make up human existence. The rules which implicitly govern our way of living and speaking, while being flexible, are not arbitrary. They are part of the fabric of our lives, and to ask which comes first, reality or language, is like asking which comes first, the warp or the woof.[4]

In many ways J. L. Austin's most recent work, especially in the later chapters of *How To Do Things With Words,* can be viewed as an extension of Wittgenstein's work. The main thrust of Austin's thought aims at overcoming the hard-and-fast dichotomies between the cognitive (constative) function and the non-cognitive (performative) function of language. Although he is rightfully credited with having discovered the performative function of language (in which we actually *do* things by speaking in addition to just speaking), in his later work Austin came to see that it differs only in degree and not in kind from other types of utterances. As a substitute for the dichotomized view of language, which leads to an absolute distinction between fact and value, Austin offered a dimensional view in which meaning is a function of the interaction among what is said ("locutionary force"), why it is said ("illocutionary force"), and the results of what is said ("perlocutionary force"). Every speech-act is an inextricable mixture of these three dimensions or forces, and thus meaning and truth can only be determined by an analysis of that mixture. Moreover, the neat distinction between true and false statements also

turns out to be one of degree rather than one of kind, since the
proper classification for some statements is "more or less true"
("rough").[5]

Now, the main conclusions to be drawn from the work of
Wittengenstein and Austin, by way of constructing a foundation for a fresh epistemological beginning, are three in number.
First, language as well as meaning and knowledge must be
viewed as contextual or functional in nature. If the meaning of
a statement is a function of its use within a broad (language-
game) and a narrow (instance) context, then the truth of a
statement must also be a function of its use within these contexts. Knowledge, then, far from being a static metaphysical or
psychological entity, is a flexible process which is relative to the
situation in which it arises. Cognitive experience only arises
within a given, but flexible, context. Thus the distinction between the known and the knower is only a relative one within
a specific context. Truth does not exist apart from a particular
utterance in a concrete situation, and it cannot be limited to
some Pickwickian realm of "Objectivity."

Second, both speaking and knowing are human activities.
Therefore, cognitive experience must be viewed as a process
and not as a state. Knowing is something which humans *do,*
not something which they *have.* Language is part and parcel
of human existence, something which has to be entered into to
gain significance. The same holds true for knowledge. The traditional approach has always implied that knowledge is a passive state which is brought about in the knower by the known
object. The present view is that knowledge is the result of the
interaction of the knower and his environment within certain
flexible contexts and perspectives. This view implies that both
language and knowledge are functions of the personal involve-
ment and commitments of the speaker-knower. Apart from
such "personal backing," speech-acts and cognitive experience
would be impossible. "Nothing ventured, nothing said or
known."

Thirdly, both meaning and knowledge must be viewed as
dimensional in character. That is to say, they can never be confronted as isolated aspects of experience, but are always
grasped as the result of interrelated activities and contexts.

This would suggest that experience and/or reality also have a dimensional structure. This view stands diametrically opposed to the traditional view in which the aspects of experience and/ or reality are conceived of as separate realms (e.g., Kant's phenomena and noumena). A dimensional view is more in line with the way in which cognitive experience actually takes place. Moreover, such a dimensional view implies that knowledge is always mediated in structure. In other words, one dimension of reality can be known only by means of the others; what is known is always known in relation, not in isolation.

III. THE CASE FOR TACIT KNOWLEDGE

On the basis of the foregoing clues I will now sketch out the basic distinctions (not dichotomies) which constitute the foundation for viewing knowledge as tacit in structure. In this sketch I will focus on the distinctions presented in the work of Michael Polanyi, although my way of developing and relating these distinctions is my own. My main contention is that knowledge must be viewed as the result of the interaction between two dimensions of human experience: the awareness dimension and the response dimension.

The first of Polanyi's distinctions which need to be explicated is that between "focal" and "subsidiary" awareness. In any given cognitive context there are some factors of which the knowing subject is aware because he is directing his attention to them. Such awareness is termed "focal." In the same context there are also factors of which the knower is aware even though he is not focusing on them. This is termed "subsidiary" awareness. By way of example, in the context of reading or hearing my words the reader (or the listener) is focusing his attention on their meaning, not on the letters (or phonemes) of which they are comprised, or even on the words themselves. Nevertheless, it is obvious that the reader is subsidiarily aware of both the letters (or phonemes) and the words.

It is clear that this distinction, like all contextual distinctions, is a relative one. In other words, a person can direct his attention to those factors of which formerly he was subsidiarily aware, thereby becoming focally aware of them. In like manner, one can become subsidiarily aware of those factors of which formerly he was focally aware. This is obvious with respect to the above example of letters, words, and meaning. It also is true with respect to other levels of experience such as the physical, the psychological, and the moral. In all these cases the cognitive context is brought into being by the knowing subject "attending from" that of which he is subsidiarily aware and "attending to" that of which he is focally aware. Polanyi summarizes it this way:

> When we are relying on our awareness of something (A) for attending to something else (B), we are but subsidiarily aware of A. The thing B to which we are thus focally attending, is then the meaning of A. The focal object B is always identifiable, while things like A, of which we are subsidiarily aware, may be unidentifiable. The two kinds of awareness are mutually exclusive: when we switch our attention to something of which we have hitherto been subsidiarily aware, it loses its previous meaning. Such is, briefly, the *structure of tacit knowing*.[6]

The major epistemological point to be drawn from this distinction is that cognitive awareness is not only an exclusive function of contextual significance; it is a function of a continuum between focal and subsidiary awareness as well. Thus knowledge as awareness simply cannot be limited to that of which we are focally aware. In order for there even to be a context in which one can be focally aware of some factors, there must also be some factors of which one is only subsidiarily aware. In short, one must have a "place to stand"—to attend *from*—in order to be able to attend *to* anything at all.

Polanyi's second distinction is one between the two poles of what might be called the "activity continuum." All human activity can be placed on a scale somewhere between "conceptualization," which is most often verbal, and "embodiment," which pertains to non-verbal behavior. It should be obvious that the vast majority of human behavior is an inextricable mixture of both verbal and bodily activity. Even when one is simply thinking (to say nothing of talking), certain bodily movements can be detected as integral; and when one is simply engaged in bodily action there are corresponding conceptual (and even.

verbal) efforts which are part of the activity. Athletes talk to themselves or to their opponents, sailors and workcrews sing as they work, and lovers feel it necessary to "whisper sweet nothings" to each other. There is a sense in which every activity on this continuum can be said to involve the making of a judgment. In addition to assertions and thought processes, which obviously involve judgment-making, it can be shown that even so-called non-cognitive verbalizations such as "hello" and "oh!" imply the making of a judgment concerning the situation in which they are uttered. Even exclamations have a "depth grammar." At the other end of the continuum, even such almost totally bodily behavior as reflex actions implies the making of a judgment about the situation in which they are performed. This is why we say that a ballplayer "misjudged" the ball, or that a motorist "misjudged" the speed of the other car. Any given human act is performed within a context which renders it an act of judgment in relation to that context.

An important corollary to this "activity continuum" is that any human behavior, to the extent that it implies the making of a judgment, involves a knowledge claim. There are two sides of this corollary which need explanation. One side is that all activity, whether verbal or non-verbal, involves the actor in a knowledge claim, and can be evaluated as either appropriate (true) or inappropriate (false). Thus there is no room for a hard-and-fast distinction between "saying" as a cognitive activity and "doing" as a non-cognitive activity. Whether a particular act is verbal or non-verbal is always a question of degree, but there is no question of whether or not an act implies a cognitive judgment. To some extent all acts do!

The other side of this corollary is that all knowledge claims involve the commitment, or "personal backing," of the one making the claim. The point is simply that even though a knowledge claim is implicit in a given action, be it verbal or non-verbal, the person involved is nonetheless responsible for substantiating his claim. We hold people accountable for their reflex actions as well as for their verbal promises. All human activity is predicated upon the reality of responsible commitment.

Now I shall bring these two distinctions together. The first distinction was between focal and subsidiary awareness and the second was between conceptual and bodily activity. When these two sets of distinctions are related to one another, the result is yet a third distinction between *explicit* and *tacit* knowledge. The relationship can be visualized by imagining the "awareness continuum" and the "activity continuum" as dimensions which intersect each other. When the poles of focal awareness and conceptual activity are related, the result is "explicit knowledge." When the poles of subsidiary awareness and bodily activity are related, the result is "tacit knowledge." As every awareness and activity is a mixture of its respective poles, so every form of knowledge is a mixture of both explicit and tacit elements. In other words, relating the first two continua in this way produces yet a third continuum—the knowledge continuum—between the explicit and tacit poles.

To put this distinction another way: every context in which cognitive significance is present is comprised of both tacit and explicit factors. That is, the context exists somewhere on the continuum between these two poles. The interaction between those factors of which the subject is focally aware and his conceptual response gives rise to explicit knowledge. Such is the case when a person attends to and names an object in his perceptual field. The interaction between those factors of which the subject is subsidiarily aware and his more non-verbal, bodily response gives rise to tacit knowledge. Such is the case when the person attending to and naming an object in his perceptual field is not conscious of but still must be said to know the functioning of his senses and discriminatory powers which render his explicit knowledge possible. That he knows these tacit factors can be made clear by asking him to focus on them, whereupon he may become quite articulate about the movement of his head and hands, and about the rational steps necessary in identifying an object. But then, some other factors will be supplying the tacit context within which this new focusing is taking place.

There are two further points about the relation between explicit and tacit knowledge which need to be discussed by way of coming to a firmer understanding of the latter. Both of these points are made in the following paragraph from Polanyi:

Things of which we are focally aware can be explicitly identified; but no knowledge can be made *wholly explicit*. For one thing, the meaning of language, when in use, lies in its tacit component; for another, to use language involves actions for our body of which we have only a subsidiary awareness. Hence, tacit knowing is more fundamental than explicit knowing; *we can know more than we can tell and we can tell nothing without relying on our awareness of things we may not be able to tell.*[7]

Polanyi's main thesis is that tacit knowledge is not only a legitimate form of knowledge, but that it is logically prior to explicit knowledge. In any situation the subject tacitly relies upon a large variety of factors in order to know any factors explicitly. Moreover, although what is known tacitly in one context may well be known explicitly in another context, Polanyi insists that some forms of tacit knowledge can never be known explicitly. In short, as not all words can be defined, so not all knowledge can be explicated.

What sort of things can be said to be examples of tacit knowledge? Polanyi often discusses bodily and perceptual skills as exemplifying tacit knowledge. All of us walk, swim, shoot basketballs, and the like, without being able to articulate fully this knowledge in words. In addition, we all are able to recognize another person's face in a crowd of thousands without being able to say how we do it. A more complex and much more important example of tacit knowledge would be the ability to grasp the concept of meaning. Child and philosopher alike are unable to be fully explicit about the meaning of the term "meaning," but it is obvious that they each know what it means. In fact, one must know what "means" means before one can ask the question "What does 'means' mean?"—and then the question is unnecessary! One way of accounting for this "logical primitiveness" of meaning is in terms of the concept of tacit knowledge.

The difficulty of the seeming circularity of the concept of meaning is similar to that which has traditionally arisen concerning the concept of knowledge. This latter difficulty received its classic statement in Plato's *Meno,* and as there stated provides strong substantiation for Polanyi's position on the necessity of tacit knowledge.

The *Meno* shows conclusively that if all knowledge is explicit, i.e., capable of being clearly stated, then we cannot know a problem or look for its solution. And the *Meno* also shows, therefore, that if problems nevertheless exist, and discoveries can be made by solving them, we can know things, and important things, that we cannot tell.[8]

One aspect of tacit knowledge which bears special mention is that which pertains to the role of the body. As was emphasized at the outset, it is necessary to view bodily activity as a form of cognitive judgment. Another way of putting this is to maintain that our bodies function as instruments for the attainment of knowledge which is often tacit in nature. This tacit knowledge is of necessity more closely related to bodily awareness and activity. Motor knowledge, for instance, can only be obtained by means of what Polanyi calls "indwelling." The only way to know some things is to indwell or participate in them. Now, since all knowledge is to some extent tacit, it becomes apparent that indwelling is an important aspect of every cognitive situation. There is always a sense in which the process of coming to know anything, be it an object or a person, is dependent upon empathetic indwelling. As Polanyi puts it:

> We know another person's mind by the same integrative process by which we know life. A novice trying to understand the skill of a master will seek *mentally* to combine his movements to the pattern to which the master combines them *practically*. By such exploratory indwelling the novice gets the feel of the master's skill. Chess players enter into a master's thought by repeating the games he played. *We experience a man's mind as the joint meaning of his actions* by dwelling in his actions from outside.[9]

A summary of the case for tacit knowledge thus far presented is now in order. Knowledge is to be viewed as a continuum between the tacit and explicit poles. "All cognitive situations involve a blending of these two polar factors." Explicit knowledge is defined as a function of focal awareness and conceptual (or verbal) activity. As such it exhibits such characteristics as: precise analysis, verbal articulation, descriptive identification, observational objectivity, and a clear distinction between the knower and the known (subject and object). Tacit knowledge, on the other hand, is defined as a function of subsidiary awareness and bodily activity. As such it exhibits such characteristics as: intuitive discovery, bodily expression, holistic recognition, embodied subjectivity, and a contextual distinction between the knower and the known. It should be clear that the concept of tacit knowledge renders extinct the common and comfortable dichotomy between "knowing how . . ." and "knowing that. . . ."

IV. RELIGIOUS EXPERIENCE

On the basis of the foregoing distinctions it is possible to construct a case for the philosophical legitimacy of religious knowledge. The following construction of such a case will consist of three phases: religious experience, religious knowing, and religious confirmation.

The foundation has been laid for attempting to understand experience in terms of the model of simultaneously interpenetrating dimensions. This model is offered as a replacement for the traditional model of a hierarchy of isolated realms. The difference between these two ways of viewing experience and reality is especially crucial with respect to the question of revelation. The more traditional realm-model forces one to conceive of revelation as something which comes from a realm which is totally distinct from, and in some sense foreign to, our own world. Thus when the question of identifying revelation arises, the religious person is forced either to maintain the necessity and reality of miraculous events and/or infallible communications (since these alone can serve as marks of the divine realm), or to give up the claim that revelation takes place. In this latter case religion becomes identified with humanism, while in the former it becomes identified with the bizarre. The realm-model offers little if any place to stand between these alternatives.

The dimension-model, on the other hand, makes it possible to conceive of revelation as the mediation of the religious dimension through the other dimensions of experience. Moreover, this way of viewing experience is more in line with the way the various aspects of reality are, in fact, experienced. The physical, moral, personal, and religious aspects of life are not experienced as separate blocks or compartments, but as vitally interrelated areas of concern and focus. Thus to conceive of experience as dimensional in structure is in harmony both with cognitive experience and with the possibility of a more adequate conception of revelation. This would indicate that the first step toward an understanding of religion and theology is to think of man as existing within a multi-dimensional universe where the knowledge of the various dimensions, including and especially the religious dimension, is mediated through the others.

To my mind the thinker who has developed this dimensional view of religious experience most fruitfully is John Hick. A presentation of his thought on this subject should serve to clarify my overall point. Hick addresses himself to the question "How is religious knowledge possible?" by maintaining

> . . . that "mediated" knowledge, such as is postulated by this religious claim, is already a common and accepted feature of our cognitive experience. To this end we must study a basic characteristic of human experience, which I shall call "significance," together with the correlative mental activity by which it is apprehended, which I shall call "interpretation." We shall find that interpretation takes place in relation to each of the three main types of existence, or orders of significance, recognized by human thought—the natural, the human, and the divine; and that in order to relate ourselves appropriately to each, a primary and unevidenceable act of interpretation is required which, when directed toward God, has traditionally been termed "faith." Thus . . . while the object of religious knowledge is unique, its basic epistemological pattern is that of all our knowing.[10]

The term "significance" is used by Hick to refer to that which gives order, or intelligibility, to the whole of experience. It involves the ability to differentiate between, and gather together, the various particulars of experience. Indeed, it might be defined as the very capacity to have what we call human experience. Hick seems to be saying that this "significance" is objective in that it is "built in" to the very structure of experience. Another way to characterize it is to call it that quality which enables the various aspects of experience to be brought into focus, reorganized, compared, and contrasted. The obvious similarities between the concept of significance and the contextual view of cognitive awareness developed in Section Three should not go unnoticed.

The concept of "interpretation" is introduced by Hick to specify the subjective correlate of significance. Thus it represents the activity, or response, of the mind in perceiving, or becoming aware of, significance in experience. On the object level, for instance, one becomes aware that the sense datum of his present experience can be interpreted, or responded to, in a variety of ways, such as: a red patch, a red thing, and a red book. Interpretations of significance in the various aspects of experience can occur on increasingly inclusive levels, depending on the extent and nature of one's past experience. Thus, to use Hick's example, a piece of paper with writing on it will be one thing to an illiterate savage, quite another to a literate person who does not know that particular language, and still another to someone who does know the language. In each case the person involved can be said to perceive both what the previous person perceives and something more as well. Here again there are obvious similarities between Hick's "interpretation" and the emphasis on knowledge as response in Section Three which must be noted. It is here that the personal commitment comes into play, as has been pointed out. On the religious level, such commitment or interpretation is termed "faith."

Hick goes on to suggest that this pattern of significance-interpretation works itself out on three levels of human experience—namely, the object level, the personal (or moral) level, and the religious level. The significance of personal experience is mediated through, but is not reducible to, object-significance. In like manner, the significance of religious experience is mediated through, but is not reducible to, object and personal experience.

Our inventory, then, shows three main orders of situational significance, corresponding to the threefold division of the universe, long entertained by human thought, into nature, man, and God. The significance for us of the physical world, nature, is that of an objective environment whose character and "laws" we must learn, and toward which we have continually to relate ourselves aright if we are to survive. The significance for us of the human world, man, is that of a realm of relationships in which we are responsible agents, subject to moral obligation. This world of moral significance is, so to speak, superimposed upon the natural world, so that relating ourselves to the moral world is not distinct from the business of relating ourselves to the natural world but is rather a particular manner of so doing. And likewise the more ultimately fateful and momentous matter of relating ourselves to the divine, to God, is not distinct from the task of directing ourselves within the natural and ethical spheres; on the contrary, it entails (without being reducible to) a way of so directing ourselves.

In the case of each of these three realms, the natural, the human, and the divine, a basic act of interpretation is required which discloses to us the existence of the sphere in question, thus providing the ground for our multifarious detailed interpretations within that sphere.[11]

As the last sentence of this quotation makes clear, Hick is concerned to point out that even on the physical (object) level of experience an act of interpretation is needed before any significance can be apperceived. Until some active, organizing response is made one does not have "experience" at all, only a "booming, buzzing confusion." Logically speaking, even a solipsistic interpretation of experience as a dream is a live option, and is by nature an interpretive act. Thus our disposition to interpret the sense-data of our experience in terms of the point of view of realism is pragmatically, but not logically, necessary. In a word, it is part of our form of life.

The apperception of significance on the moral level of experience is very similar to that of the physical level. A sense of moral obligation is the result of an interpretive response to an awareness of the significance of personal experience. It is, of course, possible to be unaware of, or to refuse to respond to, the significance of personal experience, and thereby fail to sense moral obligation. Such a situation is, in reality, simply the giving of another interpretation to personal experience. The difference between the interpretive apperception of physical and moral significance is that while the former is pragmatically necessary, the latter is not. It is less difficult to refuse to interpret personal experience as having moral significance than it is to refuse to interpret sensory experience as having physical (or real) significance. Nonetheless, for most human beings, moral interpretation is also part of the human form of life.

Hick is especially interested in the relation of mediation which exists between the physical and moral levels of significance. He maintains that moral significance is mediated through physical experience in such a way as to be dependent on it, but not reducible to it. The discernment of moral obligation is sensed *in* the experience of physical situations, but it is clearly more than an objective description of such situations would indicate. Noting this is of importance, since the same relation is held to exist between the apprehension of religious significance and moral and physical experience. Hick argues:

> Has this epistemological paradigm—of one order of significance superimposed upon and mediated through another—any further application? The contention of this essay is that it has. As ethical significance interpenetrates natural significance, so religious significance interpenetrates both ethical and natural. The divine is the highest and ultimate order of significance, mediating neither of the others and yet being mediated through both of them.
>
> Thus the primary religious perception, or basic act of religious interpretation, is not to be described as either a reasoned conclusion or an unreasoned hunch that there is a God. It is, putatively, an apprehension of the divine presence within the believer's human experience. It is not an inference to a general truth, but a "divine–human encounter," a mediated meeting with the living God.[12]

Such an apprehension of mediated, divine presence results in a total interpretation of all of human experience in terms of the religious dimension. This interpretation is not based on some knowledge of "outside reality," but is rather a perspective which a religious person takes toward the totality of his experience. Hick offers a reason why religious experience and knowledge have the rather open-ended structure which has been outlined above. His suggestion is that only this type of mediated structure safeguards human freedom and responsibility in relation to the religious dimension.[13] Any other structure either would make religious belief a necessity or would render it impossible. The concept of mediated knowledge avoids the extremes of infallibility and skepticism. To the crucial question concerning "What induces a man to experience the world religiously?" Hick says:

> The general nature of the answer is I think clear enough. Religious interpretations of human experience arise from special key points within that experience which act as focuses of religious significance. These key points both set going the tendency of the mind to interpret religiously and also act as patterns guiding the forms which such interpretations take. Among the infinite variety of life's phenomena some moment or object or person stands out as uniquely significant and revealing, providing a clue to the character of the whole. Some item of experience, or group of items, impresses the mind so deeply as to operate as a spiritual catalyst, crystallizing what was hitherto a cloud of relatively vague, amorphous feelings and aspirations, and giving a new and distinctive structure to the "apperceiving mass" by which we interpret our stream of experience.
>
> In Christianity the catalyst of faith is the person of Jesus Christ. It is in the historical figure of Jesus the Christ that, according to the Christian claim, God has in a unique and final way disclosed himself to men.[14]

V. RELIGIOUS KNOWING

With the dimensional and mediational structure of religious experience firmly established, it is now necessary to discuss its two-fold contextual nature in terms of awareness and response. The basic thrust of the claim to religious knowledge is that the person involved discerns (by means and in the midst of his everyday experience in the physical and moral dimensions of life) yet another dimension of reality which bestows an enriched appreciation upon his understanding of the more common dimensions. The discernment which takes place in such a disclosure especially enhances the person's moral sensitivity and his own self-understanding. In response to this disclosure-discernment situation, which corresponds to the "awareness continuum" discussed in connection with Polanyi's thought, the person's life becomes characterized by a profound sense of commitment which penetrates every aspect of his behavioral and conceptual existence. This response corresponds to the "activity continuum" discussed in connection with Polanyi's position.

Within the fabric provided by various cognitive contexts, the religious person discerns and responds to a dimension of reality which mediates itself through the other dimensions as that which gives existence and meaning to them. In this sense the religious person maintains that this new dimension is ultimate or "divine." Of course, for the Christian person the life and teachings of Jesus are taken to provide the context within which this ultimate dimension of reality is most clearly and deeply focused. Although not every context actually does disclose the religious dimension, every context would seem to be capable of such disclosure. Religious discernment and commitment can occur on all levels and in all aspects of human experience.

No one has done more to explicate the two-fold contextual structure of religious experience as awareness and response than Ian Ramsey, the present Bishop of Durham and former professor at Oriel College, Oxford.[15] Beginning by laying the groundwork of contextual disclosures which are not religious in nature, he proceeds to build a most helpful vantage point from which to appreciate the possibility and structure of religious disclosure. Beginning with perceptual disclosures, such as those discussed by Gestalt psychology, Ramsey moves through instances of increasing complexity wherein the knower can be said to know more than the sum of the "bare facts." He offers scientific laws, mathematical axioms, moral duty, and self-knowledge as examples of things which are known as mediated through other, more straightforward factors. Ramsey concludes his analysis of preliminary examples of disclosure with a discussion of our knowledge of other persons. Our knowledge of close friends and loved ones is related to, but is more than the sum of, our observations of their behavior. In fact, it is often the case that our knowledge of them as persons makes it possible for us to observe and understand certain aspects of their behavior more adequately. In Ramsey's words:

When such a disclosure occurs around a human pattern we speak of knowing people as they "really are," of there being "deep" affection between us, of loving them "for themselves." . . . "Husband," "mother," "father," "friend"—these are words which while they are undoubtedly associated with certain characteristic behavior patterns have a transcendent reference as well—and are grounded in disclosures.[16]

Having laid the groundwork for understanding the concept of disclosure by means of the foregoing examples, we can now move to a consideration of the concept of religious disclosure proper. Ramsey often uses the term "cosmic disclosure" in his discussion of this type of experience. It is absolutely essential to be perfectly clear at the outset about the one most important characteristic of religious, or cosmic, disclosure. Even as the disclosures discussed above are always mediated through empirical situations, religious disclosures are always so mediated as well. Moreover, and this is equally as important, one must view religious disclosures as mediated through the above-mentioned disclosures themselves! That is to say, disclosures of what may be called "the divine dimension" do not occur in an experiential vacuum, but rather arise out of perceptual, conceptual, moral, and personal disclosures, which in turn arise out of empirical settings.

> It is, I hope, evident that on this view when we appeal to "cosmic disclosures" we are not just talking about ourselves, nor merely of our own "experience," we are not just appealing to our own private way of looking at the world. . . . On the contrary a cosmic disclosure reveals something of whose existence we are aware precisely because we are aware of *being* confronted. Indeed we speak of a disclosure precisely when we acknowledge such a confrontation, something declaring itself to us, something relatively active when we are relatively passive.[17]

It is in this way, then, that one best understands what has been traditionally classified as religious experience. When one speaks of experiencing God he is calling attention to a discernment in which there has been disclosed to him a cosmic dimension of reality by means of the more common disclosures arising out of experiential situations. A person's awareness of God is similar to his awareness of objects (as opposed to "sense data"), moral obligation, and persons (including himself). All of this, of course, is not to say that the claimed awareness of God is as common as these other awarenesses, nor that it is necessarily a veridical experience. What has been discussed up to this point is the "empirical fact-and-more" nature of natural and religious disclosure. Religious experience is seen to be continuous with certain important aspects of everyday experience, when these aspects are understood in terms of their disclosure nature.

One other very important aspect of this interpretation of religious experience remains to be discussed. In every disclosure situation, on whatever level of experience, there is an element of "commitment." That is to say, whenever a disclosure "dawns," it gives rise to a corresponding commitment to act in a way which is appropriate to that which is being disclosed. In fact, it is possible to say that such commitment is what distinguishes a disclosure-situation from one which is routine or "flat." Thus it is through people's actions that their commitments are known, and through their commitments that their disclosures are known.

The universality of this element of commitment in all disclosure-situations can be seen by re-examining briefly the examples of disclosure already discussed. The grasping and using of words, sentences, and class-terms obviously involve a commitment in the sense that one's entire linguistic behavior is based upon the disclosure of this type of meaning. In this case, as in those which are to follow, it is important to avoid thinking of commitment exclusively in terms of an explicit, conscious response. As often as not, the commitments accompanying disclosures are tacit, but nonetheless real. The perception of objects and patterns also involves a tacit commitment which is appropriate to what is disclosed, as is evidenced by our ability to navigate among pieces of furniture and to master highly difficult skills.

As one moves up the scale of increasingly complex disclosures the corresponding commitments become more and more explicit and conscious. Grasping concepts like "axiom," "infinite," "causation," and "probability" involves a commitment to a certain procedure in the disciplines of mathematics and science. Seeing the point of moral discourse and relating to others as persons involve disclosures which express clear-cut commitments to that which is disclosed therein—namely, duty and personality. In the same way, our personal knowledge of ourselves results in a commitment, however implicit, concerning our own free activity and first-person discourse. On whatever level of human experience they occur, disclosures give rise to attitudinal and behavioral commitments which are commensurate with that which is disclosed therein.

The cosmic discernment which bears religious significance also evokes a commitment appropriate to its object. Although religious commitment is similar in certain respects to that of other forms of discernment, it has its own unique characteristics as well. At the very least it is more comprehensive and carries more depth than any other commitments. Ramsey puts it this way:

> So far we have seen two kinds of discernment-commitment—
> "mathematical" commitment and "personal" or "quasi-personal"
> commitment. Religious commitment, I suggest, partakes of both. It
> combines the total commitment to a pastime, to a ship, to a person,
> with the breadth of mathematical commitment. It combines the
> "depth" of personal or quasi-personal loyalty—to a sport, a boat,
> a loved one—with the range of mathematical and scientific devotion.
> It is a commitment suited to the whole job of living—not one just
> suited to building houses, or studying interplanetary motion, or even
> one suited to our own families, and no more.[18]

It is common knowledge that religious experience often brings about this high sense of commitment which, when properly interpreted, sheds light upon the totality of a person's heretofore non-religious commitments and experiences. What is not common knowledge, and what Ramsey is concerned to point out, is that the experiential logic of religious commitment is essentially similar to that of commitments involved at other levels of experience. Such an emphasis helps in the understanding of both religious commitment and non-religious commitment. The religious person's talk about God is to be understood as arising out of a disclosure-commitment situation which, in turn, both results from, and sheds light upon, the rest of his experience. Such talk will be related to object-language and will go beyond it as well.

> So our conclusion is that for the religious man "God" is a key
> word, an irreducible posit, an ultimate of explanation expressive of
> the kind of *commitment* he professes. It is to be talked about in terms

of the object-language over which it presides, but only when this object-language is qualified; in which case this qualified object-language becomes also currency for that odd *discernment* with which religious *commitment,* when it is not bigotry or fanaticism, will necessarily be associated.[19]

This, then, is the pattern of religious experience according to Ramsey's interpretation. It remains to be said that he associates revelation with cosmic disclosure. It should be noted once again that this approach to revelation stands midway between those which view it as strictly informational, on the one hand, and those which view it as strictly existential, on the other. The same relationship obtains with regard to the more extreme views of religious experience. The view discussed above will do justice to both the mystery and the empirical nature of religious experience.

One final point needs to be made before this discussion of the contextual, awareness-response nature of religious knowledge can be brought to a close. As was indicated in some detail at the close of Section Three, it is the interaction between the awareness and the response continua which gives rise to human knowledge. It is in this way that claims to religious knowledge are to be understood as well. As in the case of knowledge in general, religious knowledge may take a variety of forms along the continuum between the tacit and explicit poles. When one is focally aware of the religious dimension and responds conceptually, then religious knowledge as explicit occurs. When, on the other hand, one is subsidiarily aware of, and makes a more bodily response to, the religious dimension, then religious knowledge as tacit occurs.

Although throughout this and previous Sections it has been necessary to speak of these two interacting continua one at a time, it should always be borne in mind that the relationship between them is not one of sequence. That is, a person does not usually become aware of a dimension or context and *then* respond to it. Although this is a convenient way of speaking, and harmless if not carried too far, the whole drive of this paper has focused in the effort to establish the simultaneous interaction between these two continua within the various contexts and dimensions of existence. There is a sense in which one does not become aware of certain realities until he responds in certain ways. The dynamic and contextual structure of cognitive experience cannot be subjected to a more thorough analysis in terms of the "given" and the response. Awareness and activity occur simultaneously. Together they give rise to knowledge. The intricacies of the relation between these two aspects of the knowing situation cannot be made explicit. Nevertheless, they can be known tacitly since they lie at the base of the very possibility of all other knowledge.

The foregoing considerations render it necessary to conclude that, at least for the most part, religious knowledge is tacit in structure. This follows first from the fact that the awareness of the religious dimension is always mediated by means of two other dimensions. This is why, in both traditional and contemporary theology, there is always a certain emphasis placed on the concept of the "hiddenness of God." To come at the point from the other side, religious knowledge is primarily tacit because the deepest religious response is always a matter of action as distinguished from concepts. This is not to suggest that the two can ever be separated from one another. It is to suggest that the more profoundly something affects us the less adequate is our attempt to conceptualize it.

Thus out of the interaction of subsidiary awareness of God with an indwelling response to God arises the tacit knowledge which forms the foundation of all religious knowledge. There are, to be sure, degrees to which certain aspects of tacit religious knowledge can be rendered more or less explicit. Indeed, such rendering is necessary because man is a linguistic being. Nevertheless, the most essential aspects can never be made explicit.

VI. RELIGIOUS CONFIRMATION

Finally, the question of the confirmation of religious knowledge must be dealt with. The basis for dealing with this question was set forth in Section Two where it was argued that truth is a function of the purpose and setting for which and within which a given utterance is made. In this broad sense, truth is determined pragmatically. Moreover, in Section Three I maintained that as the cognitive context shifts from the more explicit end of the knowledge continuum to the more tacit end, the criteria for judging truth also become increasingly tacit. As these criteria become increasingly tacit, they become more a function of pragmatic indwelling than of analytic conceptualizing. Thus the truth of a tacit claim to knowledge can only be adjudicated by tracing the overall harmony and fruitfulness of the claim as it is embodied in the behavior and linguistic posits of the person making the claim.

It is on this basis, then, that the criteria for judging claims to religious knowledge must be understood. There are, to be sure, certain standard (although not absolute) criteria for judging certain explicit claims. Historical, sociological, and psychological statements often form part of one's claim to religious knowledge, and these are to be treated in the same way as other such statements and claims. However, as this type of explicit talk begins to shade off into more properly theological discourse, the situation becomes more tricky. Here the explicit and tacit factors become inextricably mixed and must be dealt with simultaneously. Finally, when the claims to religious knowledge operate entirely beneath the threshold of explicit knowledge, then they can be judged only in terms of activity and styles of life. Nonetheless, it is possible to evaluate such claims in terms of their overall consistency and fruitfulness.

The approach to the criteria of religious truth here being defended is in large measure based upon the insights of Max Black, as suggested in the following quotation in which Black calls attention to the necessity of viewing the "models" upon which theoretical frameworks are built as cognitive in nature.

We have seen that the successful model must be isomorphic with its domain of application. So there is a rational basis for using the model. In stretching the language by which the model is described in such a way as to fit the new domain, we pin our hopes upon the existence of a common structure in both fields. If the hope is fulfilled, there will have been an objective ground for the analogical transfer. For we call a mode of investigation rational when it has a rationale, that is to say when we can find reasons which justify what we do and that allow for articulate appraisal and criticism. The putative isomorphism between model and field of application provides such a rationale and yields such standards of critical judgment. We can determine the validity of a given model by checking the extent of its isomorphism with its intended application. In appraising models as good or bad, we need not rely on the sheerly pragmatic test of fruitfulness in discovery; we can, in principle at least, determine the "goodness" of their "fit." [20]

Following Black, we must realize that high-level models in both physical and social science are "analogue models" and not "picture models." By this I mean that such models do not simply represent the parts of a certain aspect of reality, like a model ship or cell. Rather, they integrate and illuminate the functional and structural relationships between the parts and the whole, and between the particular aspect of reality in question and human experience. Thus they are closer to metaphor in nature than they are to exact pictures. The confirmation of this type of model is not based on a one-to-one correspondence between its elements and those of an external reality. The analogue model is confirmed or disconfirmed in terms of its ability to organize, integrate, and illuminate past and present experience, and to predict and suggest new possibilities concerning future experience. Such confirmation is pragmatic and experiential, but is also extremely complex and flexible. In addition, there will always remain a certain element of mystery and uncertainty. The purpose of making this point is to underline the fact that the theoretical sciences are not as straightforwardly "empirical" as many empiricists maintain.

More to the point, it must be seen that the type of models employed in theological discourse are also analogical in nature. Moreover, since they are meant to help us to map the complex mysteries of personal and ultimate reality, they will of necessity be even more complex and flexible than those of the theoretical sciences. Nevertheless, they are still based upon, and must be confirmed by, human experience. Each and every model must be scrutinized, not in terms of its ability to make strict, deductive predictions about carefully controlled experiments, but in terms of its broad "empirical fit" with the facts of every area of human experience. As Ramsey puts it:

> These will be the models whose links with observable facts are not predictive, after the fashion of scientific models. These models will work in terms of what in the first lecture I called empirical fit. For it is empirical fit, rather than deductive verifications, which characterizes models which are distinctively personal. Let me illustrate. From "a

loves b" nothing can be rigorously deduced which permits of appeal to experiment and consequent verification or falsification. For instance, someone might allege that if "a loves b" there will be some occasion when a will be found planning for b's happiness; but a might some day plan for b's happiness simply in the hope of favours to come—and apparent experimental verification would be wholly deceptive. Alternatively, from "a loves b" someone might suppose that a would never be seen for example in any sort of way which might cause b even momentary unhappiness. But this would be a far too shallow view of human relationships; love indeed is "deepened" through tensions lived through and redeemed. In brief, "a loves b" will only be verified in terms of what I called in the last lecture "empirical fit" and the test will be how stable the assertion is as an overall characterization of a complex, multi-varied pattern of behavior which it is impossible in a particular case to specify deductively beforehand.[21]

This same concept of empirical fit must be applied to the question of the criteria of religious truth, especially in its more tacit forms. Furthermore, this is about all that can be said about the confirmation of claims to religious knowledge. Each person must look to his own experience and must seek to do justice to it in the most responsible way possible. Because of the necessarily tacit roots of religious knowledge, the degree of agreement will never be as great as that in other areas of knowledge. Nevertheless, there will be, and indeed always has been, much more agreement than many thinkers have been willing to admit. There is a large amount of "intersubjectivity" achieved, in spite of the diversity, among those within various religious traditions. Although it is very difficult, judgments can be and are made concerning claims to religious knowledge. There is a difference between a person who believes certain religious claims for all the wrong reasons (because his parents did, because it is comforting, etc.) and the person who believes as a result of profound existential struggle and honest cognitive searching. This difference is best accounted for in terms of the concept of religious knowledge as tacit.

One final facet of the nature of religious confirmation needs to be emphasized. As has been maintained all along, the more tacit the knowledge the more it is expressed in terms of active embodiment of indwelling. This is especially true of religious knowledge. Thus the most appropriate criterion for evaluating claims to religious knowledge is that of the quality of life embodied in the claim. In other words, there is a sense in which only by participating in, or indwelling, the religious way of life, can a person come to know the force and value of its claims. This is, of course, true of any other "form of life" as well. Only to the degree that one participates in such realities as friendship, marriage, democracy, scientific or philosophic activity, will he be able to ascertain the value of the knowledge which pertains to them. In the final analysis, all knowledge is based upon commitment. In the words of my former colleague, Carl F. Walters:

> There may be some questions which are not adequately answered merely by continued speculation and discussion. Some knowledge is not available to us simply through abstract conception and oral or written language. Although we may have technical knowledge of the factual data of tone, timing, and rhythm pattern, we may not *know* Handel's *Messiah* in the fullest sense until we give ourselves to it and take a part in singing it. Similarly, we cannot say that we truly dig James Brown's music until we let ourselves go and dance to it. You will not really know your wife or husband (if ever) until you embrace her or him in committed, responsible, and vulnerable love. In analogous fashion, we may not really know the God of Jesus until we identify with him and participate in his self-giving, life-giving, action—wherever it is. Even then the elements of uncertainty and risk, the possibility of doubt, and the necessity of faith, will not be excluded.[22]

Section One of the present paper was devoted to an analysis of the contemporary stalemate between empiricism and existentialism resulting from their mutual acceptance of the fact–value dichotomy. In particular, this epistemological dualism was seen to lie at the heart of the difficulty over the possibility of religious knowledge. In short, if the knowledge of God is related to the factual realm too exclusively, it is impossible for it to meet the requirements for cognitivity; if it is related to the valuational realm too exclusively it loses its cognitive significance. Sections Two and Three were devoted to replacing the contemporary dichotomy between fact and value with a view of language and knowledge based upon dimensional and contextual significance. In this way knowledge was seen to be a continuum stretched between the tacit and explicit poles, which in turn are the function of the interaction between awareness and response.

In the final three sections it has been argued that this contextual epistemology, and especially its concept of tacit knowledge, has provided a way of approaching the possibility of religious knowledge in a highly fruitful fashion. An understanding of knowledge as tacit combines the factual and valuational dimensions in such a way as to make the concept of religious knowledge a viable possibility.

NOTES

1. Cf. for example *Critique of Pure Reason*, A 636/B 664. Also see John Smith, *Reason and God* (New Haven: Yale University Press, 1961), pp. 18–19.

2. For a more detailed account cf. my "Kant, Kierkegaard, and Religious Knowledge," *Philosophy and Phenomenological Research*, 28 (1967), 188ff.

3. Cf. L. Wittgenstein, *Tractatus Logico-Philosophicus* (London: Routledge, 1961). Two brief quotations will have to suffice: (1) "One name stands for one thing, another for another thing, and they are combined with one another. In this way the whole group—like a *tableau vivant*—presents a state of affairs" (#4.031); (2) "In order to tell whether a picture is true or false we must compare it with reality" (#2.223).

4. Cf. L. Wittgenstein, *Philosophical Investigations* (New York: Macmillan, 1953). See especially #23, #12, #241, #242.

5. J. L. Austin, *How To Do Things With Words* (Cambridge: Harvard University Press, 1961). See especially pp. 147–148.

6. *Personal Knowledge* (Chicago: University of Chicago Press, 1958), p. x (Preface).

7. *Ibid.*

8. *The Tacit Dimension* (New York: Doubleday, 1966), p. 22.

9. "The Logic of Tacit Inference," *Philosophy*, 41 (1966), 14.

10. *Faith and Knowledge* (Ithaca: Cornell University Press, 1957), p. 110.

11. *Ibid.*, pp. 121–122.

12. *Ibid.*, pp. 127, 129.

13. *Ibid.*, p. 172.

14. *Ibid.*, pp. 196, 197.

15. Cf. especially Chapter One of *Religious Language* (New York: Macmillan, 1955) and Chapter Two of *Prospect for Metaphysics* (New York: Philosophical Library, 1961).

16. "Towards the Relevant in Theological Language," *The Modern Churchman*, 8 (1964), 50.

17. "Talking About God: Models, Ancient, and Modern," in *Myth and Symbol*, ed. F. W. Dillistone (London: SPCK Press, 1966), p. 87.

18. *Religious Language*, p. 39.

19. *Ibid.*, p. 53.

20. *Models and Metaphors* (Ithaca: Cornell University Press, 1961), p. 238.

21. *Models and Mystery* (New York: Oxford University Press, 1964), p. 38.

22. "Where the Action Is," *Theology Today*, 24 (1967), 207.

19

On the Observability

of the Self

RODERICK M. CHISHOLM

Brown University

I

A traveller of good judgment may mistake his way, and be
unawares led into a wrong track; and while the road is fair
before him, he may go on without suspicion and be followed
by others; but when it ends in a coal-pit, it requires no great
judgment to know that he hath gone wrong, nor perhaps to find
out what misled him.—THOMAS REID, *Inquiry into the Human
Mind.*[1]

THE TWO GREAT TRADITIONS OF CONTEMPORARY WESTERN
PHILOSOPHY—"phenomenology" and "logical analysis"—seem
to meet, unfortunately, at the extremes. The point of contact
is the thesis according to which one is never aware of a *subject*
of experience. The thesis in question does not pertain to the

Reprinted from *Philosophy and Phenomenological Research,* 30 (1969), 7–21,
with the permission of the author and the publishers.

perception of one's *body*. If we are identical with our bodies
and if, as all but skeptics hold, we do perceive our bodies, then,
whether we realize it or not, we also perceive ourselves. The
thesis has to do, rather, with what we find when we consult the
data of our immediate experience, or when, as Hume puts it,
we enter most intimately into what we call ourselves. Thus
Sartre seems to say that, although we may apprehend things
which are *pour-soi*, things which are manifested or presented
to the self, we cannot apprehend the self to which, or to whom,
they are manifested—we cannot apprehend the self as it is in
itself, as it is *en-soi*.[2] And Russell has frequently said that the
self or subject is not "empirically discoverable"; Carnap expressed what I take to be the same view by saying that "the
given is subjectless."[3] I say that it is unfortunate that the members of the two great philosophical traditions happen to meet
at this particular point, of all places. For at this particular
point, if I am not mistaken, both groups have lost their way.

Both traditions trace their origins, in part, to Hume.[4] I suggest that, if we are to find out what went wrong, we should
turn back to the doctrines of Hume, where we will find a number of obvious, but disastrous, mistakes.

II

The first mistake was a very simple one. Consider the following remark which may be found in Hume's "Abstract of a
Treatise of Human Nature." Hume wrote: "As our idea of
any body, a peach, for instance, is only that of a particular
taste, color, figure, size, consistency, etc., so our idea of any
mind is only that of particular perceptions without the notion
of anything we call substance, either simple or compound."[5]
This seems to me to be very obviously false, but many philosophers, I am afraid, tend all too easily and unthinkingly to assume that it is true.

Is it true that our idea of a peach is an idea only of a particular taste, color, figure, size, consistency, and the like, and
analogously that our ideas of such things as ships, trees, dogs,
and houses are ideas only of the particular qualities or attributes which these things are commonly said to have? One is
tempted to say instead that our idea of a peach is an idea of

something which *has* a particular taste, color, figure, size, and consistency; and analogously for the other familiar physical things. But even this is not quite right. Our idea of a peach is not an idea of something which *has* the particular qualities, say, of sweetness, roundness, and fuzziness. It is an idea of something which *is* sweet and round and fuzzy.

More pedantically, our idea of a peach is an idea of an individual x such that x is sweet and x is round and x is fuzzy. By thus using variables and adjectives, we express the fact that the object of our idea is not the set of qualities sweetness, roundness, and fuzziness, but the concrete thing which *is* sweet and round and fuzzy. We also make clear, what is essential to our idea of a peach, that the thing which is round is the *same* thing as the thing which is sweet and also the *same* thing as the thing which is fuzzy.

Leibniz saw the point very clearly when he criticized Locke's *Essay Concerning Human Understanding.* When we consider any person or thing, he said, what comes before the mind is always a *concretum* and not a set of abstract things or qualities; we may consider something as knowing, or something as warm, or something as shining, but we do not thereby consider knowledge, or warmth, or light. The abstract things, he noted, are far more difficult to grasp than are the corresponding *concreta.*[6]

I cannot help but think that the point is a simple-minded one. "Our idea of a peach is not an idea of sweetness, roundness, and fuzziness . . . ; it is an idea of something which is sweet and also round and also fuzzy. . . ." One would not have even thought of mentioning it, had not philosophers denied it and constructed fantastic systems on the basis of its negation. A small mistake at the outset, as the Philosopher said, turns out to be a great one in the end.

If the first part of Hume's observation is wrong, then so is the second. Our idea of "a mind" (if by "a mind" we mean, as Hume usually does, a person, or a self) is not an idea only of "particular perceptions." It is not the idea of the perception of love or hate and the perception of cold or warmth, much less an idea of love or hate and of heat or cold. It is an idea of that which loves or hates, and of that which feels cold or warm (and, of course, of much more besides). That is to say, it is an idea of an x such that x loves or x hates and such that x feels cold and x feels warm, and so forth.

III

I would say that a second error which we find in Hume's writings, and in the writings of those who follow him with respect to the observability of the self, has to do with the interpretation of certain data or evidence. Hume argued, it will be recalled, that he and most of the rest of mankind are "nothing but a bundle or collection of different perceptions." And in support of this "bundle theory," he cites a kind of *negative* evidence. He tells us, with respect to a certain proposition, that he *has* certain evidence for saying that he has *no* evidence for that proposition. But when he cites the evidence he *has* for saying that he has *no* evidence for the proposition, he seems to presuppose, after all, that he *does* have evidence for the proposition.

What Hume said was this: "For my part, when I enter most intimately into what I call *myself*, I always stumble on some particular perception or other, of heat or cold, light or shade, love or hatred, pain or pleasure. I never can catch *myself* at any time without a perception, and never can observe anything but the perception." [7] As Professor Price once observed, it looks very much as though the self which Hume professed to be unable to find is the one which he finds to be stumbling—to be stumbling onto different perceptions. [8] How can he say that he does not find himself—if he is correct in saying that he finds himself to be stumbling and, more fully, that he finds himself to be stumbling on certain things and not to be stumbling on certain other things?

We must take care not to misinterpret the difficulty. The difficulty is *not* that, in formulating his evidence for the "bundle theory" of the self, Hume presupposes that there *is* a self. For this presupposition, that there is a self, is not contrary to what Hume wishes to say. The "bundle theory," after all, is not intended to *deny* that there is a self. It is intended merely to say *what* the self is and what it is not. There is a self, or there are selves, according to Hume, and what selves are are "bundles of perceptions."

The difficulty is that Hume appeals to certain evidence to show that there are only perceptions, and that when he tells us what this evidence is, he implies not only (i) that there is, as he puts it in his example, heat or cold, light or shade, love or hatred, but also (ii) that there is *someone* who finds heat or cold, light or shade, love or hatred, and moreover (iii) that the one who finds heat or cold is *the same as* the one who finds love or hatred and *the same as* the one who finds light or shade, and finally (iv) that this one does not in fact stumble upon anything but perceptions. It is not unreasonable to ask, therefore, whether Hume's report of his fourth finding is consistent with his report of the second and the third. If Hume finds what he says he finds—that is to say, if he finds not only perceptions, but also that *he* finds them and hence that there is *someone* who finds them—how can his premises be used to establish the conclusion that he never observes anything but perceptions?

One may protest: "But this is not fair to Hume. It is true that, in reporting his data, he used such sentences as 'I stumble on heat or cold' and 'I never observe anything but perceptions.' He did not need to express himself in this way. Instead of saying 'I stumble on heat or cold' or 'I find heat or cold,' he could have said, more simply, 'Heat or cold is found.' And instead of saying 'I never observe anything but perceptions,' he could have said, more simply, 'Nothing but perceptions are found.' He could have reported his data in this way; and had he done so, he would not have presupposed that there exists an x such that x succeeds in finding certain things and such that x fails to find certain others."

But *could* Hume have reported his data in this selfless way? Let us recall that his findings are both positive and negative and let us consider just the negative ones. It is one thing to say, modestly and empirically, "I find nothing but impressions or perceptions." It is quite another thing to say, rashly and nonempirically, "Nothing but perceptions or impressions are found." The point will be clearer, perhaps, if we consider another type of example. I may look around the room and, from where I stand, fail to see any cats or dogs in the room. If I express this negative finding modestly and empirically, I will simply say "I do not see any cats or dogs." But if I say, solely on the basis of my negative observation, "No cats or dogs are seen," then I will be speaking rashly and nonempirically and going far beyond what my data warrant. How do I know what other people or God may find? And how can I be sure that there are no unseen dogs or cats? Clearly Hume would not have been justified in saying, "Nothing but impressions are to be found." And in fact he made no such subjectless report. He said, referring to himself, that *he* found nothing but impressions.

The difficulty may be put briefly. It is essential to Hume's argument that he report not only what it is that he finds but also what it is that he fails to find. But the two types of report are quite different. The fact that a man finds a certain proposition p to be true does warrant a subjectless report to the effect that p is true. For, finding that p is true entails that p is true. But the fact that he fails to find a certain proposition q to be true does not similarly warrant any subjectless report about q. For one's failure to find that q is true entails nothing about the truth of q. The fact that a man fails to find that q is true entitles him to say only that *he,* at least, does not find that q is true. And this would not be a subjectless report.

What Hume found, then, was not merely the particular perceptions, but also the fact that *he* found those perceptions, as well as the fact that *he* failed to find certain other things. And these are findings with respect to himself.

Referring to the view that the self is a substance persisting through time, Hume said that we have no "idea of self, after the manner it is here explain'd. For from what impression could this idea be derived?" Given our first two general points, could the proper reply be this—that one may derive the idea of such a self from any impression whatever?[9]

IV

Why, then, is it so tempting to agree with Hume in his report of his negative findings?

I think we tend to reason as follows. We suppose—mistakenly, it seems to me—that if we do perceive or apprehend ourselves in our immediate experience, then such perception or apprehension must resemble in essential respects the way in which we perceive or apprehend the familiar external things around us. And then we find, in fact, that we do *not* perceive or apprehend ourselves in our immediate experience in the way in which we apprehend or perceive the familiar external things around us.

Thus whenever we perceive—say, whenever we *see*—a spatial object, then the object which we perceive has certain proper parts which we perceive and certain proper parts which we do not perceive. Suppose, for example, that I see a cat. Then we may say of that side of the cat which faces me that I see certain parts of *it*. But I do not see *all* the parts of the side which faces me (I do not see those parts I would see if I took a closer look or used a microscope), and I do not see *any* of the parts of the insides or any of the parts of the sides which face away. One of the results in changes of spatial perspective is that certain parts become seen which had not been seen before and certain parts cease to be seen which had been seen before. And so, if the distance between our body and the perceived object is not too great, we may now look over this part and now look over that. We may look more closely and scrutinize —and this means that we may now see smaller parts which we had not seen before. And analogously for the nonvisual senses. But whatever our perspective upon the perceived object may be, there will always be certain parts of the perceived object which we do perceive and certain other parts of the perceived object which we do not perceive. Moreover, and this is the important point about external perception, if we know that we are perceiving a certain physical thing, then we are also capable of knowing that we are perceiving something which is just a proper part of that thing. But the situation is different when we perceive ourselves to be thinking.

I may perceive myself to be thinking and know that I am doing so and yet be unable to know whether I am perceiving any proper part of anything which I am perceiving. It may be, for all anyone knows, that whenever I perceive myself to be thinking, I *do* perceive some part of myself. This would be the case, for example, if I could not perceive myself to be thinking without perceiving some part of my body, and if, moreover, I were identical with my body or with that part of my body. But it is not true that, whenever I perceive myself to be thinking, I thereby perceive what I can *know* to be a part of myself. (Whether or not I am identical with my body or with some part of my body, I do not *know* that I am.) In short, to know that I perceive the cat to be standing, I must know that I perceive a proper part of the cat, or of the cat's body; but to know that I perceive myself to be thinking I need *not* know that I perceive what is a proper part of myself. Sartre said that the ego is "opaque"; I would think it better to say that the ego is "transparent." [10]

Ordinarily if a man can be said to perceive *that* the cat is standing, then he may also be said, more simply, to perceive *the cat*. But the locution "S perceives that *a* is F" does not entail the simpler locution, "S perceives *a*." [11] Compare "Jones perceives that Smith is no longer in the room" and "Jones perceives that the lights are on next door." Could it be, then, that a man might be aware of himself as experiencing *without* thereby being aware of himself? Let us approach this question somewhat obliquely, by recalling still another familiar source of philosophical perplexity.

During the first third of this century, British and American philosophers were perplexed about the status of what they called "sense-data" or "appearances." They thought, for example, that if a man were to walk around a table, while focusing upon the white tablecloth on the top, he could experience a great variety of sense-data or appearances. Some of these entities would be rectangular like the table-top itself; they would be the ones he would sense if he were able to get his head directly above the table and then look down. Most of them, however, would be rhomboids of various sorts. If the lighting conditions were good and the man's eyes in proper order, most of the appearances would be white, like the tablecloth. But if the man were wearing rose-colored glasses, he might sense appearances which were pink, or if he were a victim of jaundice, he might sense appearances which were yellow. The other senses, as well as imagination, were thought to bring us into relation with still other types of appearances or sense-datum.

The nature and location of these strange entities, as we all know, caused considerable puzzlement, and imposing metaphysical systems were constructed to bring them together with the rest of the world. I am sure that it is not necessary now to unravel all the confusions which were involved in this kind of talk, for the sense-datum theory has been ridiculed about as thoroughly as any philosophical theory can be ridiculed. But we should remind ourselves of one of these confusions—another very simple mistake. It was the mistake which H. A. Prichard had in mind, I think, when he used the expression, "the sense-datum fallacy." [12]

It was assumed that, if a physical thing appears white or rhomboidal or bitter to a man, then the man may be said to sense or to be aware of an appearance which *is* white, or an appearance which *is* rhomboidal, or an appearance which *is* bitter. It was assumed that if a dog presents a canine appearance, then the dog presents an appearance which *is* canine. (Thus Professor Lovejoy wrote: "No man doubts that when he brings to mind the look of a dog he owned when a boy, there is something of a canine sort immediately present to and therefore compresent with his consciousness, but that it is quite certainly not that dog in the flesh." [13]) And then it was assumed, more generally, that whenever we have a true statement of the form " Such-and-such a physical thing appears, or looks, or seems - - - to Mr. Jones," we can derive a true statement of the form "Mr. Jones is aware of an appearance which is in fact - - - ." But this assumption is quite obviously false.[14] Consider the following reasoning, which would be quite sound if the assumption were true: "I know that Mr. Simione is an Italian and that he is also old and sick. I saw him this morning and I can assure you that he also appeared Italian, and he appeared old and sick as well. Therefore Mr. Simione presents an appearance which, like himself, really is Italian, and he also presents an appearance which, like himself once again, is old and sick." It is absurd to suppose that an appearance, like a man, may be Italian or old or sick; it is absurd to suppose that an appearance may be a dog; and, I think, it is equally absurd to suppose that an appearance, like a tablecloth, may be rectangular, or pink, or white.

When the philosophers thus talked about sense-data or appearances, they were, however inadequately, reporting *something* which is very familiar to us all, and we should not let their philosophical theories blind us to the fact that there is such a going-on as sensation and that the experiences we have when we observe the familiar things around us may be varied merely by varying the conditions of observation. Suppose now that we were considering this fact on its own, and without any thoughts about Hume's theory or about Hume on the observability of the self. How would we describe it if we are to avoid the absurdities of the sense-datum fallacy?

I think that we would do well to compare the "grammar" of our talk about appearances with that of our talk about feelings. Consider the sentence "I feel depressed." It does not imply that there is a relation between me and some other entity; it simply tells one *how* I feel. The adjective "depressed," in other words, does not describe the *object* of my feeling; rather, if I may put the matter so, it describes the *way* in which I feel. It could be misleading, therefore, to use the longer sentence "I have a depressed feeling" in place of the shorter "I feel depressed." For the longer sentence, "I have a depressed feeling," has a syntactical structure very much like that of "I have a red book." Hence one might be led to suppose, mistakenly, that it implies the existence of *two* entities, one of them *had* by the other. And taking "a depressed feeling" as one would ordinarily take "a red book," one might also be led to suppose, again mistakenly, that the feeling which the person is said to have resembles the person in being *itself* depressed. I say one *might* be misled in these ways by the sentence "I have a depressed feeling," though I do not know of anyone who ever *has* been misled by it.

It is quite obvious, I think, that in such sentences as "I feel depressed" the verb is used to refer to a certain type of *undergoing*. This undergoing is what traditionally has been called being in a conscious state, or being in a sentient state. And the adjective, in such sentences as "I feel depressed," is used to qualify the verb and thus to specify further the type of undergoing to which the verb refers. The adjective could be said to function, therefore, as an adverb. Thus the sentences "I feel depressed" and "I feel exuberant" are related in the way in which "He runs slowly" and "He runs swiftly" are related, and not in the way in which "He has a red book" and "He has a brown book" are related. In short, *being depressed* is not a predicate of the feeling; rather, *feeling depressed* is a predicate of the man.

I suggest that the sentences "I am aware of a red appearance" and "I am experiencing a red sensation" are to be interpreted in the way in which we interpreted "I have a depressed feeling" and "I feel a wave of exuberance." Despite their grammatical or syntactical structure, neither sentence tells us that there are *two* entities which are related in a certain way. They, too, ascribe a certain type of undergoing to the person. The adjective "red," in "I am aware of a red appearance" and "I am experiencing a red sensation," is used adverbially to qualify this undergoing.[15] It would be useful, at least for the purpose of philosophy, if there were a verb—say, the verb "to sense"—which we could use to refer to this type of undergoing. Then we could say that such a sentence as "I am aware of a red appearance" tells us *how* the subject is sensing. Or, better perhaps, it tells us in what *way* he is sensing. For to be aware of "a red appearance," presumably, is to sense in one of the ways that people do when, under favorable conditions, they look at objects which are red.[16] (If we may say that a man "senses redly," may we also say that he "senses rhomboidally" or "senses rectangularly"? There is no reason why we may not—especially if we can identify one's sensing rhomboidally, or one's sensing rectangularly, with one of the ways in which a person might be expected to sense if, under favorable conditions, he were to observe objects which are rhomboidal, or rectangular.)

We may summarize this way of looking at the matter by saying that so-called appearances or sense-data are "affections" or "modifications" of the person who is said to experience them.[17] And this is simply to say that those sentences in which we seem to predicate properties of appearances can be paraphrased into other sentences in which we predicate properties only of the self or person who is said to sense those appearances. If this is correct, then appearances would be paradigm cases of what the scholastics called *"entia entis"* or *"entia per accidens."* These things are not entities in their own right; they are "accidents" of other things. And what they are accidents *of* are persons or selves.

It is interesting to note, in passing, that Hume himself criticizes the view that appearances are modifications of persons or selves—and that, in doing so, he provides us with an excellent example of the sense-datum fallacy. First he notes the absurdity of Spinoza's view, according to which such things as the sun, moon, and stars, and the earth, seas, plants, animals, men, ships, and houses are in fact only "modifications" of a single divine substance. And then he argues that, if this Spinozistic view is absurd, then so, too, is the view that "impressions" or "ideas" are only modifications of the self. But the reason he cites for this seems clearly to be based upon the sense-datum fallacy. For, he says, when I consider "the universe of thought, or my impressions and ideas," I then "observe *another* sun, moon, and stars, and earth, and seas, covered and inhabited by plants and animals; towns, houses, mountains, rivers. . . ." [18] In other words, if a real dog cannot be a modification of God, then an appearance of a dog cannot be a modification of me!

Why this way of interpreting appearances? For one thing, it seems to me, we multiply entities beyond necessity if we suppose that, in addition to the person who is in a state of undergoing or sensing, there is a certain *further* entity, a sense-datum or an appearance, which is the object of that undergoing or sensing. And for another thing, when we do thus multiply entities beyond necessity, we entangle ourselves in philosophical puzzles we might otherwise have avoided. ("Does the red sense-datum or appearance have a back side as well as a front side? Where is it located? Does it have any weight? What is it made of?")

And now we may return to the question which brought us to this consideration of appearances: "Could it be that a man might be aware of himself as experiencing without thereby being aware of himself?" If what I have suggested is true, then the answer should be negative. For, in being aware of ourselves as experiencing, we are, *ipso facto,* aware of the self or person—of the self or person as being affected in a certain way.

This is not to say, of course, that we do not *also* perceive or observe external physical things. It is in virtue of the ways in which we are "appeared to" by the familiar things around us, of the ways in which we are affected or modified by them, that we perceive them to be what they are. If, under the right conditions, the fields should appear green to me, then I would *see* the fields to be green.[19] And at the same time I could become directly aware of—immediately acquainted with—the fact that I myself am modified or affected in a certain way.

If what I have been saying is true, then there are two rather different senses in which we may be said to apprehend ourselves.

The first type of apprehension was what Hume himself reported—that *he* found heat or cold, that *he* found light or shade, and that *he* did not find himself, at least in the sense in which he found heat or cold and light or shade. He found, to repeat, that there was *someone* who found heat or cold, that this same someone found light or shade, and that this same someone did not in the same sense find himself. That we apprehend ourselves in this first sense would seem to be clear whatever view we may take about the nature of appearances, or of being appeared to.

And if the particular view of appearances which I have proposed is true, then we apprehend ourselves in still another sense. For if appearances, as I have said, are "accidents" or "modifications" of the one who is appeared to, then *what* one apprehends when one apprehends heat or cold, light or shade, love or hatred, is simply oneself. Whether one knows it or not, one apprehends *oneself* as being affected or modified.

The two points may be summarized by returning to the figure of the bundle theory. One may ask, with respect to any bundle of things, what is the nature of the bundle and what is the nature of the bundled. What is it which holds the particular items together, and what are the particular items which are thus held together? Now, according to the second of the two points which I have just made, the items within the bundle are nothing but states of the person. And according to the first point, as we may now put it, what ties these items together is the fact that that same self or person apprehends them all. Hence, if these two points are both correct, the existence of particular bundles of perceptions presupposes in two rather different ways the existence of selves or persons who are not mere bundles of perceptions.

VI

And there is one more simple mistake which we may note briefly.

One may grant everything which I have said ("Yes, there are those senses in which one may be said to observe the self") and yet insist, at the same time, that we really know nothing about the self which we do thus observe ("Knowing what states the self is in does not entitle you to say that you know anything about the self"). What kind of reasoning is this?

Let us recall what Kant says about the subject of experiences —about the I which, as he puts it, we "attach to our thoughts." Whenever we find ourselves thinking or judging, he said, we attach this I to the thinking or judging, and then we say to ourselves, or think to ourselves, "I think" and "I judge." Yet, although we manage somehow to "attach" the I to the thinking or judging, we do so "without knowing anything of it, either by direct acquaintance or otherwise." The I is known, he says, "only through the thoughts which are its predicates, and of it, apart from them, we cannot have any concept whatever." [20]

Kant seems to be telling us this: even if there is a subject which thinks, we have no acquaintance with it at all and we can never know what it is. And his *reason* for saying that we have no acquaintance with it all and can never hope to know what it is, would seem to be this: the most we can ever hope to know about the subject is to know what predicates it has—to know what properties it exemplifies; and apart from this— apart from knowing what predicates it has or what properties it exemplifies—we can never know anything of it at all.

During the latter part of the nineteenth century and the early part of the twentieth century, there were philosophers in the idealistic tradition who reasoned in a similar way. They seemed to say that we can never hope to have any genuine knowledge of reality. The most we can hope to know about any particular thing is to know what some of its properties or attributes are. But, they said, we can never know what the thing is which has those properties or attributes.[21] In the present century, Jean-Paul Sartre has despaired because we seem to have no access to the *en-soi*—to the self as it is in itself. Whatever we find is at best only *pour-soi*—the self as it manifests itself to itself.[22]

Despite the impressive tradition, should we not say that this is simply a muddle? The reasoning seems to be as follows.

It is noted (i) that a person can be acquainted with the subject of experience to the extent that the subject manifests itself as having certain properties. (And this we can readily accept—provided that we take care not to commit at this point the first of the errors on our list above. What we should say is not merely that the subject manifests certain qualities; it is rather that the subject manifests *itself as having* certain qualities.)

Then one adds an "only" to what has just been said. One now says (ii) that a person can be acquainted with the subject of experience *only* to the extent that the subject manifests itself as having certain qualities. The "only" is thought to express a limitation. (But consider the limitation expressed by the "only" in "One can see what is only an object of sight" and "Trees are capable of growing only below the timberline.")

From these two premises one then deduces (iii) that no one has acquaintance with the self as it is in itself.

But it is not difficult to see, it seems to me, that (ii) does not add anything to (i), and that (iii), moreover, does not follow from (i) and (ii). Indeed I would say, not only that (iii) does *not* follow from (i) and (ii), but also that the *negation* of (iii) *does* follow from (i) and (ii). From the fact that we are acquainted with the self as it manifests itself as having certain qualities, it follows that we are acquainted with the self as it is in itself. Manifestation, after all, is the converse of acquaintance: x manifests itself to y, if and only if y is acquainted with x. How can a man be acquainted with *anything* unless the thing manifests or presents itself to him? And how can the thing manifest or present itself unless it manifests or presents itself as having certain qualities or attributes? [23]

The muddle was neatly put by Wittgenstein. We are all naked, he said, underneath our clothes.

NOTES

1. Chapter I, Section VIII.

2. Jean-Paul Sartre, *L'Être et le Néant* (Paris: Gallimard, 1943), pp. 134, 145, 652–653.

3. Bertrand Russell, *Logic and Knowledge* (London: Allen & Unwin, 1956), p. 305; Rudolf Carnap, *Der logische Aufbau der Welt* (Berlin: Weltkreis-Verlag, 1928), pp. 87–90.

4. Husserl wrote of Hume: "Dessen genialer *Treatise* hat bereits die Gestalt einer auf strenge Konsequenz bedachten struckturellen Durchforschung der reinen Erlebnissphäre, [ist] in gewisser Weise also der erste Anhieb einer 'Phänomenologie'" (*Phänomenologische Psychologie* [The Hague: Nijhoff, 1961], p. 264). The members of the Vienna Circle traced the "scientific world-outlook" to the same source; see *Wissenschaftliche Weltauffassung* (Vienna: Wolf, 1929), p. 12.

5. The passage may be found on page 194 of Charles W. Hendel's edition of Hume's *An Enquiry Concerning Human Understanding* (New York: Liberal Arts Press, 1955).

6. *New Essays Concerning Human Understanding*, Book II, Ch. xxxiii, sec. 1: ". . . c'est plutôt le *concretum* comme savant, chaud, luisant, qui nous vient dans l'esprit, que les *abstractions* ou qualités (car se sont elles, qui sont dans l'object substantiel et non pas les Idées) comme savoir, chaleur, lumière, etc. qui sont bien plus difficiles à comprendre" (Erdmann's edition of Leibniz' *Opera Philosophica*, p. 272).

7. *A Treatise of Human Nature*, Book I, Part iv, Section vi ("Of Personal Identity").

8. H. H. Price, *Hume's Theory of the External World* (Oxford: Clarendon, 1940), pp. 5–6. Compare P. F. Strawson, *Individuals* (London: Methuen, 1959), pp. 96–97.

9. Compare Brentano's remark about the concept of substance: "Those who say that this concept is not included in any perception are very much mistaken. Rather it is given in every perception, as Aristotle had said . . ." (Franz Brentano, *Versuch über die Erkenntnis* [Leipzig: Meiner, 1925], p. 30). Referring to the thesis according to which we know only "phenomena" and not "things in themselves," he wrote: "But what does it mean to say that one apprehends something as a *phenomenon*? Simply that one apprehends it as a phenomenon to the one for whom it is a phenomenon. This means, in other words, that one apprehends that one is presented with or intuits the phenomenon in question and hence that one apprehends the one to whom it is presented, the one who intuits. But this is a thing which one apprehends in itself" (*Die Vier Phasen der Philosophie* [Leipzig: Meiner, 1926], p. 92; my italics). But Brentano also held, unfortunately, that so-called external perception is "blind."

10. Jean-Paul Sartre, *The Transcendence of the Ego,* trans. Forrest Williams and Robert Kirkpatrick (New York: Farrar, Straus and Cudahy, 1957), p. 51.

11. I am indebted to Keith Lehrer for this point. I am also indebted to him and to Charles Caton for criticisms enabling me to correct an earlier version of this paper.

12. See H. A. Prichard, *Knowledge and Perception* (Oxford: Clarendon, 1950), p. 213. Compare his much earlier *Kant's Theory of Knowledge* (Oxford: Clarendon, 1909) and his "Appearances and Reality," first published in *Mind* in 1906 and republished in Roderick M. Chisholm, ed., *Realism and the Background of Phenomenology* (Glencoe, Ill.: Free Press, 1960), pp. 143–150.

13. A. O. Lovejoy, *The Revolt against Dualism* (New York: Norton, 1930), p. 305.

14. "The general rule which one may derive from these examples is that the propositions we ordinarily express by saying that a person A is perceiving a material thing M, which appears to him to have the quality x, may be expressed in the sense-datum terminology by saying that A is sensing a sense-datum s, which really has the quality x, and which belongs to M" (A. J. Ayer,

292   RODERICK M. CHISHOLM

The Foundations of Empirical Knowledge [New York: Macmillan, 1940], p. 58).

15. Compare Thomas Reid: "When I am pained, I cannot say that the pain I feel is one thing, and that my feeling of it is another thing. They are one and the same thing and cannot be disjoined even in the imagination" (*Essays on the Intellectual Powers* [Cambridge: M.I.T., 1969], Essay I, Chapter 1).

16. But there are still two alternative interpretations of such expressions as "sensing red" or "sensing redly." (i) We might define "sensing redly" in such a way that our definiens makes explicit reference to things which are red. Using the expression in this way, we may say that no one can *know* that he is sensing redly unless he *also* knows something about red things and the ways in which they appear. Or, more empirically, (ii) we might take "sensing redly" as undefined, in which case we may say that a man who knows nothing about red things may yet know that he is sensing redly. For in this second case, the proposition connecting his sensing redly with one of the ways in which people are appeared to by things which are red would be a proposition which is synthetic.

17. And so are "thoughts." Consider a man who is thinking about a unicorn. We may say, if we choose, that he has a thought and that his thought is about a unicorn. Whether or not we say, as Meinong did, that the situation involves a relation between an existent man and a nonexistent unicorn, we should not say that the situation involves a relation between a man and a certain independent entity which is his thought. There is not *one* relation between a man and a thought, and then a *second* relation between the thought and a nonexistent unicorn. Though we say, quite naturally, that the unicorn is the object of the man's thought, it would be less misleading to say that the unicorn is the object of the man to the extent that he is thinking. For thinking, like feeling and like what we may call "sensing," is an affection, modification, or state of the man. Compare Leibniz' assertion that ideas are "affections or modifications of the mind" in his "Thoughts on Knowledge, Truth, and Ideas" in Erdmann's edition of the *Opera Philosophica*, p. 81. Sartre, too, has said that the appearance is "the manner in which the subject is affected [la manière dont le sujet est affecté]," but he adds, unfortunately, that "consciousness has nothing of the substantial [la conscience n'a rien de substantiel]" (*L'Être et le Néant*, pp. 13, 23).

18. *Treatise of Human Nature*, Book I, Part IV, Section 5; my italics.

19. I have tried to say what these conditions are in *Theory of Knowledge* (Englewood Cliffs: Prentice-Hall, 1966), Chapter Three, and in *Perceiving: A Philosophical Study* (Ithaca: Cornell University Press, 1957). An excellent summary of this view of perception may be found in Keith Lehrer, "Scottish Influences on Contemporary American Philosophy," *The Journal of Philosophy*, 65 (1968), 34–42.

20. "Durch dieses Ich oder Er oder Es (das Ding), welches denkt, wird nun nichts weiter als ein transcendentales Subject der Gedanken vorgestellt = X, welches nur durch die Gedanken, die seine Prädicate sind, erkannt wird, und wovon wir abgesondert niemals den mindesten Begriff haben können. . . . Es ist aber offenbar, dass das Subject der Inhärenz durch das dem Gedanken angehängte Ich nur transcendental bezeichnet werde, ohne die mindeste Eigenschaft desselben zu bemerken, oder überhaupt etwas von ihm zu kennen oder zu wissen" (*Kritik der reinen Vernunft*, A346, A355; see N. Kemp Smith's edition, pp. 331, 337).

21. Compare A. E. Taylor: "What we call one *thing* is said, in spite of its unity, to have many *qualities*. It is, *e.g.*, at once round, white, shiny, and hard, or at once green, soft, and rough. Now, what do we understand by the *it* to which these numerous attributes are alike ascribed, and how does it possess them? To use the traditional technical names, what is the substance to which

the several qualities belong or in which they inhere, and what is the manner of their *inherence?* . . . The notion *that* things have a that or substance prior to their *what* or quality . . . is thus unmeaning as well as superfluous" (*Elements of Metaphysics,* 5th ed. [London: Methuen, 1920], pp. 128, 133).

22. "Ainsi le Pour-soi en tant qu'il n'est pas *soi* est une présence à soi qui manque d'une certaine présence à soi et c'est en tant que manque de cette présence qu'il est présence à soi" (*L'Être et le Néant,* p. 145).

23. Compare Leibniz again: "En distinguant deux choses dans la substance, les attributs ou prédicats et le sujet commun de ces prédicats, ce n'est pas merveille, qu'on ne peut rien concevoir de particulier dans ce sujet. Il le faut bien, puisqu'on déjà séparé tous les attributs, où l'on pourroit concevoir quelque détail. Ainsi demander quelque chose de plus dans ce pur *sujet en général,* que ce qu'il faut pour concevoir que c'est la même chose (p. e. qui entend et qui veut, qui imagine et qui raisonne) c'est demander l'impossible et contrevenir à sa propre supposition, qu'on a faite en faisant abstraction et concevant separément le sujet et ses qualités ou accidens" (*New Essays Concerning Human Understanding,* Book II, Ch. 23, sec. 2; Erdmann, *Opera Philosophica,* p. 272).

20

Re-examining Kierkegaard's "Teleological Suspension of the Ethical"

JOHN DONNELLY

Fordham University

> But . . . when I have to think of Abraham, I am as though
> annihilated. I catch sight every moment of that enormous para-
> dox which is the substance of Abraham's life, every moment I
> am repelled, and my thought in spite of all its passion cannot set
> a hairs-breadth further. I strain every muscle to get a view of
> it—that very instant I am paralyzed.[1]

ANGLO–AMERICAN PHILOSOPHERS OFTEN MAKE A FETISH
out of avoiding "primary-source material," particularly when
evaluating or more properly criticizing the work of a "Con-
tinental philosopher." Carnap's well-known criticism of Heidegger's "das Nichts selbst nichtet" can well serve as a paradigm case for such effrontery. A somewhat similar derisive
treatment is accorded Sören Kierkegaard's "teleological sus-

pension of the ethical" which is often dismissed as irrational-
ism, "crisis theology," or at best an extreme example of
situational religious ethics.[2] Even a potential Kierkegaardian
sympathizer, George Schrader, agrees with the cynics:

> In *Fear and Trembling*, Kierkegaard makes the trenchant point that
> . . . insofar as a person is ever called upon to act as an individual,
> he stands outside the ethical sphere, and thus can find no justification
> for his action. If ethical justification is equated with rational justifica-
> tion, then the action of the individual *qua* individual must presumably
> go without any justification whatever.[3]

However, after a number of readings of *Fear and Trembling*
which by Kierkegaard's own admission was his most "perfect
work," it still occurs to me that a more positive case can be
established against such dismissals, which both the critics and
perhaps even Kierkegaard himself might have refused to consider or just failed to realize. That is, I believe that "the teleological suspension of the ethical" raised issues which are of
interest to the philosopher, issues which merit not being simply
assigned to "crisis theology." My motivation is then to provide, not an intrinsically interesting, exegetical exercise in the
history of ideas, but rather an attempt to restore some sem-
blance of consistency and coherence to a work of literature
generally considered most philosophically unrespectable. Accordingly, I would suggest that the analytic philosopher take
seriously Kierkegaard's invitation to investigate

> . . . whether in this story there is to be found any higher expression
> for the ethical such as would ethically explain his conduct, ethically
> justify him in suspending the ethical obligation toward his son, with-
> out in this search going beyond the teleology of the ethical.[4]

Kierkegaard in *Fear and Trembling* relates the Biblical
story of Abraham, and poses the question whether there can
be any ethical justification for Abraham's conduct, and, in particular, whether there can be any moral explanation for the intended action of killing his own son, Isaac, out of obedience
to a divine command. Such a probing involves the famous "teleological suspension of the ethical," a phrase which indicates,
if affirmed, that any justification of Abraham's conduct, if not

blatantly immoral, is clearly amoral, and a defense of a distinctly religious sort.

> Faith is precisely this paradox, that the individual as the particular is higher than the universal, is justified over against it, is not subordinate but superior—yet in such a way be it observed, that it is the particular individual who, after he has been subordinated as the particular to the universal, now through the universal becomes the individual who as the particular is superior to the universal, for the fact that the individual as the particular stands in an absolute relation to the absolute. This position cannot be mediated, for all mediation comes about precisely by virtue of the universal; it is and remains to all eternity a paradox, inaccessible to thought.[5]

Critics, potential sympathizers, and apparently Kierkegaard himself concur in their respective views that at best one can provide a religious justification for Abraham's conduct, but surely any ethical, rational, or philosophical explanation of his conduct is out of the question (Blanshard speaks of the "dysteleological" suspension of the ethical!). Much as the mother *qua* Christian Scientist, who allows her only child to die of first-degree burns when proper medical treatment could have prevented such a result, can be said to have a religious explanation for her action, albeit not a moral one, so too it is argued that this is the best which can be said for Abraham's plight *qua* knight of faith. Indeed, it might even be said that the cases are not even strictly analogous, for the mother can justify her conduct by recourse to the religious institution of Christian Science, but Abraham *qua* knight of faith plays a non-institutional role in life, and thus forfeits such a defense.

However, I wish to suggest that these critics, potential sympathizers, and even Kierkegaard himself have failed to realize that a plausible defense can be mounted for Abraham *qua* knight of faith, a defense which is not just of a religious sort, but rather a distinctly moral, rational, and philosophical justification. In the light of the above-mentioned quotation from *Fear and Trembling,* I would wish to suggest that: (i) one can affirm with Kierkegaard that "the individual as the particular is higher than the universal," where "universal" here connotes our conventional socio-ethical standards; yet, (ii) also claim with Kierkegaard that "through the universal becomes the individual who as the particular is superior to the universal";

that is, affirm (ii) by noting the equivocation in the term "universal," where the former use connotes that which is distinctly moral, and the latter use connotes our conventional socio-ethical standards, as in (i); so that (iii) one can affirm with Kierkegaard that "the individual . . . stands in an absolute relation to the absolute," wherein a unique relationship is established between the knight of faith and his God, a relationship within the moral sphere; but (iv) one can deny Kierkegaard's assertion that "this position [i.e., knighthood of faith] cannot be mediated," in that I can mount a moral, rational, and philosophical defense for the knight of faith; so that (v) I can also deny that the conduct of Abraham is "a paradox inaccessible to thought."

To commence our investigation into the complexities of Abraham's plight in *Fear and Trembling*, I suggest that we consider the "classic" article by an analytic philosopher on the subject of the "teleological suspension of the ethical." James Bogen takes seriously the possibility of finding a philosophical analysis of Abraham's conduct which will allow us to grant him a moral justification, so that there never would be a "teleological suspension of the ethical." This much is to Bogen's credit! That is, Bogen seeks to determine if the philosopher cannot assign a negative answer to Kierkegaard's "Problem One: Is there such a thing as a teleological suspension of the ethical?" while granting an affirmative answer to Kierkegaard's "Problem Two: Is there such a thing as an absolute duty to God?" But, Bogen's investigation yields the conclusion that there can be no moral defense of Abraham's conduct, so that there was a "teleological suspension of the ethical" involved in *Fear and Trembling*. Bogen answers "Problem One" in the affirmative and "Problem Two" in the negative. I wish to compliment Bogen on his initial resolve, but to disagree with his resultant conclusion. That is, I wish to claim that we can answer "Problem One" in the negative, and "Problem Two" in the affirmative.

I

James Bogen proposes the thesis that Kierkegaard regarded morality as a system of duties ("Throughout his discussion of Abraham, Kierkegaard speaks as though morality were a system of duties" [6]), such that one's moral duties are tied to the position, office, role, or station (i.e., these terms are used as intensional equivalents herein) one plays in life (" . . . statements of the form 'Y has a duty to do X' can be verified by appeal to nothing else but the position of the agent" [7]). Bogen presents us with no formal argument *per se* in his article; however, to show that this is what duty consists of in *Fear and Trembling,* we might faithfully argue his case as follows: (1) If X is a duty of moral agent A, then X is derivable from position(s) P_1 v P_2 . . . v P_n which A occupies in life; (2) It is not the case that X is derivable from either P_1 v P_2 v P_n which A occupies in life; (3) Therefore, it is not the case that X is a duty of A.

Applying this line of ratiocination to Abraham's situation in *Fear and Trembling,* we get the following argument: (1.1) If the act of sacrificing one's son is a duty of Abraham, then the act of sacrificing one's son is derivable from position(s) P_1 v P_2 . . . v P_n which Abraham occupies in life; (2.1) It is not the case that the act of sacrificing one's son is derivable from the respective positions (i.e., husband, father, head of household, etc.) which Abraham occupies in life; (3.1) Therefore, it is not the case that sacrificing one's son is a duty of Abraham's.

Bogen proceeds to make two further claims, namely, (i) a denial of any legitimacy to a sense of duty *qua* man, allowing him (ii) the option to argue for the logical connection between duties and positional contexts.

> (i) . . . We do not speak of the duties of human beings *qua* human beings. The everyday concept of duty is such that we are said to acquire duties not . . . simply by being born into the species *homo sapiens*—but by occupying definite positions in society.[8]
> (ii) . . . arguments over whether a person acting in a particular capacity has a particular duty must . . . be arguments over the nature of the position he occupies.[9]

Given the above claims, we might present Bogen's next argument to read: (4) If there are only duties of a positional nature, then any ethical justification of Abraham's conduct must lie in the establishment of a case for citing positional contexts such that Abraham's conduct can be morally explained therein;

(5) There are only duties of a positional nature; (6) Therefore, any ethical justification of Abraham's conduct must lie in the establishment of a case citing positional contexts such that Abraham's conduct can be morally explained therein; (7) But there is no possible establishment of a case for citing positional contexts such that Abraham's conduct can be therein explained; (8) Therefore, there is no ethical justification of Abraham's conduct; (9) Therefore, the action of Abraham would involve a "teleological suspension of the ethical."

> . . . it would make no sense to say either that Abraham acted out of duty, or that his action was morally right. Because of Abraham's position, none of the moral considerations made relevant to the evaluation of his conduct by the circumstances of his case, justify his conduct. . . . One cannot speak in his case of a duty toward God which conflicts with his duty toward his son in the way in which we can speak of Agamemnon's having a duty (as king) which conflicted with his duties as a father.[10]

It seems to me that there is a twofold way to counter Bogen's basic theme, by presenting an argument either to establish a position for Abraham, such that this position calls for Abraham's sacrificing his son, and/or to establish a case for speaking of duties *qua* man, and show how the recognition of such a type of duty will allow us to speak favorably of the conduct of Abraham. Both approaches as methods of defending Abraham, if successful, would thereby prevent "the teleological suspension of the ethical" from occurring.

I shall opt for the former line of defense of Kierkegaard's account in *Fear and Trembling,* so that I will deny Bogen's premise (2) and (2.1), thereby making the respective conclusions (3) and (3.1) false. I will express some misgivings with premise (4) because of its limited conception of duty, yet recognize it for the purposes of more fully extending its logic to allow for a novel defense of Abraham. Quite obviously, I will deny the truth claim for (7) and (8), and, paradoxically enough, for (9) as well.

It might be suggested that the latter of the twofold approach previously mentioned—that is, the possibility of establishing a case for the recognition of duties *qua homo sapiens* —would be the more feasible. So why not adopt this method of vindication? I quite agree that Bogen is clearly mistaken in maintaining that there are no duties *qua* man, and that while one might establish a case for introducing such duties into our ethical structure, it seems to me that ultimately this procedure will prove unsuccessful. For, suppose that it were argued: (10) God created all of mankind; (11) We are all creatures of God; (12) The role of creature has certain tasks and responsibilities associated with it as a result of the consequences of (10); (13) One of these tasks and responsibilities is obeying the commands of God; (14) Therefore, all men *qua* creatures of God ought to obey the commands of God.

I shall not argue at any length against this choice of supporting the case of Abraham, for Bogen himself does not consider it, and I most want to meet his challenge. Nonetheless, a few brief remarks seem in order. First of all, there is the obvious descriptive fallacy of deriving an "ought" in (14) from descriptive premises in (10)–(13). Perhaps, more importantly, the argument seems prone to the accusation that all men would now be called upon to assimilate their conduct to Abraham, so that sacrificing one's son out of respect to God's wishes would become a duty for all men. At best, it would seem odd to suggest such lines of conduct as any more than supererogatory, and one cannot help wondering what many moral agents would have to do in order to compensate for their lack of having any children!

Accordingly, it seems a more fruitful approach, in attempting any justification of Abraham's conduct, to counter Bogen through the establishment of a positional context for Abraham. However, if we are to avoid the naturalistic weaknesses of Bogen's concept of duty, it will be incumbent upon us to introduce a more enlightened (and, it is hoped, more ethical) concept of duty.

It is not at all clear to me, after a great deal of textual exegesis, exactly what Kierkegaard's own views on morality were. To be sure, it would seem that Kierkegaard did not simply limit the ethical to a system of duties, as that expression is understood by Bogen. Bogen's account is, accordingly, too narrow in scope both textually and, as we shall see, philosophically. Indeed, one wonders how a passage like the following can be so structured that it incorporates a specific duty only for a specific position.

The ethical as such is the universal, and as the universal it applies to everyone, which may be expressed from another point of view by saying that it applies every instant.[11]

Although Bogen's claim then is textually underextended in scope, as well as philosophically limited, it by no means follows that Kierkegaard did not also employ a type of duty much akin to Bogen's analysis. The following passages give substance to Bogen's thesis, although as we shall see the concept of duty and that of position need to be further delineated. The passages refer respectively to the situations of Agamemnon, Jephtha, and Brutus, and cite the need for the recognition of certain sorts of tasks and responsibilities as required by the respective positions of king, military leader, and Roman consul.

> When an undertaking in which a whole nation is concerned is hindered, when such an enterprise is brought to a standstill by the disfavor of heaven, when the angry deity sends a calm which mocks all efforts, when the seer performs his heavy tasks and proclaims that the deity demands a young maiden as a sacrifice—then will the father heroically make the sacrifice. . . . the whole nation . . . will be also cognizant of his exploit, that for the welfare of the whole he was willing to sacrifice her. . . .[12]

> When the intrepid judge who saved Israel in the hour of need in one breath binds himself and God by the same vow . . . all Israel will lament her maiden youth, but every free-born man will understand, and every stout-hearted woman will admire Jephtha, and every maiden in Israel will wish to act as did his daughter.[13]

> When a son is forgetful of his duty, when the state entrusts the father with the sword of justice . . . then will the father heroically forget that the guilty one is his son, but there will not be a single one among the people, not even the son, who will not admire the father, and when the law of Rome is interpreted, it will be remembered that many interpreted it more learnedly, but none so gloriously as Brutus.[14]

II

I have already alluded to the philosophical limitations of Bogen's concept of "duty," and to such an analysis I now wish to turn. We have just seen Bogen's proposal that Kierkegaard regarded morality as a system of duties. This implies that the rightness or wrongness of acts depends upon whether or not it is the case that the moral agent has a duty to perform X-action or to refrain from X-action. Moreover, the interesting aspect of Bogen's thesis is that a particular moral agent acquires certain duties only by occupying a particular definite position in life. I take it that such an intimate association between the concept of "duty" and the particular status or role maintained by the moral agent commits Bogen to contending that if A claims to be morally justified in doing X because it is A's duty to do X, then this entails that A is acting in K-capacity such that K calls for A's doing X. Agamemnon held the position of "King of the Achaeans," and since his country's welfare depended upon his sacrificing his daughter Iphigenia, it is his duty so to sacrifice her.

Here to question whether A in fact has a duty to do X is to be reduced to asking on Bogen's account if the legitimacy of the inference from A occupies K-position, and, if A so acts in accordance with K, then is not A obliged to do X? Surely we need not deny that it is the moral duty of rulers to act in their country's best interests, but such an assertion need not be analytic, as Bogen insinuates. Indeed it is often appropriate to ask the Moorean question: "But should kings really always act in their country's best interests?" This appears to be a fair and appropriate question, although Bogen considers it to be closed: "It would then be unreasonable to ask whether Agamemnon was morally bound to sacrifice his daughter *just because* he was military leader, and the invasion depended upon his sacrificing her." [15]

Now, Bogen considers the above to be a nonsensical question because of: (*a*) the soundness of the deductive inference from (i) A occupies K; (ii) K calls for action X; (iii) therefore, A ought to do X; and (*b*) the definitional equivalence of "A has a duty to do X" with "A occupies K and K requires X." However, while it may be the case that the assertions (i)–(iii) are true, so that one condition of soundness is satisfied, it surely is not the case that the inference is valid, for (iii) contains an "ought" and the premises (i) and (ii) contain only descriptive terms. Also, quite clearly the definiens in (*b*) can be satisfied, without the definiendum's being satisfied, so that this connotational linkage is rendered somewhat dubious. That is, A may occupy a role or office, in a specific organization or in a particular social system, which requires performances X of A, yet it need not be the case that A has a moral duty to do X (i.e., Eichmann in the Nazi organization could not be said to have had a moral duty to kill millions of Jews). Bogen presumably overlooked Kierkegaard's admonition that "It is only the lower natures which find in other people the law for their actions, which find the premises for their actions outside themselves." [16] There appear, then, to be good grounds for disavowing any claim, such as Bogen's, that to say "X is right" or "X is my duty" is logically equivalent to saying "X is required by position K," for clearly the evaluation of moral conduct depends not only on the agent's position but also on the circumstances and motives under which the action in question was performed.

Bogen further contends that Kierkegaard's conception of morality viewed as a system of duties need make no allowances for moral rules or principles (e.g., temptations can be more adequately described as tending to keep one from doing one's duty, rather than as tending to make one break a moral rule). But, I find such a conception of duties to be too limited. That is, the requirement of a duty for Bogen has simply the stringency of a claim of law, custom, taste, etc. I suggest that to say B occupies position F, and B freely accepts the requirements of F, entails that B thereby subscribes (at least implicitly) to the following moral principles (P_1, P_2 . . . P_n) defining that position. Jephtha is King of the Jews and freely accepts the requirements of that office, so that he accordingly submits to uphold such a moral principle as "kings ought always to act in their country's best interests."

Now, there is strong textual evidence to support a thesis that Kierkegaard did recognize a hierarchy of duties. Agamemnon is a father, and so has the duty to care for his daughter's welfare, but he is also a king, and so he has the duty in a higher sense to sacrifice his daughter for the sake of his country's successful invasion against Troy. But Bogen wishes to maintain that, in such cases of conflict between fatherly duties and kingly duties, Kierkegaard is forced to resort to the quite arbitrary claim that kingly duties override fatherly duties, a resolution procedure Bogen finds acceptable. However, if there is a sense of "good reasons" in ethics, then clearly the decision what action is to be performed must be justified by invoking either prudential or utilitarian considerations, or at least by appealing to an overriding supreme principle. But this is precisely what Bogen's analysis of Kierkegaard has ruled out in claiming that statements such as (1) "It is A's duty to do X" are entirely distinct from and logically prior to statements such as (2) "It is A's duty to do X in accordance with the dictates of moral principle P to which A freely subscribes." That is, Bogen has erroneously maintained that the connection between one's position and the rules he must obey is different from that between one's position and one's duties, and that indeed the former is decidedly un-Kierkegaardian. Whereas Bogen's reading would claim that (3) "A may know what A is to do and do X because A knows X is his duty to do," I would contend that this needs to be reformulated to read (4) "A may know what A is to do and do X because A holds X to be his duty in light of moral principle P." Bogen leaves us with the thesis that the concept of duty is bound to positional usage; but I wish to maintain that such a thesis is philosophically inadequate as the concept of duty is more properly related to the subscription to certain moral principles and their accompanying secondary rules, which principles and rules serve in turn to define the very role or position which an agent is to play in life. Whereas Bogen's account recognizes only a *descriptive* sense of duty, tying it down to certain roles or positions one plays *in society,* my account recognizes a more properly normative sense of duty, tying it down to certain roles or positions one plays *in life.* Accordingly, Bogen's analysis of morality as a system of duties in *Fear and Trembling* is fraught with naturalistic shortcomings, limitations which prevent any appreciable understanding of the conduct of the knight of faith.

III

We have seen where, on Bogen's analysis, Agamemnon, the prototype of the tragic hero, is morally justified in causing the death of his daughter, because his duties as king take precedence over all other relevant moral considerations. My interpretation would claim that Agamemnon is morally justified in his action because the moral principles governing the posi-

tion of a king—more properly defining that position—and its correlative duties override those governing the position of a father. But how are we to handle the case of Abraham, which by Kierkegaard's own admission involves the subordination of the very moral principles upon which a moral evaluation of his conduct could be based? Bogen at this point maintains—quite erroneously, I believe—that Abraham's act would not be performed under circumstances in which the various positions he occupied (i.e., father, husband, tribal leader, etc.) involved duties calling for the killing of Isaac. In one respect, Bogen is quite correct in this matter, for, given even an amended rendition of Bogen's concept of "duty" to avoid his naturalistic assumptions, it still does not follow that such a concept of "duty," what I call "duty-proper," will allow us to explain morally the conduct of Abraham. By "duties-proper" I refer to those assigned tasks which attach to stations, offices, and roles in society, and which are generally of an institutional sort, so that one can be in Sartre's "bad faith," or be living what Heidegger termed an "inauthentic existence," and yet still fulfill the requirements of one's duties-proper. To be living an authentic mode of life, as I understand and employ the expression, is to be the individual in full possession of oneself, Heidegger's "eigentlich," which Richard Schmitt translates as "genuinely self-possessed." [17] On the other hand, to be inauthentic, to be living an inauthentic mode of existence, is to be fallen away from oneself (Heidegger's "uneigentlich"), alienated from self. Likewise, I understand Sartre's "bad faith" to be the practice of self-deception, so that in being "uneigentlich" one is also acting in bad faith. More specifically, "Y is a duty-proper act of moral agent A" if and only if: (a) Y is an action required by moral principles $P_1, P_2 \ldots P_n$, and moral rules $R_1, R_2 \ldots R_n$, (b) these principles and rules in turn characterize A's position in the life of the society, and (c) these principles and rules require a specific performance if A is to satisfy the obligatory functions enjoined by such moral principles and rules.

Some rules are extremely precise in specification, as in certain institutional associations which speak of "duties of members," which on my terminology are duties-proper. The tragic hero and the ecclesiastical hero fall into this type of role, in that, being functionaries, their respective duties are determined by the set of rules which establish the character and structure of the institution as a whole. Here there is no allowance for a *moral* usurper, and the knight of faith is such a person.

If Abraham had acted out of duty, his action, Bogen claims, would be morally right, but as Bogen wishes to deny a concept of duty which applies to Abraham *qua* knight of faith, he claims that Abraham acted in no special capacity before God so that his action is not only not called for by duty, but morally reprehensible as well—in fact, "absurd." For Bogen to say that A is not in K-position, and K-position calls for doing X-action, entails that A is not obliged to do X. But this is surely false. A may not be a social worker but this need not imply that A is not obliged in some minimal sense to help the cause of social justice.[18] Incidentally, this is not an inconsistency on my part to invoke here a concept of "basic duty," or duties incumbent on man *qua homo sapiens,* for I do not wish to tie duty down to positional contexts in the restrictive manner Bogen does. Rather I merely want to explore his mistaken suggestion, amend it, and then develop a rational defense for the conduct of Abraham.

Suppose that we accept Bogen's challenge. Can we then establish a special capacity or position for Abraham, such that his action was called for by duty? It seems to me that we can. Whereas Bogen's account allows only for a "limited" notion of "position," tying it down to "fathers," "kings," etc.—the sort of institutional offices sanctioned by society—I see no logical obstruction preventing us from giving the term a more "extended" meaning, and thereby employing it to designate certain mental attitudes, in which a position is a way of looking at something, taking a certain perspective on life. Such an extended sense of "position" allows the term to designate a point of view adopted with reference to a particular subject, such as a certain benevolent attitude toward God. In such an extended sense of the term, "position" clearly transcends man's more objective, vocational situation in life as a policeman, father, taxpayer, etc.—the sort of offices listed in the *Dictionary of Occupational Titles.* Moral agent A occupies my extended notion of position whenever A has a certain mental

attitude or outlook on life such that: (1) A voluntarily subscribes to a certain overriding supreme principle and the more
subordinate rules and maxims emanating from it, (2) the
conjunction of which serves to characterize A as a moral agent
of a special sort. That is to say: for every moral agent A, there
is a description F and certain definite moral principles and
rules PR, such that under F, A may be said to subscribe to PR,
which in turn demarcate A as occupying a certain position in
life.

My extended notion of "position" accordingly serves to designate a sense in which the term connotes man's more personal
role or station in life. Now, if we accept Bogen's use of the
term "duty" wherein there are certain positive performances
recognized as pertaining to a role or situation in life, which
performances are deemed necessary for a satisfactory fulfill-
ment of one's position, then it is likewise incumbent on us to
recognize a certain set of activities to which a knight of faith
commits himself in accepting a certain station in life. That is
to say, in both the limited (Bogen's use) and extended sense
of the term "position" there is a list of tasks and responsibilities associated with such positions. It strikes me that doing
what one ought to do entails doing what one thinks one ought
to do if one is intent upon fulfilling one's obligations and dis-
charging one's duties. Such an extended rendition of position
does justice to Kierkegaard's attack against the sort of moral
and religious institutionalism in which moral standards are
not a matter of personal decision by the individual agent in
deciding his own destiny, but are to be found instead in the
church or moral code into which the individual is inducted as
a participant position-bearer.

Quite obviously, the introduction of an extended meaning of
position raises several difficulties, and to these I now turn.
First of all, it might be argued that this extended notion of
position seems to apply *sui generis* to the knight of faith, so
that I am guilty of subtly stipulating the introduction of a
novel expression simply to eradicate any difficulties to an understanding of Abraham's situation. In reply to this possible
objection, I would say that it does seem to be the case that this
extended notion of position applies uniquely to the knight of
faith, but this is not to say that this definite description may

not apply equally to proper names other than Abraham who may assume the knighthood of faith. Furthermore, such *sui generis* application is but a contingent matter of fact, for a hermit need not be a knight of faith, and yet fulfill the conditions of the extended notion of position. Indeed, oftentimes it is the case that such roles which are created by application of this extended notion of position, such as "civil-rights worker," become immediately codified and pressed into the institutional framework. To argue that social recognition grants moral appropriateness where heretofore it did not exist, seems question-begging at best. Also by way of reply: the distinctly institutional role President of the United States of America applies by definition to one person, and indeed this definite description cannot simultaneously be applied to other than one proper name; yet we feel no hesitation in granting this role a list of incumbent tasks and responsibilities. Given such considerations, I cannot feel the force of this first objection to my extended use of position.

Secondly, it might be objected that the allowance of an extended use of position into our ethical categories will give license to certain agents to justify their immoral way of life, and this can only serve as a *reductio ad absurdum* of my analysis. In reply, I would add that, in fulfilling my extended notion of position, and adopting a self-chosen role in life, this be consistent with (*a*) the total subscription to a way of life so that it is never a momentary stage in one's life (". . . he is too proud to be willing that what was the whole content of his life should be the thing of a fleeting moment" [19]), as well as (*b*) a distinctly moral outlook on life. That is, one cannot justify being a conscientious objector by recourse to this extended notion of position, for this role clearly fails to be anything other than a momentary outlook in life, and oftentimes the role itself is institutionalized. More important than the condition of temporal delimitation is that my extended rendition of position will not allow an Eichmann to claim moral justification for his conduct as "savior of the Aryan race from the Jewish menace," for this fails to meet the moral requirement of the position involved.

Thirdly, although this is not an objection to my view, I do not wish to suggest that roles such as "pope," "Trappist monk," or "spiritual adventurer" are exact analogues of my extended notion of position.[20] This is so, because the first two are institutional roles of an ecclesiastical sort, whereas the last is but a duty-plus way of viewing a distinctly institutional role such as physician or missionary—although it comes the closest to capturing (and may in some situations actually satisfy) the spirit of my extended concept of position.

Kierkegaard wishes to say that a man is not only the self which he appears to be by his role in society, but also the one he aspires to be *simpliciter*. In Heideggerian terms, man is characterized not only by "facticity" but by "transcendence" as well, so that truly authentic existence demands the synthesis of an actualized possibility and an idealized actuality. And this is precisely the sort of role my analysis of an extended version of position will allow us to recognize.

Some philosophers (e.g., Schrader[21]) would claim that to be an individual in my sense of occupying an extended notion of position in life would be inauthentic. Although he does not clarify what he means by "inauthentic," I suspect that Schrader has in mind the Heideggerian sense of "uneigentlich," a state of fallen-awayness from self, alienation from self. Schrader might then appeal to the only apparent authenticity of Abraham *qua* knight of faith, arguing that he is but an individual who is only apparently genuinely self-possessed. That is, Schrader might say that to occupy a limited concept of "position" and "be what we are occupied with" may be more authentic than to "rummage around extravagantly in one's psyche" by occupying an extended notion of "position" in life. If so, then Schrader could be construed as raising two distinct claims against my analysis: (*a*) the *conceptual* point of questioning what it means to occupy a role or position in life; and/or (*b*) the *normative* point of asking what it means to be authentic.

However, given the preceding analysis, Schrader would appear ill-advised to be questioning (*a*), so this leaves us with the point of (*b*). His argument might now read: I agree with your conceptual point's coherency, but it seems to me that to instantiate it would be to invite moral or institutional havoc (i.e., for Schrader, as for Bogen, both qualifications of "havoc" are synonymous). Suffice it to say that such institutional or moral havoc does not occur as a result of my recognition of an extended notion of position, and even Kierkegaard was clear on this point:

> People . . . are afraid that the worst will happen as soon as the individual takes it into his head to comport himself as the individual. Moreover they think that to exist as the individual is the easiest thing of all, and that therefore people have to be compelled to become the universal. I cannot share either this fear or this opinion. . . . He who has learned that to exist as the individual is the most terrible thing of all will not be fearful of saying that it is great, but then too he will say this in such a way that his words will scarcely be a snare for the bewildered man, but rather will help him into the universal. . . .[22]

Accordingly it seems to me that Schrader is simply mistaken in his apprehensions concerning any recognition of my extended notion of position. We can grant Schrader that the knight of faith is "geworfen," that he is characterized by facticity, but still deny a contradiction in the following two assertions: (1) A and B live in the same world; (2) It is not the case that A and B live in the same world.

Here, the seeming contradiction is eliminated by noticing the equivocation of the expression "same world," such that the two assertions can become the compatible: (1.1) A and B live within the same space–time boundaries, environment, and community; (2.1) A and B do not live (share) in the same perspective through which all the cosmological aspects in (1.1) become one's own (for the knight of faith lives within the city of Jerusalem, as well as that of Babylon).

Whereas Schrader recognizes assertions (1) and (2) to be incompatible, my analysis will allow them to be the compatible conjunction of (1.1) and (2.1). Accordingly, I cannot share Schrader's insinuation that Abraham acting in the capacity of a knight of faith is a Quixotic figure. Rather, it seems to me to be the case that the knight of faith neither "rummages around in his psyche" nor causes any moral havoc to occur in performing the tasks associated with his non-institutional role in life. My introduction of an extended notion of position, and its incumbent recognition of "duty-plus" acts, to be shortly elucidated, will show Abraham as an individual to be playing a role which anticipates his very possibilities; yet such a projection need never outrun the categories of the ethical; for it may be a projection in, of, and with the world.[23]

Another objection which arises is whether talk of "knighthood of faith" is not simply a "category mistake." That is, Abraham is just a father, husband, tribal leader, etc. He occupies only these limited notions of position, so that he can be spoken of as a knight of faith only in the sense of the manner in which he views these respective institutional roles he plays in life. Much as, when you have toured the constituent colleges of Oxford, you have toured the university, so too when you are aware of the institutional roles a man plays in life, you are aware of his knighthood of faith. This objection arises from consideration of the following passage from *Fear and Trembling*:

> . . . he [the knight of faith] knows the bliss of the infinite . . . and yet finiteness tastes to him just as good . . . as though the finite life were the surest thing of all.[24]

In reply, I wish to answer that there is a sense in which this objection is partly correct, but also partly erroneous. That is, there is a sense in which it is a category mistake to speak of knighthood of faith, and also a sense in which it is not a category mistake. Let me explain this seemingly Kierkegaardian reply!

First of all, it might be argued that to ascribe knighthood of faith to Abraham is a "category mistake," although I do have some hesitation here in allowing the objection to be judged partly correct. For, it seems a bit queer to have such a supreme moral principle as "One ought to obey the commands of God" determining the institutional roles of husband, father, etc., although Kierkegaard himself in *Fear and Trembling* did speak of a bookkeeper as a knight of faith: "One might suppose that he was a clerk who had lost his soul in an intricate system of bookkeeping, so precise is he." [25] Kierkegaard also spoke of a tax-collector, professor of philosophy, and a servant girl as knights of faith—the last at least showing that the role is not limited to the male species. Furthermore, if one is to allow such considerations to deem it a "category mistake" to speak of a precise role of knighthood of faith, then one must qualify this ascription by granting that the awareness of these institutional roles which led to the identification of a knight of faith is to be viewed from the perspective of duty-plus.

Secondly, it seems that there is a stronger sense in which it is not a "category mistake" to speak of the distinct role of a knight of faith, consonant with my extended notion of position. For, consider the case of a "hermit" who can be said to occupy no institutional roles (i.e., he has "no ties with the world") whatsoever, and who furthermore fulfills the conditions of being a knight of faith. Here, I believe, we cannot speak simply of knighthood of faith as being just a way of viewing one's institutional roles, or putting them in a certain perspective, for, *ex hypothesi,* knighthood of faith is the sole role he plays in life. It is important also to note that in this case, at least, our hermit plays a distinctly moral role, for he is not a derelict or a misanthrope, which would be non-institutional roles also, albeit non-moral ones.

IV

The introduction of such an extended meaning of position will then allow us to recognize such a role as knight of faith. And, if there is some legitimate sense in referring to the position of a "knight of faith," as I have been contending, then clearly certain duties are conferred by such a role in life. And, if this further implies the subscription to certain moral principles, then it is proper to speak of the knight of faith as recognizing such supreme principles as "One ought to offer all things to God" or "One ought always to obey the wishes of God"; for, as Kierkegaard said, such is the principal duty (the "absolute duty") of the knight of faith.[26]

Now, it might be granted that there is a sense in which such a religious man has certain duties to God, for he may occupy a certain office in some religious organization, and such an institution deems it mandatory for such a person to be duty-bound to obey God. But—and I think that Kierkegaard is correct in here insisting that such an "ecclesiastical hero" is not a knight of faith—he has not gone far enough to recognize an absolute duty to God alone, which is not mediated by the ethical or religious institution in which he finds himself. However, if we can appreciate the distinction between those tasks which are ordinarily thought essential by social consensus to a certain duty, and those tasks which go beyond the ordinary implications of duty, although not beyond duty itself, then we can begin more fully to understand Kierkegaard's knight of faith. To the extent that the individual allows himself to be directed by the standards of what existentialists call the "One" (i.e., impersonal collectivity), he never becomes a true self. Indeed, to become an individual is precisely to begin to formulate one's own principles of conduct and to act resolutely in accordance with them. But this is precisely the sort of "personal universalizability" (i.e., moral principles formed out of regard to Kant's first formulation of the categorical imperative which are applicable *sui generis* to oneself alone) which Kierkegaard is driving at, although it need not be gained at the expense of the "absurd" (e.g., "Either the individual becomes a knight of faith by assuming the burden of the paradox, or he never becomes one. In these regions partnership is unthinkable" [27]). The knight of faith, I would claim, can legitimately make a claim to universal recognition of his special status, and at least implicitly a claim to the recognition that what he did was a justified action for himself, since his own account of "special status" is such that it logically excludes anyone else from sharing that very same status (e.g., Buber's "I–Thou" relationship).

. . . he [the knight of faith] becomes God's intimate acquaintance, the Lord's friend, and (to speak quite humanly) that he says "Thou" to God in heaven, whereas even the tragic hero only addresses Him in the third person.[28]

Certain philosophers (e.g., Feinberg, Urmson) have too long lingered in the error of supposing that the moral or religious code must not be in part too far beyond the capacity of the ordinary man in normal circumstances, or else a feared general non-compliance with such moral codes would result. Urmson comments: "The basic moral code must not be in part too far beyond the capacity of the ordinary man on ordinary occasions or a general breakdown of compliance with the moral code would be an inevitable consequence; duty would seem to be something high and unattainable, and not for 'the likes of us'." [29] This has engendered the result that strictly dutiful acts (e.g., Kant's "hard duties") which require a great deal of self-restraint and suppression of basic desires have been classified as non-dutiful, but meritorious supererogatory acts. Feinberg says: "The sacrificial element in supererogatory actions does not necessarily exceed that in the performance of a duty; what it exceeds is the sacrifice normally involved in the doing of a duty." [30] By his "infinite resignation of faith" and his "leap" to the religious stage of life, so these sympathizers might argue, Abraham has so obligated himself to sacrifice Isaac; but surely he has no duty to do so, for this is plainly "beyond the call of duty." But, it is clearly false that some heroic and saintly acts cannot be classified as morally required acts within the sphere of duty (to be further specified in the realm of "duty-plus"). It is also equally erroneous to infer that supererogatory acts must be better in the moral scale than certain obligatory acts, for surely it is often the case that acts of dutiful heroism are better than heroic acts of supererogation. I am not suggesting that one could formulate complicated rules to determine in just what situation an act is obligatory or not, but I am suggesting that there are some basic requirements in the form of rules or principles which are necessary features of a position and which, should one consider oneself to be in such a position, one is bound thereby to subscribe to in due fashion.

If we are to preserve the conduct of Abraham within the moral sphere, then it is incumbent upon us to delineate further what Kierkegaard means by "absolute duty." If not, then surely Urmson is correct in saying that by any ordinary appeal to our conventional moral standards, it is absurd to claim that Abraham has a duty to sacrifice his son; and Feinberg is also correct in his questioning of the excessive sacrificial element involved in the performance of such a presumed duty.

I suggest that we speak of a "duty-plus" act (i.e., what Kierkegaard refers to as an "absolute duty") whenever the following situation obtains: X is a duty-plus act of moral agent A if and only if: (a) X is an action required by moral principles P_1, P_2 ... P_n and moral rules R_1, R_2 ... R_n; (b) A has voluntarily chosen to subscribe to such moral principles and rules; (c) these principles and rules in turn characterize A's position in life; and (d) they require a specific performance if A is to satisfy the obligatory functions enjoined by such moral principles and rules.[31] For instance, it is not normally considered by our ordinary ethical standards a duty of a particular person to refrain from eating meat, to pray some eight hours a day, or to forbear from speaking to other human beings. Indeed, if there were such a Christian who did consider it his duty to do the above tasks, then surely our normal ethical standards would tell us that it is only a "false modesty" which prompts such a man to say "I only did my duty," for philosophers tell us that such a person has done more than duty requires. J. O. Urmson makes such a claim, and in so doing an error, in my view, when he remarks: ". . . though he [the hero] might say to himself that so to act was a duty, he could not say so even beforehand to anyone else, and no one else could ever say it. Subjectively at the time of action, the deed presented itself as a duty, but it was not a duty." [32] However, this seems to me to be a clearly inadequate account of the moral life, and hence the need to speak of "duty-plus acts" which form a bridge as it were between our ordinary moral duties and those supererogatory acts which go beyond the "call of duty." Moreover, there is (was) a moral agent, namely, Thomas Merton (the author of *Seven-Storey Mountain*) who occupies the position of Trappist monk, who plays the solitary role of "hermit," so that, should he willingly perform the above-listed acts, it would be only a "misguided modesty" which would have us say "Thomas Merton is living beyond the call of duty." Bogen, Urmson, and other philosophers holding similar ethical theories have then fallen into the mistake of failing to recognize the equivocation of the term "duty" in the locution "X is a duty of A." That is, they have failed to realize that X may refer to duties-plus as much as it is normally construed as referring to duties-proper. However, in failing to draw the proper distinction between types of duties, Bogen, Urmson, etc., have mistakenly been led to infer that if X is not a duty-proper it is not a duty *simpliciter*. But this conclusion belies the complexity of the moral life. We do not ordinarily expect the average moral agent by our conventional ethical standards to act like Merton, or in an even more extreme case like Abraham, but the resultant psychological disequilibrium should not cause us to list their actions as "beyond the call of duty."

> The fortunate chance in life is that the two correspond, that my wish is my duty and vice-versa, and the task of most men in life is precisely to remain within their duty, and by their enthusiasm to transform it into their wish. . . . [But if the knight of faith] would remain within his duty and his wish, he is not a knight of faith, for the absolute duty requires precisely that he should give them up.[33]

V

There then seems to be a sense in which we can keep Kierkegaard's knight of faith within the ethical sphere, although in the class of duty-plus acts. Much as the premises of an argument are not established by that argument but must be justified elsewhere, or accepted as self-evident, so too the use of "good reasons" to justify a particular moral decision are not established by that decision, but are justified in terms of previous decisions. However, in moving to what Kierkegaard somewhat misleadingly characterized as the "religious stage of life," the fundamental decision to subscribe to the rules governing faithful knighthood cannot be established by recourse to previous decision, but must be "created" in the very making of such a decision. Accordingly, a particular moral judgment such as "Abraham ought to sacrifice Isaac" would be then derivable from the supreme moral principle to which Abraham has subscribed, namely that "One ought to obey the mandates of God in all situations, however demanding." I would suggest that the knight of faith's conduct need not be reduced to irrationality, but might be instead explained by the following moral syllogism:[34] (1) A knight of faith ought to obey the mandates of God in all situations, however onerous; (2) Abraham chooses to be a knight of faith; (3) Therefore, Abraham ought to obey the mandates of God in all situations, however onerous; (4) God commands that Abraham sacrifice Isaac; (5) Therefore, Abraham ought to sacrifice Isaac.

One's moral duty and obligation can then be either what one must do to act consistently with the general institutional principles governing the particular role and contractual situation in which one finds oneself placed in society, or else it can be what one must do if one is to fulfill the requirements of what one feels one ought to do, consistent with the general moral principles governing the particular role and contractual situation in which one chooses to place oneself, as opposed to what the moral code dictates that one ought to do. Agamemnon and the ecclesiastical hero chose the first horn of this either/or situation, whereas Abraham chose the latter, and with "passionate inwardness" resolved to carry out his self-given prescription. This is why I can find no paradox in the conduct of Abraham, for it is surely no logical contradiction for an individual to remain consistently self-reliant within his chosen set of moral ideals. Kierkegaard himself was somewhat aware of this, but he did not bring it to its logical culmination, so that the paradox of Abraham's life would become annihilated.

> . . . the significance of the lofty dignity which is assigned to every man, that of being his own censor, is a far prouder title than that of Censor General to the whole, Roman Republic.[35]

Moreover, it does not strike me as a strong objection to remark that Abraham's proposed act is simply absurd, because there might not be a God. This objection seems to me to be weak, for often we have self-imposed duties and obligations, as when I declare myself a trustee of property for a yet unborn child, and then assume certain duties and obligations consonant with such a declaration. It might be objected here, and rightly so, that my example as stated admits of sufficient disanalogous features to make it unable to offset the objection. For, to be sure, it is questionable whether the unborn child is not already an existing person, and even if we grant it the status of a mere biological entity *qua* fetus, the example is still deficient, for as soon as the "child" comes-into-being there exists a person to whom I have such and such obligations and duties. With this criticism I agree. But, the initial objection still does not hold; for my example now slightly amended might still hold and indeed be legally precedential in cases in which a father declares himself a trustee of property for a yet unborn child of his daughter, and the daughter never becomes pregnant before her father's death. Here, *ex hypothesi*, the father had duties and obligations *qua* trustee to a person who did not exist. So too, it might also be argued in my defense, that a wife can be said to have duties to her missing husband, although it is questionable whether her husband is living or not. If we are to judge Abraham's conduct as absurd, we must *mutatis mutandis* judge the conduct of our hypothetical father and wife to be equally absurd.

> From this, however, it does not follow that the ethical is to be abolished, but that it acquires an entirely different expression, the paradoxical expression—that love to God may cause the knight of faith to give his love to his neighbor the opposite expression to that which, ethically speaking, is required by duty.[36]

VI

We have now seen how a plausible philosophical defense can be established for the conduct of Abraham *qua* knight of faith. This defense allows us to give a negative answer to Kierkegaard's "Problem One: Is there such a thing as a teleological suspension of the ethical?" while allowing an affirmative answer to his "Problem Two: Is there such a thing as an absolute duty to God?" I now wish to make an exegetical point, the philosophical ramifications of which allow diverse interpretations to our re-examination of the "teleological suspension of the ethical."

Throughout *Fear and Trembling,* Kierkegaard uses the terms "temptation" and "trial" in describing the complexities of Abraham's life. Although any distinction is generally overlooked by philosophical critics of Kierkegaard, so that the two terms are rendered intensional equivalents,[37] it seems to me that such an analysis is most unsatisfactory; a discovery of this unsatisfactoriness will uncover, I believe, poignant exegetical evidence to support my analysis of the logic of "position" and "duty," and the preceding defense of Abraham. Kierkegaard himself hints at such a distinction, when he writes:

> But if he does not love like Abraham, then every thought of offering Isaac would be not a trial (fristelse) but a base temptation (anfechtung).

It seems that we may speak of ϕ as a "temptation" provided that: (a) ϕ is an action of enticing a person to evil by presenting inducements to his passion or human frailties; or, (b) ϕ is a severe challenge against a person in the attempt to confute him intellectually in regard to some moral issue; or, (c) ϕ is an attempt to offset one from his chosen plan of life.

Now, we may speak of ψ as a "trial" provided that: (d) ψ is a test of one's beliefs in a certain set of moral principles and rules; or, (e) ψ is an action of testing, "putting to the proof" the moral fitness of some proposed line of conduct; or, (f) ψ is an inquiry to ascertain a certain practical decision; the search for evidence by the examiner to prove a certain set of qualifications in the examinee, such as the endeavor to establish a person's moral commitment to a certain role in life.

The critic might argue here: (1) that if temptations can be so described as those actions which attempt to entice a person (either by appeal to his passions or intellectually) from performing his moral duty, and (2) "temptation" means the same as "trial," then (3) trials can also be described as those actions which attempt to entice a person from performing his moral duty, so that (4) to describe the testing of Abraham by use of the term "trial" is to cast aspersions on any considerations offered to show that he may have a moral duty to sacrifice his son. The critic might proceed by citing Kierkegaard to show that the most one can claim for Abraham's proposed line of conduct, given the univocal sense of "trial" and "temptation," is some sort of religious justification; but, on no account can there be any moral justification of his action. That is, if "trial" $\overset{df}{=}$ "temptation," then to characterize the testing of Abraham as a "trial" is to imply that God's command seeks to direct Abraham away from his moral and rational responsibilities (qua father, husband, etc.), in favor of a religious decision (qua knight of faith). But, if it is the case, as I wish to suggest, that "trial" $\overset{df}{\neq}$ "temptation," then to characterize the testing of Abraham as a "trial" is to imply that God's command seeks to direct Abraham to act morally [in the sense of (f)] out of respect for the responsibilities of his role qua knight of faith.

Why then did Abraham do it? For God's sake and for his own sake.
. . . The unity of these two points of view is perfectly expressed by

the word which has always been used to characterize this situation: it is a trial, a temptation (fristelse). A temptation—but what does that mean? What ordinarily tempts a man is that which would keep him from doing his duty, but in this case the temptation is itself the ethical . . . which would keep him from doing God's will.[38]

. . . to the question, "Why," Abraham has no answer except that it is a trial, a temptation (fristelse). . . .[39]

I certainly do not propose to refute the critic's charge that the issue is not always so well-defined, nor will I deny that Kierkegaard himself gets into certain muddles with his "passionate use of language." Therefore, the two above-mentioned textual references, cited as evidence against my claim for the distinction between "trial" and "temptation," I shall not deny. However, I will not accept the critic's conclusion that the terms "trial" and "temptation" have the same connotation. Furthermore, I would reply to the critic that he had simply failed properly to consider the possible uses of Kierkegaard's "dialectical method"; that is, the way in which he goes about presenting issues in "desultory fashion." [40]

First of all, Kierkegaard borrowed from his antagonist, Hegel, the belief that from the thesis and antithesis of conflicting claims may well come the synthesis of understanding. This is what he means in saying that like the lyricist he goes about things "dialectically." [41] This procedure is closely associated with his "desultory manner," an expression used by Kierkegaard to indicate the presentation of an issue from all points of view, so that the reader may draw his own conclusions, having seen, as it were, the issue illuminated from all opposing viewpoints. Kierkegaard as the philosopher is simply raising the issues; he is the Socratic gadfly, but the reader must make his own personal decision. I would suggest, then, that an appreciation for this manner of doing philosophy will yield the result that the texts cited by our critic may be construed as simply illustrating a particular point of view, but by no means a definitive solution to the problem.

Secondly, for such a fusion of the two terms as synonymous, there are passages which clearly repudiate such a connotational linkage, and which, moreover, support my analysis, in favor of the distinction.

. . . the whole of life is a trial.[42]

Would not his contemporary age . . . have said of him, "Abraham is eternally procrastinating. Finally he gets a son . . . now he wants to sacrifice him. So is he not mad?—but he always says that it is a trial." [43]

The relief of speech is that it translates me into the universal. Now Abraham is able to say the most beautiful things any language can express about how he loves Isaac. But it is not this he has at heart to say, it is the profounder thought that he would sacrifice him because it is a trial. This latter thought no one can understand, and hence everyone can only misunderstand the former.[44]

Every instant Abraham is able to break off, he can repent the whole thing as a temptation (anfechtung), then he can speak, then all could understand him—but then he is no longer Abraham.[45]

Lastly, in reference to the critic's argument, I would simply deny premise (2), citing the linguistic evidence presented in (a)–(f), so that the definitional equivalence of (3) fails to be satisfied, thereby rendering (4) a poorly drawn philosophical conclusion.

VII

Having drawn the above distinctions among types of duties, I now wish to clarify for the reader some possible, lingering difficulties concerning my analysis of the logic of "duty." I wish to claim (1) that duties are tied down to positional contexts, in the sense of duties-proper, duties-plus, and oftentimes ultra-duties (i.e., supererogatory acts). But, (2) unlike duties-proper, duties-plus (i.e., what Kierkegaard calls "absolute duties") and ultra-duties are tied down to positional contexts of both a limited and an extended sort, the latter not recognized as applicable to ascriptions of duties-proper. So that, (3) to affirm a duty of Abraham in order to meet Bogen's challenge successfully, it is necessary by (1) to argue for a positional context for Abraham's proposed action, or else to establish a case by recourse to basic duties. However, (4) to argue for a defense of Abraham grounded on basic duties is doomed to failure, as we have seen. In addition, (5) to argue for a defense of Abraham based on duties-proper is also doomed to failure, inasmuch as duties-proper pertain only to institutional roles, and the knight of faith occupies a non-institutional role in life.

Moreover, (6) to argue for a defense of Abraham grounded on ultra-duties is also doomed to failure. No doubt, some philosophers might wish to agree with me that a case cannot be made for establishing duties of a basic duty and/or duty-proper nature for the knight of faith; yet also wish to disagree with me that a case can be established for allowing the duty of a knight of faith to be in the class of the duty-plus. But these philosophers would seem to have overlooked Kierkegaard's claim that Abraham *qua* knight of faith had a prescriptive right to be a great man, although his proposed action would be a sin (i.e., morally wrong) for another to do—an assertion which seems to imply that Abraham's action was not supererogatory (as they suggest), but rather in the line of duty-plus.

These philosophers might proceed by defining "X is a supererogatory act for A" provided that: (i) X ought to exist; (ii) A is permitted to do X; and (iii) A is permitted not to do X.[46] They would accordingly claim that the proposed line of conduct of Abraham fulfills these conditions, and so may be spoken of as a supererogatory act. However, I wish to dispute such a charge; moreover, when we apply these three necessary and jointly sufficient conditions to the case of the knight of faith, we see that their analysis breaks down. That is, their argument fails because: (i.1) the state of affairs of Isaac's being killed ought not to exist; (ii.1) Abraham is required to do X, not just permitted to do X; and lastly (iii.1) since it is forbidden for Abraham not to do X, it follows that Abraham is not permitted not to do X. Accordingly, we can say, on my analysis, that the action of slaying Isaac ought to be performed, but that it is dubious whether the object of the action ought to exist.

Our antagonists might yet claim hope for their view that Abraham's proposed action is at best supererogatory, and so beg only half-defeat, for it might be conversely argued that Abraham's action is simply *offensive,* that is, bad but not forbidden, for consider: "X is an offensive act for A" provided that: (iv) X ought not to exist; (v) A is permitted to do X;

and (vi) A is permitted not to do X. They would now claim that the proposed line of conduct of Abraham fulfills these conditions, and so may be spoken of as "offensive." But again their analysis is seen to break down. For, while we might agree with condition (iv), surely conditions (v) and (vi) are not satisfied, for reasons already cited in regard to (ii.1) and (iii.1), so that those would-be sympathizers of Kierkegaard who would allow Abraham to have intended to have committed an act of permissive ill-doing, although not a morally wrong act, have failed to provide such a line of defense.

Equally, (7) it is mistaken to assume that I introduced an extended notion of position to justify duties-plus, for they apply as well to institutional roles of a limited sort. It seems that a person may assume a role which is well-delineated by conventional social standards, such as that of a teacher, yet conceive of this descriptive office in such a way that it takes on a prescriptive quality, and with it the incumbent duties which go beyond the requirements of our ordinary moral standards. For instance, the following assertion seems blatantly contradictory: (a) "Professor Smith ought to teach his students to the best of his abilities and it is not the case that Professor Smith ought to teach his students to the best of his abilities."

Moral philosophers, like Bogen and Urmson, would no doubt argue here that there is no moral conflict involved in (a), for either Smith ought to teach his students to the best of his abilities or it is not the case that Smith ought to teach his students to the best of his abilities. But such a conclusion bespeaks ignorance of the moral nature of the case. It seems that the first conjunct in (a) could be uttered by an educational progressivist (e.g., Dewey), while the latter conjunct could be what society expects of him *qua* teacher, viewing his role as that of an educational traditionalist (e.g., Locke). Here we have an institutional role (teacher) which presents Smith with conflicting duties, and with the practical problem of deciding wherein his actual duty lies. With the view to reaching a "way out" of our newly discovered conflict, I suggest that the seeming contradiction of (a) begins to dissolve when it is reformulated to read: (a.1) "Professor Smith [conceives his role in life to be such that he] ought to teach his students to the best of his abilities; but [viewed *publici juris*] it is not the case that

Professor Smith ought to teach his students [i.e., he need not be acquainted with their psychological and social problems of adjustment to the curriculum structure] to the best of his abilities."

That is, viewed *publici juris,* viewed from the perspective of duty-proper, to say "It is not the case that Professor Smith ought to teach his students to the best of his abilities" implies that teaching is a self-justifying activity, so that it need not attain the achievement status of education (i.e., learning) ; that is, "teaching" may be, as Ryle points out, simply a "task verb." However, viewed from the perspective of duty-plus, to say "Professor Smith ought to teach his students to the best of his abilities" implies that Smith's teaching is not intrinsically worthwhile in itself unless it attains the appropriate state of learning in the pupils under Smith's tutelage. Accordingly, two people may fit the same descriptive role in society, yet conceive of their role in such a manner that the position itself demands dissimilar performance, often even conflicting duties for them. My normative solution to the above conflict is that Smith's duty-plus requirement takes precedence over his duty-proper. Unfortunately, what is a duty-plus act for Smith, viewed from the perspective of duty-proper, becomes a supererogatory act *publici juris.*

However, (8) I do need an extended notion of position to allow us to speak of Abraham's non-institutional role in life, *qua* knight of faith; and (9) because non-institutional roles are not recognized by conventional moral standards, and since society applies duties-proper only to its institutionally recognized roles, it follows that only duties-plus can be ascribed to certain non-institutional roles in life.

VIII

I wish to claim that, although there is a supreme moral principle in Abraham's ethical categories—namely, "One ought to obey the commands of God above all else"—we might nonetheless also agree with 1 John 4:20 that such a principle "contextually implies" "One ought not to perform unjust injuries to one's neighbors" (cf. 1 John 4:20: "If a man says, I love God, and hates his brother, he is a liar").

What do I mean by "contextual implication"?[47] Suppose that we speak of statement S as contextually implying S^1 if and only if: for any person P, if P knew the normal conventions of language L, P would be able to infer S^1 from S in the context in which S and S^1 occur. That is, all I wish to maintain is that if a moral agent subscribes to the moral principle "One ought to obey the commands of God," as does the knight of faith, then in all probability (i.e., there is strong inductive evidence to suggest) he also subscribes to the moral principle "One ought not to perform unjust injuries to one's neighbors"—albeit, conversely, this is not the case.[48]

To illustrate further the difference between logical entailment (LE) and contextual implication (CI), consider the following assertions: (1) One ought to obey the commands of God; (2) It is not the case that one ought not to obey the commands of God; (3) One ought not not obey the commands of God; and (4) Non-commands of God ought not to be obeyed. Now (1) $\overset{CI}{\rightarrow}$ (2), although it does not $\overset{LE}{\rightarrow}$ (2); (1) also $\overset{LE}{\rightarrow}$ (3); and (3) neither $\overset{LE}{\rightarrow}$ nor $\overset{CI}{\rightarrow}$ (4).

IX

It is often asserted by moral philosophers that, because a particular ethical theory entails that (1) "One ought to do X" and also (2) "One ought not to do X," this is sufficient evidence to destroy the plausibility of the ethical theory in question. It could be pointed out by these same moral philosophers that the situation outlined in (1) and (2) fits Abraham's case, in that: (1.1) "Abraham ought to obey the command of God"; (2.1) "Abraham ought not to obey the command of God."

It might be pointed out that the above two assertions, (1.1) and (2.1), are elliptical for: (1.11) "Abraham [*qua* knight of faith] ought to obey the command of God [to sacrifice Isaac]"; (2.11) "Abraham [*qua* father] ought not to obey the command of God [to sacrifice Isaac]."

The situation(s) pointed out by these critics is indeed serious, if allowed to stand, but I believe that certain remarks might be made in behalf of Kierkegaard. First of all, it should be pointed out that the basic schemata of (1) and (2) are ethical contraries, yet they may both be true at the same time, a circumstance that is absurd$_2$ from a logical perspective, albeit not a moral one. This seems to lessen greatly the charge of destructiveness of the ethical theory.

Secondly, I would want to claim that (1.11) and (2.11) equivocate on the sense of "ought" derivable from their respective duties, in that (1.11) refers to "duty-plus," (2.11) to "duty-proper," so that in Rossian terminology, (1.11) is the "actual duty"; (2.11) the "*prima facie* duty." This would be a "way out" of the dilemma, but a decision procedure of dubious moral quality, in that it enjoins Abraham to sacrifice his son. This argument from equivocation may strike one as decidedly arbitrary, if not intuitively immoral, so that we might even strengthen the argument anti-Kierkegaard by allowing the respective moral assertions to read: (1.111) "Abraham [*qua* knight of faith] ought to obey the command of God [to sacrifice Isaac]"; (2.111) "Abraham [*qua* knight of faith] ought not to obey the command of God [to sacrifice Isaac]."

Now, in (1.111) Abraham is enjoined to sacrifice Isaac; in (2.111) he is enjoined not so to sacrifice him. I would suggest that, as the two assertions now read, and given my analysis, we would indeed have two contrary assertions on both a moral and a logical perspective, in that one is obviously false, if the other is true. Since it would seem that (1.111) is true, it follows that (2.111) is false, so that we seem to be giving approval to Abraham *qua* knight of faith to sacrifice Isaac.

But I have elsewhere claimed that for (1.111) to be satisfied, it "contextually follows" that the content of such a command not run counter to treating one's neighbor in a just manner. Since the content of the command in (1.111) does run so counter, it follows that (2.111) should now be true, given that (1.111) and (2.111) are both logico/moral contraries. If (2.111) is now to be treated as true, then it needs to be qualified, in that it is dubious whether this particular forbidden command is really a God-given command which (2.111) enjoins Abraham to forbear.

Some philosophers (e.g., John Ladd) would claim that our original moral assertions (1) and (2) are "moral opposites," with the stipulation that these not be confused with logical contraries.[49] To this I have agreed! However, such philosophers would go on to suggest, although not applying an analysis *per se* to Kierkegaard's *Fear and Trembling,* that there lies a "way out" which is different from mine—namely, that while one might claim that both (1) and (2) may be true together, (1) is true for reasons $r_1 \ldots r_5$; (2) for reasons $r_6 \ldots r_{10}$. Ladd would presumably now address himself to situations (1.11) and (2.11), and claim that here he would be what Kierkegaard termed a system-man, and favor (2.11) to (1.11), for the greater moral reasons in its favor. But, it seems to me, this is to solve the knight of faith's plight by dissolving his knighthood of faith!

Should such philosophers (e.g., H. D. Aiken also) now address themselves to situation (1.111) and (2.111), they would presumably side with (1.111) [i.e., there are greater motivating and justifying reasons for a knight of faith to obey a command of God than not], but again the result, while markedly different, leaves us with certain moral apprehensions. Also, so to side with (1.111) may be no different from affirming the less-interesting, tautological assertion that "Abraham ([*qua* knight of faith] *qua* man who ought to obey the command of God) ought to obey the command of God." Given this account of the matter, (1.111) is logically true, and (2.111) self-contradictory!

Another interesting approach to our basic problem would be to argue that the situations we have envisioned have all failed to take account that both (1) and (2) may be false, on both a moral and a logical scale. Since the alternative courses of action are not mutually exclusive, then, perhaps, Abraham ought to *abstain,* where this reads: (3) "It is not the case that Abraham *qua* knight of faith ought to obey the command of God to sacrifice Isaac *and* it is not the case that Abraham *qua* knight of faith ought not to obey the command of God to sacrifice Isaac."

Ladd claims such a formulation but removes (3) from the moral sphere (i.e., he calls it "*moral* neutrality"), but I would suggest that the decision to abstain on the part of Abraham would itself be a moral decision. Note that one could not make a moral decision to: (4) "Abraham *qua* knight of faith ought not to obey the command of God *and* it is not the case that Abraham *qua* knight of faith ought not to obey the command of God."

In (4), to satisfy the first conjunct is to negate the second conjunct. That is, to be morally responsible for performing the action enjoined by the first conjunct is to be morally responsible for the failure to perform the action enjoined by the second conjunct.

It is situations like (1) and (2) which stress the "open-textureness" of "oughts," "duties," etc. Consider the mutually exclusive disjunction: (5) "A ought to do X *or* it is not the case that A ought to do X."

Now, in (5), if the first disjunct is true, the second is false, and vice versa. Logic can here have no patience with those who might claim that both might be true at the same time, or false at the same time. But, indeed, they might be both true or both false, given my distinction between types of duties. To see this, consider the following case: (6) "Policeman Jones ought (duty-plus) to apprehend criminals in his precinct *and* it is not the case that Policeman Jones ought (duty-proper) to apprehend criminals in his precinct."

Assertion (6) may be further clarified to read: (6.1) "Policeman Jones [conceives his role to be such that he] ought to apprehend criminals in his [Atwells Ave.] precinct, [but viewed *publici juris*] it is not the case that Policeman Jones ought to apprehend criminals [Mafia members on Atwells Ave.] in his precinct."

However, let us revert to assertion (3). The action in (3) results from taking seriously the question: assuming that the divine command is legitimate, why did God command Abraham to sacrifice Isaac, if there is present this contextual implication between the moral principles "One ought to obey the commands of God" and "One ought not perform unjust actions toward one's neighbors"? For us to answer this question, we must recall that I previously argued in Part VI for the need to draw a distinction between "temptation" and "trial," and argued that the latter term most aptly characterized the state of affairs surrounding the situation of Abraham. I still wish to maintain such an argument; but I now want to add that the use of "trial" to describe the relationship between Abraham and the divine mandate applies to the testing of Abraham to see whether or not Abraham understood the ramifications of his supreme moral principle "One ought to obey the commands of God" and in particular how it contextually implies "One ought not to perform unjust actions to one's neighbors." That is, the divine command is not to be acted upon with the result that Isaac is sacrificed. It is "idle" in this sense. However, it is to be acted upon to the extent that it forces Abraham to understand the principles defining his role *qua* knight of faith, and reach a moral decision about what line of moral conduct to adopt. Such a decision is found in (3).

It might be suggested that my solution (3) of Abraham's plight is too cautious; why not just affirm (2.111) instead? To such a question, I would invoke the traditional reply "that the ways of God are mysterious," so that it may be the case that God's command is not "idle," but was intended to be acted upon, so that the basic arguments of Parts I–V could now be used to justify Abraham's conduct, and (1.111) be satisfied. Nonetheless, on my interpretation of *Fear and Trembling*, I have described Abraham as betting on (3), so that even a knight of faith can be allowed to hedge.

It now becomes clear that Kierkegaard's "Problem One: Is there such a thing as a teleological suspension of the ethical" allows of a negative answer for reasons slightly more sophisticated than those previously offered. We might now agree that, viewed from a loose and popular standpoint, as well as from a strict and philosophical point of view, "Problem One" allows of a negative answer.[50]

NOTES

1. Sören Kierkegaard, *Fear and Trembling,* trans. Walter Lowrie (New York: Doubleday, 1954), p. 44. Hereafter cited as *FT.*

2. Cf. H. J. Paton, *The Modern Predicament* (London: Allen and Unwin, 1955), p. 120, and Brand Blanshard, "Kierkegaard on Faith," *The Personalist,* 49 (1968), 5–23.

3. George Schrader, "Kant and Kierkegaard on Duty and Inclination," *Journal of Philosophy,* 65 (1968), 688.

4. *FT,* p. 67.

5. *FT,* p. 66.

6. James Bogen, "Kierkegaard and the Teleological Suspension of the Ethical," *Inquiry,* 5 (1962), 306.

7. *Ibid.,* p. 312.

8. *Ibid.,* p. 308.

9. *Ibid.,* p. 311.

10. *Ibid.,* p. 314.

11. *FT,* p. 64.

12. *FT,* p. 68.

13. *FT,* p. 68.

14. *FT,* pp. 68–69.

15. Bogen, p. 312.

16. *FT,* p. 55.

17. Richard Schmitt, *Martin Heidegger on Being Human: An Introduction to Sein und Zeit* (New York: Random House, 1969), p. 265, fn. 11.

18. Mill speaks of such duties as being exacted from a person much like a debt, as a minimum requirement for social harmony.

19. *FT,* p. 55.

20. Cf. Albert Schweitzer, *My Life and My Thought,* p. 110: "Only a person who feels his preference to be a matter of course, not something out of the ordinary, and who has no thought of heroism, but just recognizes a duty with sober enthusiasm, is capable of becoming a spiritual adventurer."

21. George Schrader (ed.), *Existential Philosophers: Kierkegaard to Merleau-Ponty* (New York): McGraw-Hill, 1967), p. 24.

22. *FT,* p. 85.

23. "He constantly makes the movements of infinity, but he does this with such correctness and assurance that he constantly gets the finite out of it" (*FT,* p. 51).

24. *FT,* p. 51.

25. *FT,* p. 50.

26. Cf. John Donnelly, "Moral and Religious Assertions," *International Journal for Philosophy of Religion,* 2 (1971), 53–55.

27. *FT,* p. 82.

28. *FT,* p. 88.

29. J. O. Urmson, "Saints and Heroes," *Essays in Moral Philosophy,* (ed.) A. I. Melden (Seattle: University of Washington Press, 1958), p. 212.

30. Joel Feinberg, "Supererogation and Rules," *Ethics,* 71 (1961), 280.

31. The following passages point to the recognition of duties-plus by Kierkegaard in *Fear and Trembling*: "The absolute duty may cause one to do what ethics would forbid . . ." (*FT,* p. 84). ". . . Yea, he would be offended if anyone were to say of him . . . 'I do not remain standing by any means, my whole life is in this' " (*FT,* p. 131).

32. Urmson, p. 203.

33. *FT,* p. 88, fn. 1.

34. A particular line of defense in morals often argues that a specific moral judgment is right in that it is implied by some moral rule or set of rules, which in turn are derived from some more general ethical principle. The argument cannot continue *ad infinitum,* so that ultimately to question the basic principle involved (e.g., benevolence, utility, or Abraham's "One ought to obey the commands of God," etc.) is senseless, for such principles define the very game or position one plays in life.

35. *FT,* p. 59.

36. *FT,* p. 80.

37. "If these three men [Agamemnon, Brutus, Jephtha] had replied to the query why they did it by saying 'It is a *trial* in which we are tested,' would people have understood them better?" (*FT,* p. 69)

38. *FT*, p. 69.

39. *FT*, p. 81.

40. ". . . I entered into the . . . discussion . . . not as though Abraham would thereby become more intelligible, but in order that the unintelligibility might become more desultory" (*FT*, p. 121).

41. Cf. *FT*, p. 99.

42. *FT*, p. 63.

43. *FT*, p. 87.

44. *FT*, pp. 122–123.

45. *FT*, p. 124.

46. It needs to be pointed out that (i) and (iii) are not inconsistent, and this is so because (i) refers to the "ought to be," that is, that state of affairs which it would be desirable to bring about as the result of A's practical action in the best of all possible worlds, but because of certain contingent factors involved in the situation (e.g., time, physical incapacity, etc.), A is permitted not to do X, so that (iii) is satisfied. For example, policemen ought to protect the lives of their precinct citizens, but suppose it the case that Policeman Kopp alone is working the night shift, and is patrolling streets K, L, M, N, which conjunctively comprise his precinct, and Kopp is currently situated on street M at t_1, and a rape is taking place at t_1 on N street, and a robbery on K at t_1. Here, Kopp will probably decide that his duty lies in disrupting the rape, so that, because of the given contingencies of the situation, he is permitted not to disrupt the robbery, although ideally as in (i) it ought to be disrupted as well.

47. Cf. P. H. Nowell-Smith, *Ethics* (Baltimore: Penguin, 1954), p. 80.

48. The statement "Jones is a teacher" both logically entails and contextually implies "Jones instructs at least one pupil," but it only contextually implies "Jones instructs two pupils."

49. John Ladd, "Moral Dilemmas," an unpublished paper presented at the University of Houston (October 20, 1967).

50. I am grateful for discussions on these matters to Richard Schmitt, Vincent Tomas, John Ladd, and members of the Department of Philosophy, Michigan State University.

Index nominum